W9-ACP-696

THE COMMONWEALTH AND INTERNATIONAL LIBRARY
Joint Chairmen of the Honorary Editorial Advisory Board
SIR ROBERT ROBINSON, O.M., F.R.S., LONDON
DEAN ATHELSTAN SPILHAUS, MINNESOTA

LIBRARIES AND TECHNICAL INFORMATION DIVISION
General Editor: G. CHANDLER

HOW TO FIND OUT
ABOUT CHILDREN'S LITERATURE

THIRD EDITION

HOW TO FIND OUT ABOUT CHILDREN'S LITERATURE

THIRD EDITION

by

ALEC ELLIS, M.A., F.L.A.

*Principal Lecturer, Department of Library and
Information Studies, Liverpool Polytechnic*

PERGAMON PRESS

OXFORD · NEW YORK · TORONTO
SYDNEY · BRAUNSCHWEIG

Pergamon Press Ltd., Headington Hill Hall, Oxford

Pergamon Press Inc., Maxwell House, Fairview Park, Elmsford,
New York 10523

Pergamon of Canada Ltd., 207 Queen's Quay West, Toronto 1

Pergamon Press (Aust.) Pty. Ltd., 19a Boundary Street,
Rushcutters Bay, N.S.W. 2011, Australia

Vieweg & Sohn GmbH, Burgplatz 1, Braunschweig

First edition 1966 Second edition 1968 Third edition 1973

Reprinted 1974

Library of Congress Catalog Card No. 67–30614

Printed in Great Britain by Biddles Ltd., Guildford, Surrey

ISBN 0 08 016970 8

TO DAD AND MOTHER

Contents

List of Illustrations

Preface to the First Edition

FOR a number of years I have derived considerable pleasure from reading children's books and building a personal collection of many of them. More recently it has been necessary to gather material for lectures, and this has proved difficult because so much of the information needed is scattered, and a great deal could not be found in books of any kind.

There is a need for a brief account of the development both of children's literature in this country and abroad, and a guide to bibliographical material which is available for use in selection. This book attempts to fill these gaps and the writing of it has been an enjoyable and often illuminating task. In addition, I have included a section in which the value of books in child development is discussed. The intention has not been to treat the subject exhaustively and in many cases the result has been a personal selection. I have tried, however, to include as many of the bibliographies and criticisms as possible and trust my comments on the latter will encourage the reader to inquire further into this fascinating subject.

No reference has been made to children's periodical literature but a chapter is included which gives the sources of periodical articles about the literature, as well as a brief index of outstanding articles which have appeared during the past thirteen years.

My work has been made lighter by the very willing co-operation of my wife, who was the first Organizer of Library Work with Young People in the County of Lanark. She has read, criticized, and advised me on my often deplorably written manuscript, and discussed points as they have arisen.

I should also like to place on record my debt to Mr. A. S. Bishop, B.A., Senior Lecturer in Education, St. Katharine's College of Education, Liverpool, for reading the manuscript and being so helpful in his comments and advice in the roles of both teacher and parent.

A great deal of informal help has been provided at various times by friends and colleagues who, knowing of my interest in children's books, have brought to my attention useful information and material. Particularly to be remembered in this connection are Mrs. D. A. Lymer, F.L.A., Organizer of Work with Young People, Liverpool Public Libraries, and Mr. J. E. Vaughan, M.A., Tutor-Librarian, The University of Liverpool, Institute of Education.

Childwall   ALEC ELLIS

Preface to the Second Edition

THE reception of the first edition of this book was far more favourable than I had dared to contemplate. I should like to thank those who wrote to me in such encouraging terms, particularly Miss Berna Clark, F.L.A., Schools' Librarian, Bristol Public Libraries; Mr. Roger Lancelyn Green, B.LITT., M.A.; Mrs. L.-C. Persson of the Bibliotekstjanst, Lund, Sweden; and Mrs. Anne Wood, Editor of *Books for Your Children*. Where errors and omissions were pointed out either personally or in reviews, I have endeavoured to correct them. In the writing of this second enlarged edition I have included a substantial amount of new material, particularly in the fields of early children's literature, books from Commonwealth countries, and in the inclusion of more specimen pages from bibliographies, catalogues and indexes.

This book is intended to be complementary to my historical work *A History of Children's Reading and Literature*, and effectively demonstrates the extremely potent results of the growth of literacy in the last century. It is increasingly necessary for all who wish to contribute to the growth of literacy to be aware of the sources and availability of children's literature.

Childwall   ALEC ELLIS

Preface to the Third Edition

So MANY changes have taken place in the bibliography of literature for children since the last edition of this book in 1968 that it has been necessary in this third edition to make a considerable number of additions and amendments. The most significant change in this edition is the inclusion of a section on surveys of children's reading, the number of which has increased significantly of recent years. An ever-growing multitude of individuals is becoming interested in the field and I trust that this new edition will prove as satisfactory to them as I understand the previous ones have been.

Calderstones   ALEC ELLIS

CHAPTER 1

The Growing Importance
of Children's Books

THERE have been a number of factors in recent years which have contributed to an increased interest in literature for children on the part of an ever-growing section of the community.

The Department of Education and Science and Her Majesty's Inspectorate have done a great deal to encourage an awareness in schools and colleges of education of the importance of books in their work. As a result of this there have been startling changes in educational method since the days, well within living memory, when a whole class would read from copies of one textbook. Today it is common practice for a wide variety of books to be provided catering for all ages in a school, and reflecting not only the curriculum but also the extra-academic interests of the children. In very few instances can local education authorities be condemned for curtailing the book grant as the first of a series of economy measures, though regrettably there are still occasional lapses of this kind.

A feature of colleges of education during the past few years has been the development of model school libraries consisting of at least 7500 volumes. This was recommended in a joint pamphlet of the Library Association and the Association of Teachers in Colleges and Departments of Education entitled *Colleges of Education: recommended standards for their development* (1967). It is necessary that the model collection reflects the kind of books used in schools and in so doing it will follow rather than lead practice in the schools. The purposes of a model school library are to increase an awareness of the accepted place of school libraries in education; to further the students' knowledge of specific books for children; to foster an appreciation of quality in children's literature; and to provide a collection of material for use during school practice in the preparation of lessons. Thus, students are leaving college equipped to use books with children to an extent seldom possible in the past.

Two excellent pamphlets have been issued by the Department of Education for the guidance of teachers on the maximum utilization of books in schools. *The School Library* appeared in 1952 (revised edn., 1967) and *The Use of Books* in 1964. These demonstrate the many valuable uses to which a well-selected range of books can be put. Standards have been raised through the work of the School Library Association, in the many bibliographical works it has published since its inception in 1937, and also by the Certificate for Teacher Librarians, which encourages trained teachers to specialize in school librarianship and to learn more of books for children. The recent enterprise of Scholastic Publications and other bodies of making available to schools well-selected paperback books is also worthy of mention.

The public library movement is on the threshold of a new era due to the passing of the Public Libraries and Museums Act, 1964, which makes it "the duty of every library authority to provide a comprehensive and efficient library service for *all*". Books and other library materials are to be provided "sufficient in number, range and quality to meet the general requirements and any special requirements both of adults *and children*". It is important to remember that until the passing of the Act the provision of library facilities by a local authority was permissive, and it is anticipated that the introduction of compulsory legislation and the setting of definite standards will effect considerable improvement in the availability of children's literature in libraries. Evidence of further official interest has been seen in the Department of Education and Science courses which have taken place principally at Homerton College, Cambridge.

In order to satisfy the need for adequately qualified children's librarians, the Library Association in its syllabus of examinations has included papers in both its Post-Graduate and Final Examinations on the Bibliography and Librarianship of Literature for Children. Courses are provided in this connection in the various schools of librarianship. A nationwide improvement in library services to children will follow with the availability of librarians fully conversant with the sources of reference and the textual content of children's literature. It is not only at the academic level that the Library Association has shown interest in children's books, as it was this body which inaugurated the Carnegie and Kate Greenaway Medals, the former being awarded annually for an outstanding children's book published in the previous year, and the latter for an outstanding example of children's book illustration. Thus, standards of selection have been set, and it is more important, perhaps, in this field than in any other that there is a policy in this respect, not only on the part of librarians, but also of teachers and parents.

The publishing trade has not been slow to recognize the demand for children's books and there is an increasing flow of good-quality works by competent writers who have been stimulated to cater for this booming market. At the present time, approximately 2300 new children's books are being published annually in this country alone, and credit must go to many British publishers for the standards they have set. In 1966 the Children's Book Circle, which consists of children's book editors, inaugurated the Eleanor Farjeon Award for outstanding services to children's literature.

There is increasing evidence of well-written material being imported from the Commonwealth, the United States and other countries in Europe and elsewhere. Many of these countries have relied in the past on literature from Britain, and will continue to do so for various social and economic reasons, but now they are reciprocating in a small way for the benefit of young people in this country.

The phenomenon of the paperback book has ensured that outstanding children's titles are available at economic prices. The proprietors of Penguin Books have done much with their Puffin and Peacock series to bring children's books into the home as never before, not as material to be borrowed from a public or school library but as treasures to be kept in the reader's possession to form the basis of a worthwhile personal collection. In the last few years a wider range of paperbacks has been made available in the Armada, Collie, Dragon, Knight, Oxford and other series which do not all achieve the high standards set by the Puffin Books but which nevertheless meet a definite demand.

There are a number of good reasons why it is necessary to select books for children, because while so much is available which is of good quality, there is even more which is not; and much of this larger section may well have a detrimental effect upon its readers. It has been estimated that a child can read approximately 400 books between the ages of 7 and 14, and yet about 16,000 children's titles would be published in such a period in Britain, not taking into account the output of previous years. Surely it is not wrong to desire the best for one's children when it is realized the impressions they absorb will remain for life.

Apart from the attitudes expressed in a book there are other criteria for deciding on its quality, and there are very few books which will score well on all counts. In fiction we look for literary style, imaginative power, original plots, good characterization, authentic settings, dramatic interest, inspired and challenging episodes; and in non-fiction we are concerned with factors like accuracy, viewpoint, up-to-date information, scope of subject, reliability and usefulness of illustrations, maps, bibliographies, and indexes.

In addition, there are the qualities which make a book attractive or drab, which decide whether it will be handled with love or left to rot on a shelf. For there is no doubt that the physical appearance of a book will influence the children in selecting it. If they are helped by sympathetic adults, this will not be the sole criterion they use.

Very few librarians, parents, or teachers will have the time to scrutinize books from all the angles suggested, and there are numerous reliable bibliographies and guides to help them in selection. The following chapters survey some of the most prominent national and international organizations and collections in the field, the guides to book selection and periodical articles, and the relevant lengthier histories and criticisms. In addition, a brief study of the history of children's literature from its early development to the present has been included, of this country, of the Commonwealth, of the United States, and of some of the countries of Europe and elsewhere, and the outstanding authors in particular fields are indicated. Finally, two chapters show the value of children's literature in child development, for the benefit of all those parents, teachers, and librarians, who want to know how to find out about children's books.

CHAPTER 2

Guidance from National
Organizations and Collections

LIBRARY ASSOCIATION, 1877

The purposes of the Library Association as expressed in its Charter, while general in scope, are nevertheless relevant to library work with young people. During the present century the Association has been responsible for the publication of a great deal of literature concerned with children's books and librarianship, as well as for inaugurating the Carnegie Medal (1936) and the Kate Greenaway Medal (1955). Optional papers may be sat in the professional examinations at both Post-Graduate and Final level in the Bibliography of Children's Literature and Library Service for Young People.

The Library Association is jointly responsible with the School Library Association for the Certificate for Teacher Librarians (1958).

The activities of the Library Association in the field of children's work are usually channelled through the Youth Libraries Group. In 1937 an independent Association of Children's Librarians was commenced which was disbanded in 1947 when a special Youth Libraries Section of the Library Association was established. All "Sections" of the Association became "Groups" in the reorganization of 1962.

The aims of the Youth Libraries Group are to encourage discussion of and to promote interest in all matters relating to young people's libraries and literature, by means of meetings, publications, and in such other forms of cooperation as may be deemed desirable; to increase the efficiency of youth libraries and further the objects set forth in the Library Association Charter; to collect and disseminate information about young people's literature; to use all means in its power to raise the standards of book production and selection. Branches of the Group are active throughout the country and work is co-ordinated in *YLG News* which is issued three times yearly.

Notable publications of the Library Association related to children's literature include:

CROUCH, M. (ed.). *Chosen for Children: an account of the books which have been awarded the Library Association Carnegie Medal, 1936–1965.* New edn. 1967. (First published 1957.)

MORRIS, CHARLES H. *The Illustration of Children's Books.* 1957.

THWAITE, M. F. (comp.). *Children's Books of This Century.* 1958.

CROUCH, M. *Treasure Seekers and Borrowers: children's books in Britain, 1900–1960.* 1962. Amended edn. 1970.

THWAITE, M. F. *From Primer to Pleasure: an introduction to the history of children's books from the invention of printing to 1900.* 1963.

CROUCH, M. (ed.). *Books About Children's Literature.* 1963. 2nd edn. 1966.

First Choice: a basic book list for children. 1968.

ELLIS, ALEC. *Books in Victorian Elementary Schools.* 1971.

From 1967 the Youth Libraries Group has issued pamphlets on topics relating to children's literature, which have included:

Children's Libraries and the Book Market. 1967.

Stories to Tell. 1968.

Book Selection for Children. 1969.

An Investigation into the Physical Wear and Length of Life of Books for Young People, 1967–1969. 1970.

Special Collections of Children's Literature. 1972.

Two collections of children's material were formerly housed at the Library Association headquarters and are now located at the Manchester Polytechnic, Department of Librarianship. One collection is representative of children's books published during the present century, which has been made possible by gifts from various individuals.

The other collection consists of the history and criticism of children's literature and is based on a generous gift from H. J. B. Woodfield. The content of the collections is reflected in the booklists *Children's Books of This Century* (1958) and *Books About Children's Literature* (1963, revised 1966).

CARNEGIE MEDAL

The Carnegie Medal was founded in 1936 to commemorate the centenary of the birth of Andrew Carnegie. It is available to be awarded annually to an outstanding book for children published during the previous year, which is written in English, and was first or concurrently produced in the United Kingdom. A writer is eligible for the award on more than one occasion. Prior to 1969 eligibility was limited to British authors domiciled in the United Kingdom. Selection is made by a committee of the Youth Libraries Group from a list of recommendations submitted by members of the Library Association. In addition to the winning book, each year an honours list of other commended books is also published. The award is given publicity by means of posters and also special bookmarks.

In the selection of fiction, plot, style, and characterization are the principal criteria; whilst in the case of information books, accuracy, method of presentation, and style are taken into account. Format is an additional factor but is not of primary importance.

The wide scope of children's literature and the relative meaning of the word "distinction" mean that the award decision is seldom universally approved. If several books have distinctive qualities the subcommittee may favour an author whose previous work is admirable (for example, C. S. Lewis); an author dealing with a subject for which there has been an unsatisfied demand (I. W. Cornwall); an author who has an original approach. At the time they won the Medal, Arthur Ransome (1936), Eve Garnett (1937), and Edward Osmond (1953) all came into the latter category.

It must be admitted that Carnegie Medal winners are not always the most popular of children's authors. Good-quality literature will always require more effort in reading than poorer material. Children need guidance from librarians, parents, and teachers, who can only be of real assistance if they themselves know the books involved.

Medal Winners 1936–70

1936	ARTHUR RANSOME	*Pigeon Post* (Cape)
1937	EVE GARNETT	*The Family From One End Street* (Muller)
1938	NOEL STREATFEILD	*The Circus is Coming* (Dent)
1939	ELEANOR DOORLY	*Radium Woman* (Heinemann)
1940	KITTY BARNE	*Visitors From London* (Dent)
1941	MARY TREADGOLD	*We Couldn't Leave Dinah* (Cape)
1942	B.B.*	*The Little Grey Men* (Eyre & Spottiswoode)
1943	No award	
1944	ERIC LINKLATER	*The Wind on the Moon* (Macmillan)
1945	No award	
1946	ELIZABETH GOUDGE	*The Little White Horse* (London U.P.)
1947	WALTER DE LA MARE	*Collected Stories for Children* (Faber)
1948	RICHARD ARMSTRONG	*Sea Change* (Dent)
1949	AGNES ALLEN	*The Story of Your Home* (Faber)
1950	ELFRIDA VIPONT	*The Lark on the Wing* (Oxford U.P.)
1951	CYNTHIA HARNETT	*The Wool-pack* (Methuen)
1952	MARY NORTON	*The Borrowers* (Dent)
1953	EDWARD OSMOND	*A Valley Grows Up* (Oxford U.P.)
1954	RONALD WELCH	*Knight Crusader* (Oxford U.P.)
1955	ELEANOR FARJEON	*The Little Bookroom* (Oxford U.P.)
1956	C. S. LEWIS	*The Last Battle* (Bodley Head)
1957	WILLIAM MAYNE	*A Grass Rope* (Oxford U.P.)
1958	PHILIPPA PEARCE	*Tom's Midnight Garden* (Oxford U.P.)
1959	ROSEMARY SUTCLIFF	*The Lantern Bearers* (Oxford U.P.)
1960	I. W. CORNWALL	*The Making of Man* (Phoenix)
1961	L. M. BOSTON	*A Stranger at Green Knowe* (Faber)
1962	PAULINE CLARKE	*The Twelve and the Genii* (Faber)
1963	HESTER BURTON	*Time of Trial* (Oxford U.P.)
1964	SHEENA PORTER	*Nordy Bank* (Oxford U.P.)
1965	PHILIP TURNER	*The Grange at High Force* (Oxford U.P.)
1966	No award	
1967	ALAN GARNER	*The Owl Service* (Collins)
1968	ROSEMARY HARRIS	*The Moon in the Cloud* (Faber)
1969	K. M. PEYTON	*The Edge of the Cloud* (Oxford U.P.)
1970	LEON GARFIELD and EDWARD BLISHEN	*The God Beneath the Sea* (Longmans)
1971	IVAN SOUTHALL	*Josh* (Angus and Robertson)

*D. J. Watkins-Pitchford.

KATE GREENAWAY MEDAL

The Kate Greenaway Medal was instituted in 1955 and is awarded annually to an artist who has produced the most distinguished work in the illustration of children's books, first or concurrently published in the United Kingdom in the preceding year. In this it differs from the American Caldecott Medal which is awarded only to picture books. It has, however, been the tendency to give the Greenaway Medal to picture books with very few exceptions.

Medal Winners 1955–70

1955	No award	
1956	EDWARD ARDIZZONE	*Tim All Alone* (Oxford U.P.)
1957	VIOLET H. DRUMMOND	*Mrs. Easter and the Storks* (Faber)
1958	No award	
1959	WILLIAM STOBBS	*A Bundle of Ballads* / *Kashtanka* } (Oxford U.P.)
1960	GERALD ROSE	*Old Winkle and the Seagulls* (Faber)
1961	ANTONY MAITLAND	*Mrs. Cockle's Cat* (Constable)
1962	BRIAN WILDSMITH	*A.B.C.* (Oxford U.P.)
1963	JOHN BURNINGHAM	*Borka* (Cape)
1964	C. WALTER HODGES	*Shakespeare's Theatre* (Oxford U.P.)
1965	VICTOR AMBRUS	*The Three Poor Tailors* (Oxford U.P.)
1966	RAYMOND BRIGGS	*The Mother Goose Treasury* (Hamilton)
1967	CHARLES KEEPING	*Charley, Charlotte, and the Golden Canary* (Oxford U.P.)
1968	PAULINE BAYNES	*A Dictionary of Chivalry* (Longmans Young Books)
1969	HELEN OXENBURY	*The Quangle Wangle's Hat* / *The Dragon of an Ordinary Family* } (Heinemann)
1970	JOHN BURNINGHAM	*Mr. Gumpy's Outing* (Cape)
1971	JAN PIENKOWSKI	*The Kingdom under the Sea* (Cape)

SCHOOL LIBRARY ASSOCIATION, 1937

This Association was founded to promote the development and use of the school library as an instrument of education in schools of all kinds.

There are regional and local branches of the Association which make it possible for larger numbers of interested people to meet, establish contacts, and exchange ideas on educational, literary, and technical topics. Some of the branches issue booklists and other publications for their members, for example, Hull and East Riding, Shropshire, and Worcestershire.

Subject panels draw up booklists and often work with the appropriate subject organizations. Among the outstanding booklists published by the Association are *Books for Primary Children* (1969), *Eleven to Fifteen: a booklist of non-fiction* (new edn., 1963), *Contemporary Adult Fiction, 1945–1965* (1967), *Books of Reference for School Libraries* (2nd edn., 1968), *A Guide to Booklists and Bibliographies for the Use of Schools* (1969), *Books and the Sea* (1964), and *Social Studies* (1965, supplemented 1966). *Books and the Sea* was compiled in collaboration with the National Maritime Museum.

Other publications include the quarterly periodical *The School Librarian*, the twice yearly *Members' Newsletter*, the progressive pamphlet *School Libraries Today* (1950, new edn., 1961), leaflets on library techniques, and editions for schools of the Dewey Decimal and Bliss Bibliographical Classifications.

The Certificate for Teacher Librarians has been in existence since 1958, and the School Library Association together with the Library Association is responsible for it. This Certificate is granted to teachers with a minimum of 3 years teaching experience on the satisfactory completion of a written examination which consists of three 3-hour papers covering educational aspects of school librarianship, technical aspects of school librarianship, and practical classification and cataloguing.

NATIONAL BOOK LEAGUE, 1944

The National Book League grew out of the National Book Council (1925), and was founded to increase the use of books, increase the enjoyment of books, and give information and advice on books of all kinds.

It organizes meetings, talks, exhibitions on educational and recreational books. The touring exhibitions are on a wide range of subjects to which guides are issued. Exhibitions are graded Infant, Junior, Secondary, Sixth Forms, and Adults. Special exhibitions are available on request in addition to those advertised. Since 1966 a collection of children's books published in the previous year has been maintained at the League's headquarters.

Publications of the League include the periodical *Books* which appears six times yearly, and in addition to interesting articles, includes news of activities of both the League and the wider world of books. A variety of readers' guides are published, and more detailed booklists such as *School Library Books: Non-Fiction* (1965, new edn., 1969), *School Library Fiction Booklists* (1966–7), *Help in Reading* (1968), and *Children's Books on the Commonwealth* (1968). Kathleen Lines' excellent *Four to Fourteen* (2nd edn., 1956) was produced on behalf of the League. The guides to touring exhibitions can be used as booklists: *Reference Books for Infants*, *Religion in Primary Schools*, *Foreign Languages in the Primary School*, and others.

The National Book League does a great deal of work with schools. In 1955 it made recommendations for the provision of school libraries; in 1957 recommendations regarding the provision of textbooks; and in 1965 and 1968 compiled with the Association of Education Committees a report on school library and textbook allowances. It has a full-time Education Department which deals with inquiries from member schools and other educational bodies. A library is maintained which includes a large bibliographical collection. Three books may be borrowed at a time and material is borrowed for members from other libraries. A periodicals collection is also maintained.

NATIONAL LIBRARY FOR THE BLIND, 1882

There is a collection of children's books at the National Library for the Blind and the work of most of the well-known writers is represented in braille.

Books are lent to blind readers free of charge. Readers are entitled to as many volumes as they require and these can be exchanged at any time. The usual period allowed for reading individual volumes is 4 weeks, but this can be extended on request.

Readers are requested to ensure that the library always holds a list of not less than forty titles required by them, so that delay in dispatching volumes can be reduced to a minimum.

THE TANN COLLECTION OF BOOKS FOR USE IN PRIMARY SCHOOLS, 1949

This is a Department of Education Inspectors' Library and is named after Miss F. M. Tann, who was at one time Chief Inspector of Primary Schools.

The collection consists of representative examples of books appropriate for use in primary schools, and is divided into two evenly balanced sections. There is a periodical revision and lists are reprinted annually.

Principles which have been kept in selection are: suitability, quality of language, attractive illustrations and production. In information books the criteria are factual accuracy, clarity of diagrams, style of writing, and the presence of a table of contents and an index. In stories, right values, characterization, and plot are considered.

Paperbacks are included in the collection to draw attention to the many good books which can be obtained in inexpensive editions.

The Tann Collection is exhibited at teachers' courses and on other occasions where teachers will be able to consult it.

THE CHILDREN'S BOOK CIRCLE, 1962

Members of this organization are those employed on editorial work with children's books, and all the leading publishers are represented. It meets six times each year and discussions take place on children's literature and librarianship.

The Carnegie and Kate Greenaway Awards were announced at its annual dinner in 1963, and made a greater impact on the book trade than ever before. This has stimulated the Library Association to give more flamboyant publicity to the Awards.

The Circle has awarded an Eleanor Farjeon Award annually since 1966 for distinguished services to children's literature:

1965	MARGERY FISHER	1968	ANNE WOOD
1966	JESSICA JENKINS	1969	KAYE WEBB
1967	BRIAN W. ALDERSON	1970	MARGARET MEEK
		1971	JANET HILL

PUBLISHERS ASSOCIATION: CHILDREN'S BOOK GROUP

One of the largest groups in the Publishers Association. The Group organizes the annual Children's Book Show and co-operates closely with other bodies interested in children's books.

THE CHILDREN'S WRITERS GROUP, 1963

This group was formed within the Society of Authors and includes many well-known writers, such as Geoffrey Trease, Anthony Buckeridge, and Ian Serraillier.

Confidential surveys of children's tastes are carried out, and business matters are discussed at meetings.

FEDERATION OF BOOKS FOR CHILDREN GROUPS, 1968

This organization co-ordinates the activities of existing groups of parents and others who are engaged in the promotion of interest in the leisure reading of children. The work of the Federation and the local groups with which it is associated is publicized in the periodical *Books for Your Children*, edited by Anne Wood.

JOINT CONSULTATIVE COMMITTEE ON CHILDREN'S LITERATURE, 1969

Consists of representatives of the Library Association, the Booksellers Association, the National Book League, the Publishers Association, the Society of Authors, the School Library Association, and other bodies. The function of the Committee is to consider topics of mutual interest and matters referred to it by the constituent bodies, and deliberations are referred back to the member organizations.

THE GUARDIAN AWARD, 1966

An annual award of 100 guineas for the best novel written for children in the previous year. The judges are the literary editor of *The Guardian* and regular critics of children's books in the paper. A primary criterion of selection is literary quality.

1966	LEON GARFIELD	*Devil-in-the-Fog* (Constable)
1967	ALAN GARNER	*The Owl Service* (Collins)
1968	JOAN AIKEN	*The Whispering Mountain* (Cape)
1969	K. M. PEYTON	*Flambards, Flambards in Summer* *The Edge of the Cloud* } (Oxford U.P.)
1970	JOHN CHRISTOPHER	*The Guardians* (Hamilton)
1971	GILLIAN AVERY	*A Likely Lad* (Collins)

SCHOLASTIC PUBLICATIONS, LTD.

Aims to make it possible for every boy and girl to own and enjoy the possession of a personal collection of books, and provides a special service to schools of paperbacks with discount facilities. It makes available a wide selection of good-quality children's books from various publishers, which are selected by practising teachers with specialist knowledge of the field of paperback books. Children are encouraged to join clubs according to age ranges: Lucky Club (5–8 years), Chip Club (8–11 years), Scoop Club (11–15 years), and Student Club (15+years).

ULVERSCROFT LARGE-PRINT BOOKS

In April 1965 the publishers of Ulverscroft Books began a series of large-print books for partially sighted older children. The books were selected by a committee of head teachers of schools for the partially sighted and consist of fiction and non-fiction of general interest as opposed to textbooks.

The Ulverscroft Large Print Books are produced as a non-profit-making welfare project at £1.05 per volume. Unfortunately the demand has not been such as to encourage this venture and no further children's books are to be issued. Existing volumes include G. K. Chesterton's *The Father Brown Book*, Peter Dawlish's *Johnno the Deep Sea Diver*, Freda Dinn's *The Observer's Book of Music*, Patrick Moore's *Caverns of the Moon*, and Laura Ingalls Wilder's *Little House in the Big Woods*.

The series includes adult books which are suitable for teenagers by authors such as Agatha Christie, Edgar Wallace, Sir Arthur Conan Doyle, C. S. Forester, Daphne du Maurier, A. J. Cronin; and non-fiction includes Axel Munthe's *The Story of San Michele*, Arthur Grimble's *A Pattern of Islands*, Margaret Lane's *The Tale of Beatrix Potter*, and Gavin Maxwell's *A Ring of Bright Water*.

At a time when the standards of children's book provision are rising it is important that the needs of special groups of physically defective as well as mentally handicapped children are not neglected. The activities of F. A. Thorpe (Publishing) Ltd. in its Ulverscroft Books are a step in the right direction for a fuller coverage of material for all children. It would be a tragedy if this series were to fail due to lack of consumer interest.

COLLECTIONS OF EARLY CHILDREN'S BOOKS

Carolyn Field edited *Subject Collections in Children's Literature* (Bowker, 1969) which deals with collections in the United States and Canada. The main part of the work consists of an alphabetical subject listing of approximately 500 collections, subdivided geographically with information regarding sizes of collections, state of documentation, and availability to users. This section is followed by a directory of collections arranged by states; a bibliography of books and articles relating to the collections; and an index. A similar type of publication concerned with collections of early children's books in Britain would be of value, more broadly based than the Library Association's *Special Collections of Children's Literature: a guide to collections in libraries and other organizations in London and the Home Counties* (1972).

The most obvious libraries to possess good collections of early children's books are those national libraries in which for many years published material has been deposited under the Copyright Acts. These libraries include the British Museum in London, the Bodleian Library at Oxford University, the Cambridge University Library, and the National Library of Scotland in Edinburgh. Other collections may be instanced as follows:

LONDON: Victoria and Albert Museum

There is a large collection of early children's books, between 1500 and 2000 of which were presented by Guy Little in 1953, and approximately 50,000 by Mr. and Mrs. Fernand Renier in 1970. The books are not on open access to the public but are partially indexed in subject indexes which include acquisitions from 1905 to the present. A separate card catalogue arranged by authors and titles has been compiled of the Guy Little Collection.

LONDON: Borough of Hammersmith Public Library

This collection was presented in 1943 to the Fulham Public Library (now part of the Borough of Hammersmith) by W. C. Cater, and consisted of 300 volumes. It has been added to substantially and the Catalogue issued in 1965 listed over 1100 items. The collection is biased to nineteenth-century material and may be loaned to individuals through other public libraries or in selections for exhibition purposes.

BATH: Municipal Library

Consists of material from the eighteenth century onwards and is normally for reference only. Many of the items were presented in 1951 by General Sir Henry Jackson but the collection is added to continually.

BEDFORD: College of Education

The Hockliffe Collection of early children's books has been in the College library since 1927. A classified catalogue of over 1200 annotated items was compiled by Doreen Boggis and published in 1969.

BIRMINGHAM: Public Library

A large collection of more than 2000 items covering the late eighteenth to the end of the nineteenth century for reference only. Many of the books were originally collected by Mr. and Mrs. J. F. Parker of Bewdley.

EDINBURGH: City Museum of Childhood

Established by Patrick Murray in 1955, this is an attempt to preserve articles of culture or of general interest relating to children. The fourth floor of the Museum contains specimens of early educational and recreational children's books and periodicals. Unusual items include *The Speaking Picture Book* and various mechanical books.

GLASGOW: Public Library—Gorbals Branch

Pre-1914 material is included and was listed in a Catalogue published in 1965. Editions are not necessarily originals. The books may be borrowed on application to the librarian.

HARROGATE: Public Library

Approximately 1200 books from the eighteenth century to the early twentieth century. The emphasis is on illustrated books and the material is for loan.

KENT: County Library, Maidstone

More than 1000 items from the eighteenth and nineteenth centuries are loaned through the South Eastern Regional Library Bureau. Early school textbooks are included.

LEICESTER: University, School of Education Library

Approximately 1500 works from c. 1680 onwards, for loan. School textbooks are included, and the aim is to illustrate the history of education. A handlist was issued in 1960 and has been supplemented.

LIVERPOOL: University, School of Education Library

A collection of pre-1914 material, the nucleus of which was presented by Sir Sydney Jones. Current purchasing policy is concentrated on twelve authors including Mrs. Molesworth, Mrs. Sherwood, Hesba Stretton, and Mrs. Walton. Loans to libraries.

NEWCASTLE-UPON-TYNE: College of Commerce, Department of Librarianship

A small collection, mainly nineteenth century, including school books. For reference only.

PRESTON: Public Library

The Spencer Collection of over 1000 children's books dating from 1725 to 1914 was presented to the public library in 1948, and has since been increased substantially. The material is in four sections: eighteenth century; early nineteenth century; late nineteenth and early twentieth century; and one of the most notable collections of picture books in existence. A well-produced Catalogue was published in 1967 with an introduction by Percy Muir.

CHAPTER 3

Guidance from International and Foreign Organizations and Collections

INTERNATIONAL BOARD ON BOOKS FOR YOUNG PEOPLE, 1953

The International Board comprises representatives of national sections and private individuals from other countries. This body was set up in the belief that books for the young play an important part in international culture, and also that a good book is an aid to friendship and understanding between people. It was the first international group to be concerned exclusively with children's literature, and championed the attack on the vicious comic strips of the 1950's.

The main tasks of the Board are to:

1. Group and maintain at the international level all bodies interested in children's books.
2. Help in the publication and diffusion of good literature for youth.
3. Create institutes for scientific investigations on youth literature.
4. Bring to bear all available influence in all cultural fields where a stimulating, or retarding, action can be exercised on children's books, especially children's periodicals, radio, cinema, and television.
5. Collaborate closely with the International Youth Library and found new libraries as centres of action.

Among the publications of this organization is the periodical *Bookbird*, which is issued quarterly. It contains interesting articles, news of activities all over the world, and lists and reviews of new children's books. This periodical is edited by Dr. Richard Bamberger. Since 1965 *Bookbird* has been published jointly with the International Institute for Children's, Juvenile and Popular Literature (q.v.).

In 1953 it was decided to institute the Hans Christian Andersen Award which was first made in 1956. It is presented every 2 years to a living writer who has made a lasting contribution to children's literature. The winners have been:

1956	ELEANOR FARJEON	Britain
1958	ASTRID LINDGREN	Sweden
1960	ERICH KÄSTNER	Germany
1962	MEINDERT DEJONG	United States
1964	RENÉ GUILLOT	France
1966	TOVE JANSSON	Finland
1968	JAMES KRUSS	Germany
	J. M. SANTEZ SILVA	Spain
1970	GIANNI RODARI	Italy
1972	SCOTT O'DELL	United States

As from 1966 the Hans Christian Andersen Award may include the complete works of an illustrator:

1966	ALOIS CARIGIET	Switzerland
1968	JIRI TRNKA	Czechoslovakia
1970	MAURICE SENDAK	United States
1972	IB SPANG OLSEN	Denmark

It is difficult to make a satisfactory decision for this award. The judges cannot always read books in their original language and are bound to rely on advisers. However, it can be regarded as a focal point for arousing interest in children's books.

INTERNATIONAL INSTITUTE FOR CHILDREN'S, JUVENILE AND POPULAR LITERATURE, 1965

The aims of this organization are as follows:

1. Promotion of international research in the field of juvenile literature and its co-ordination.
2. Collection and evaluation of the results from research.

3. Development of an international bibliography of children's literature in order to ensure its accessibility by means of a card index, and the publication of *Bookbird* (in co-operation with the International Board on Books for Young People), and *Jugend und Buch* (in co-operation with the Austrian Children's Book Club), both of which are published quarterly.
4. Arrangement of conferences, exhibitions, and seminars.
5. Compilation and publication of recommended lists.
6. Establishment and development of a Documentation and Advisory Centre for all fields of juvenile book work.
7. Undertaking of studies on juvenile literature. In this connection the Institute prepared in 1966 a study on *The Influence of Literature on the Shaping of Young People's Thought and Behaviour*, for UNESCO.
8. Collaboration with publishers for the promotion of translations of outstanding material and the analysis of sales and popularity of children's books.

INTERNATIONAL ASSOCIATION FOR RESEARCH IN CHILDREN'S AND YOUTH LITERATURE, 1970

Founded to promote research into literature for young people, reading, and allied educational subjects. Membership is restricted to individuals only, but the Association co-operates with specialists in the field, both individual and institutional.

INTERNATIONAL YOUTH LIBRARY, MUNICH, 1949

This library is closely associated with the International Board on Books for Young People and has several worthwhile purposes:

1. The promotion of international understanding and education by the free exchange of cultural ideas among children and young people.
2. The provision of a centre for children, students, youth workers, educators, and publishers of the world.

3. The collection of books, periodicals, and other relevant material.
4. The provision of a centre "for the life of the mind rather than for abstract research".

Initial grants did a great deal to make the Library a success. A very generous donation was made by the Rockefeller Foundation in 1949, and other benefactors included the American Library Association and the Bavarian Government. Today, it is supported financially by the German Federal Republic, the State of Bavaria, and the City of Munich.

The Library is interested in children's paintings and picture books which are an international medium as story books can never be. Children's books are donated by publishers throughout the world, and the Library includes an international reference collection on the history of children's literature, an information centre and archive, a multi-language lending collection and a study hall for children, and a children's art studio. Book exhibitions play an important part in the work of the Library. Dramatics are promoted, conferences are sponsored, and the exchange of children's books and letters between countries is encouraged.

G. K. Hall & Co. of Boston, United States, published the catalogue of the International Youth Library in 1968. It consists of a five-volume author catalogue, a two-volume classified catalogue (Dewey), a four-volume title catalogue, and a three-volume catalogue of illustrators. The collection consists of more than 100,000 volumes and is the largest of its kind in the world, mainly being confined to literature published since 1950.

Jella Lepman has described the history of the Library in *A Bridge of Children's Books* (S. Fischer Verlag, Frankfurt am Main, 1964; Brockhampton, 1969), which was translated into English by Edith McCormick.

The International Youth Library was responsible for the book *Children's Prize Books* (1969) which lists both international and national awards for children's books in twenty-four countries.

INTERNATIONAL FEDERATION OF LIBRARY ASSOCIATIONS, 1927

A committee on library work with children was established in 1959, and has received help from the government of the Netherlands.

IFLA has produced numerous publications in the fields of children's libraries and literature. *Library Service to Children* is in three volumes published in 1963, 1966, and 1970, the first volume being issued in a second edition in 1965. Volumes 1 and 2 deal with library work with young people in twenty-six countries, whilst Volume 3 is concerned with the education and training of children's librarians in eighteen countries. Other publications include *Translations of Children's Books* (1962) by Lisa-Christina Persson, *Bibliography on Literature of Children's Library Work* (1966) by Annie Moerkercken van der Meulin, and *Public Library Service to Young Adults* (1968) by Emma Cohn and Brita Olsson.

News of IFLA activities can be read in *IFLA News* (1962–date) which is published quarterly.

UNITED NATIONS AGENCIES: THE CHILDREN'S FUND (UNICEF), 1946

Functions under the supervision of the Economic and Social Council and embraces all aspects of child welfare.

A centre of information and documentation about "all the world's children" was established in 1967 by the United States Committee of UNICEF at its headquarters in New York. The basic collection consists of books and other materials for and about children, and primary source materials for adults undertaking research projects which will benefit children.

UNITED NATIONS EDUCATIONAL, SCIENTIFIC AND CULTURAL ORGANIZATION (UNESCO), 1946

UNESCO has been a very important international influence regarding the development of children's libraries. Whenever possible its Library Department has made their development an integral part of general public libraries schemes. This has been exemplified in Ceylon, Delhi, Eastern Nigeria, Indonesia, and other places.

Numerous Arab states have been assisted with demonstration libraries, fellowships for travelling children's librarians, and the production of children's literature. UNESCO encouraged the government of Iraq to publish a manual on library work in schools.

Courses for the training of teacher-librarians have been initiated in a number of underdeveloped countries. It has been made possible for librarians from Britain and other countries to have experience in places where children's work is not well developed.

Bibliographical work is carried out. The bi-monthly *UNESCO Bulletin for Libraries* includes news of children's libraries. Lionel McColvin's *Public Library Service for Children* (1957) examined the subject from the international standpoint. Other publications include *Books for Asian Children* and *The Primary School Library and its Services.*

CANADA: BOYS' AND GIRLS' HOUSE, TORONTO, 1924

The city of Toronto has a long and distinguished history of library work with children. As long ago as 1909 a children's room was opened, and in 1912 Lillian H. Smith was appointed as librarian and began 40 years of fruitful work with children. Story hours were instituted in 1912 and story-tellers of the highest calibre were invited to present their delightful repertoires to enthusiastic audiences. From 1917 international conferences and study groups became a regular and lasting feature of the activities.

It was in 1924 that the Toronto Public Library Board acquired a private house adjoining the Library. It was remodelled and opened as a club for children, with lending-library facilities, reading rooms, story-hour rooms, a theatre, and a parent–teacher collection. This was the first building in the British Commonwealth used exclusively for children's books.

A new Boys' and Girls' House was opened in 1964 by the Director

General of the National Book League. On that occasion a "Treaty for Eternal Amity" was agreed between the Toronto Public Library and the National Book League. The new House maintains and displays the Osborne Collection of Early Children's Books, and its supplement the Lillian H. Smith Collection.

A further feature of the Toronto Library is its unrivalled tradition of publishing guides to children's reading. A well-produced example of this is Jean Thomson's *Books for Boys and Girls* (1954) and its supplements to 1958.

THE OSBORNE COLLECTION OF EARLY CHILDREN'S BOOKS, 1566–1910

Edgar Osborne was for many years the county librarian of Derbyshire, and he presented his collection of early children's books to Toronto Public Library as a tribute to the very fine standard of children's work with which the city was associated.

A Catalogue of the Osborne Collection was published in 1958 (Fig. 1). In it are listed 3000 books. Most of the items are annotated and some include biographical sketches of authors. Books, periodicals, and annuals are included and a chronological list of editions from 1566 to 1799 is given. The index is of authors, titles, series, editions, and translations. This is the fullest catalogue of early children's books in existence.

The Osborne Collection is supplemented by the Lillian H. Smith Collection which consists of material published since 1911. In 1966 a Society of Friends of the collection was established, and from 1968 the Johnson Reprint Corporation began to produce reprints of books in the collections.

NETHERLANDS LIBRARY ASSOCIATION: BUREAU OF BOOKS FOR YOUTH, 1952

This body receives financial help from the government of the Netherlands. Its primary function is to supply information on all matters relating to children's books and libraries. The services are not

JARVIS, MARY ROWLES. The sliding panel; or, The miser of Raynham Farm. By Mary Rowles Jarvis. London: The Religious tract society [1890]. Pp. 80. 12.8x9.1cm.

JEFFERIES, RICHARD, 1848-1887. Bevis, the story of a boy. By Richard Jefferies,. . . London: Sampson Low, Marston, Searle, & Rivington, 1882. Three volumes. 17.4x11.7cm.

In *Bevis* the author, a novelist and a naturalist, recaptures the boyhood adventures of himself and his brother in the Wiltshire countryside.

KATIE SEYMOUR; or, How to make others happy. London: The Religious tract society [1860]. .Pp. 136. 14.1x9cm.

Illustrated with three Kronheim plates.

[KEDDIE, HENRIETTA] 1827-1914. A loyal little maid, a story of Mar's rebellion. By Sarah Tytler [pseud.] . . . With four illustrations by Paul Hardy. London [etc.] Blackie and son, limited [1899]. Pp. 240. 17.8x12.3cm.

The inscription on the fly-leaf is dated Xmas, 1900.

[KEDDIE, HENRIETTA] 1827-1914. A young Oxford maid in the days of the King and the Parliament. By Sarah Tytler [pseud.] . . . London, The Religious tract society [1890]. Pp. vi, 320. 18x11.5cm.

KING-HALL, EDITH. Fairy fancies and fun. By Edith King-Hall . . . Frontispiece illustration by Miss Alice B. Woodward . . . London: Syd. H. E. Foxwell, 1902. Pp. 120. 18x11.8cm.

Ten stories printed within red decorative borders.

KINGSLEY, CHARLES, 1819-1875. The water-babies; a fairy tale for a landbaby. By the Rev. Charles Kingsley. With two illustrations by J. Noel Paton. London & Cambridge: Macmillan and co., 1863. Pp. 350. 20.1x15.4cm.

First published serially from August, 1862, to March, 1863, in *Macmillan's magazine*. Complete with the rare leaf at signature B₁ with the poem "L'Envoi", which Kingsley suppressed during the printing, on the recto. The story was written for the author's youngest son, Grenville Arthur. Kingsley himself wrote about this book, which was to become a nursery

FIG. 1. Specimen entries from *The Osborne Collection of Early Children's Books, 1566–1910: a catalogue.* 1958. (By courtesy of the Public Library, Toronto, Canada.)

only provided to those connected with library work with young people, but the general public is requested to make use of them too.

The Bureau of Books for Youth co-operates closely with book-sellers' and publishers' associations, and compiles lists of books for schools and public libraries. In addition, reviews are supplied to editors of educational journals, librarians, and the general public. In 1965 a central catalogue of juvenile literature was commenced. An extensive bibliography, *Professional Literature on Library Work with Children*, was issued in 1966, which lists books on the history and organization of children's libraries, children's reading, and book reviewing in sixteen countries.

Meetings are organized together with book weeks and exhibitions at both national and local levels.

SWEDEN: BIBLIOTEKSTJANST, 1960

Btj grew out of the Swedish Library Association (1915) and since 1960 has operated as a joint stock company, the profits of which are used for the development of the enterprise.

It provides a number of centralized services to libraries such as library bound books, printed catalogue cards, library furniture and equipment, the dissemination of practical and bibliographical information to librarians.

This organization selects from the output of children's books published in Sweden each year a number which are included in the binding programmes, and lists are circulated to Swedish libraries. Booklists of children's literature on a variety of subjects and informative bookmarks are issued.

A scheme is in operation by which small collections of outstanding foreign books are circulated to subscribing libraries, and there is a talking book service for blind children. Sweden is one of the few countries where talking books are loaned through public libraries.

The Nils Holgersson Medal for outstanding children's books was established in 1950 and has been awarded to such outstanding writers as Astrid Lindgren (1950), Harry Kullman (1955), Hans Peterson

(1958), Maria Gripe (1963) and Max Lundgren (1968). In addition an Elsa Beskow Medal has been awarded to picture books since 1958.

The example of Btj and also the previous passage on the Netherlands Books for Youth Bureau have been included as examples of what can be done for children's work and what could well be followed in other countries, including Britain, subject to the necessary aid being available.

The activities of a number of countries in work with children can be studied in the IFLA publication *Library Service to Children* which has been mentioned earlier.

AMERICAN LIBRARY ASSOCIATION, 1876

Interest in library work with children in the United States was fairly widespread by the beginning of the present century, and in 1905 the Children's Library Association was founded. In 1929 a Young People's Reading Round Table was established in recognition of the growing importance of literature and library services for teenagers. In 1948 the two organizations were amalgamated to become the Division of Libraries for Children and Young People. Since 1957 the Division has been separated into two parts: the Children's Services Division and the Young Adults' Services Division.

The aim of the Divisions is the "improvement and extension of services to children in all types of libraries" and they are "responsible for the evaluation and selection of books and non-book materials for, and the improvement of techniques of library service to children, from pre-school through the eighth grade or junior high school age".

There are numerous committees of the two Divisions. The Children's Services Divison has committees for service to exceptional children, and for the selection of foreign children's books. The Young Adults' Services Division has, among other committees, one which selects books for slow readers in high schools.

Top of the News is the mouthpiece of the Divisions and is issued quarterly. In it activities of young people's libraries are reported, recommended books are listed, and information given regarding sectional activities. Conferences are held on two occasions in each year.

Occasional articles on children's and school libraries are printed in *American Libraries*, and children's books are reviewed in the *Booklist*.

The Children's Services Division and the Young Adults' Services Division are responsible for the Newbery, Caldecott, Laura Ingalls Wilder, and Mildred L. Batchelder Awards. The choice of winners is decided by specially appointed committees such as the Newbery-Caldecott Awards Committee.

NEWBERY AND CALDECOTT MEDALS

Frederic G. Melcher proposed the inauguration of the Newbery Medal at the American Library Association annual conference in 1921. The Medal has since been awarded each year to the most distinguished book for children. The author must be a citizen or a resident of the United States, and the Medal is only given for an original work. Reprints and compilations are ineligible.

Some years later Melcher suggested a similar award for picture books, and the first Caldecott Medal was awarded in 1938.

Until 1957 the vote of the Newbery–Caldecott Awards Committee had to be unanimous for an author to receive the Medal more than once, and under these circumstances such an event did not occur. The rule was waived in 1957 since which date two authors have received the Newbery Medal for a second time: Joseph Krumgold (1954 and 1959) and Elizabeth G. Speare (1958 and 1961). Three illustrators have been awarded the Caldecott Medal for a second time, namely Robert McCloskey (1941 and 1957), Marcia Brown (1954 and 1961), and Nonny Hogrogian (1965 and 1971).

It is of interest at this point to draw some comparisons between the American and the British awards:

1. Historical novels predominate in the Newbery but not in the Carnegie.
2. Geographical novels are represented in the Newbery but not in the Carnegie.

3. Three works of non-fiction have won the Newbery since 1921, while four in this group have won the Carnegie since 1936.
4. No author has won the Carnegie Medal on more than one occasion but many have received honourable mention in other years for outstanding work.
5. The Greenaway Medal is wider in scope than the Caldecott as it is awarded for book illustration and not for the more specific "picture book".

Three other American awards are the Laura Ingalls Wilder Award which has been presented every 5 years from 1954 to date to an author or illustrator who has made a lasting contribution to children's literature; the Aurianne Award, which from 1958 to 1966 was given annually (except in 1959) to the author of a children's book on animals which adopted a humane attitude; and the Mildred L. Batchelder Award, which was established in 1966 to be made annually to an American publisher for a children's book considered to be the most outstanding of those originally published in a foreign language, in a foreign country, and subsequently published in the United States.

Newbery Medal Winners, 1921–70

1921	H. W. VAN LOON	*The Story of Mankind*
1922	HUGH LOFTING	*The Voyages of Doctor Dolittle*
1923	CHARLES B. HAWES	*The Dark Frigate*
1924	CHARLES J. FINGER	*Tales From Silver Lands*
1925	A. B. CHRISMAN	*Shen of the Sea*
1926	W. R. JAMES	*Smoky*
1927	D. G. MUKERJI	*Gay-Neck: the story of a pigeon*
1928	ERIC P. KELLY	*The Trumpeter of Krakow*
1929	RACHEL L. FIELD	*Hitty: her first hundred years*
1930	ELIZABETH COATSWORTH	*The Cat Who Went to Heaven*
1931	LAURA ADAMS ARMER	*The Waterless Mountain*
1932	ELIZABETH F. LEWIS	*Young Fu of the Upper Yangtse*
1933	CORNELIA L. MEIGS	*Invincible Louisa* (L. M. Alcott)
1934	MONICA SHANNON	*Dobry*
1935	CAROL R. BRINK	*Caddie Woodlawn*
1936	RUTH SAWYER	*The Roller Skates*
1937	KATE SEREDY	*The White Stag*
1938	ELIZABETH ENRIGHT	*Thimble Summer*

1939	JAMES H. DAUGHERTY	*Daniel Boone*
1940	ARMSTRONG SPERRY	*Call It Courage*
1941	WALTER D. EDMONDS	*The Matchlock Gun*
1942	ELIZABETH JANET GRAY	*Adam of the Road*
1943	ESTHER FORBES	*Johnny Tremain*
1944	ROBERT LAWSON	*Rabbit Hill*
1945	LOIS LENSKI	*Strawberry Girl*
1946	CAROLYN S. BAILEY	*Miss Hickory*
1947	WILLIAM P. DU BOIS	*Twenty-one Balloons*
1948	MARGUERITE HENRY	*King of the Wind*
1949	MARGUERITE DE ANGELI	*The Door in the Wall*
1950	ELIZABETH YATES	*Amos Fortune, Free Man*
1951	ELEANOR ESTES	*Ginger Pye*
1952	ANN NOLAN CLARK	*The Secret of the Andes*
1953	JOSEPH KRUMGOLD	*And Now Miguel*
1954	MEINDERT DEJONG	*The Wheel on the School*
1955	JEAN LEE LATHAM	*Carry on Mr. Bowditch*
1956	VIRGINA SORENSEN	*The Miracles on Maple Hill*
1957	HAROLD KEITH	*Rifles for Watie*
1958	ELIZABETH G. SPEARE	*The Witch of Blackbird Pond*
1959	JOSEPH KRUMGOLD	*Onion John*
1960	SCOTT O'DELL	*The Island of the Blue Dolphin*
1961	ELIZABETH G. SPEARE	*The Bronze Bow*
1962	MADELEINE L'ENGLE	*A Wrinkle in Time*
1963	EMILY CHENEY NEVILLE	*It's Like This Cat*
1964	MAIA WOJCIECHOWSKA	*Shadow of a Bull*
1965	ELIZABETH B. DE TREVIÑO	*I, Juan de Pareja*
1966	IRENE HUNT	*Up a Road Slowly*
1967	ELAINE L. KONIGSBURG	*From the Mixed-up Files of Mrs. Basil E. Frank-weiler*
1968	LLOYD ALEXANDER	*The High King*
1969	WILLIAM H. ARMSTRONG	*Sounder*
1970	BETSY BYARS	*Summer of the Swans*
1971	ROBERT C. O'BRIEN	*Mrs. Frisby and the Rats of NIMH.*

Caldecott Medal Winners, 1937–70

	Illustrator	*Title*	*Author if different*
1937	DOROTHY P. LATHROP	*Animals of the Bible*	H. D. Fish, sel.
1938	THOMAS HANDFORTH	*Mei Li*	
1939	I. and E. P. D'AULAIRE	*Abraham Lincoln*	
1940	ROBERT LAWSON	*They Were Strong and Good*	
1941	ROBERT MCCLOSKEY	*Make Way for the Ducklings*	
1942	VIRGINIA LEE BURTON	*The Little House*	
1943	LOUIS SLOBODKIN	*Many Moons*	James Thurber

	Illustrator	*Title*	*Author if different*
1944	ELIZABETH ORTON JONES	*A Prayer for a Child*	Rachel Field
1945	MAUD and MISKA PETERSHAM	*The Rooster Crows*	
1946	LEONARD WEISGARD	*The Little Island*	G. MacDonald
1947	ROGER A. DUVOISIN	*White Snow, Bright Snow*	A. Tresselt
1948	B. H. and E. S. HADER	*The Big Snow*	
1949	LEO POLITI	*The Song of the Swallows*	
1950	KATHERINE MILHOUS	*The Egg Tree*	
1951	NICOLAS MORDVINOFF	*Finders Keepers*	Will Lipkind
1952	LYND WARD	*The Biggest Bear*	
1953	LUDWIG BEMELMANS	*Madeline's Rescue*	
1954	MARCIA BROWN	*Cinderella*	Charles Perrault
1955	FEODOR ROJANKOVSKY	*Frog Went A-Courtin'*	John Langstaff
1956	MARC SIMONT	*A Tree is Nice*	J. M. Udry
1957	ROBERT MCCLOSKEY	*Time of Wonder*	
1958	BARBARA COONEY	*Chanticleer and the Fox*	
1959	M. H. ETS and A. LABASTIDA	*Nine Days to Chistmas*	
1960	NICOLAS SIDJAKOV	*Baboushka and the Three Kings*	Ruth Robbins
1961	MARCIA BROWN	*Once a Mouse*	
1962	EZRA JACK KEATS	*Snowy Day*	
1963	MAURICE SENDAK	*Where the Wild Things Are*	
1964	BENI MONTRESOR	*May I Bring a Friend?*	B. S. de Regniers
1965	NONNY HOGROGIAN	*Always Room for One More*	S. Nic Leodhas
1966	EVALINE NESS	*Sam, Bangs and Moonshine*	
1967	ED EMBERLEY	*Drummer Hoff*	Barbara Emberley
1968	URI SHULEVITZ	*The Fool of the World and the Flying Ship*	Arthur Ransome
1969	WILLIAM STEIG	*Sylvester and the Magic Pebble*	
1970	GAIL HALEY	*A Story, A Story*	
1971	NONNY HOGROGIAN	*One Fine Day*	

Laura Ingalls Wilder Award, 1954–70

1954 LAURA INGALLS WILDER
1960 CLARA INGRAM JUDSON (posthumous award)
1965 RUTH SAWYER
1970 ELWYN BROOKS WHITE

The Aurianne Award, 1956–64

Only books published 2 years previously were eligible for this Award, which was presented annually. Thus the first award in 1958 was to the best animal story of 1956.

1956	JEAN and JOHN GEORGE	*Dipper of Copper Creek*
1957	No award	
1958	MEINDERT DEJONG	*Along Came a Dog*
1959	AGNES SMITH	*An Edge of the Forest*
1960	JACK SHAEFER	*Old Ramon*
1961	SHEILA BURNFORD	*The Incredible Journey*
1962	EMIL LIERS	*A Black Bear's Story*
1963	STERLING NORTH	*Rascal*
1964	WILSON GAGE	*Big Blue Island*

This Award was discontinued in 1966.

Mildred L. Batchelder Award, 1966–9

	Author	Title	Publisher
1966	ERICH KÄSTNER	*The Little Man*	Knopf
1967	BABBIS FRIIS-BAASTAD	*Don't Take Teddy*	Scribner
1968	ALKI ZEI	*Wildcat Under Glass*	Holt
1969	HANS BAUMANN	*In the Land of Ur*	Pantheon
1970	HANS PETER RICHTER	*Friedrich*	Holt

All the books which have been awarded these testimonials are either available in British editions or can be obtained from the United States through any bookseller. It should be the policy of children's departments of public libraries to hold copies of these books.

The memory of Frederic G. Melcher is perpetuated in a Scholarship which is available annually to young people who wish to work with children in libraries. The Scholarship assists them through Library School.

A further division of the American Library Association is the American Association of School Librarians. In Britain the School Library Association is quite independent and publishes its own booklists and guides. In the United States all such material appears under the imprint of the parent organization.

UNITED STATES: CHILDREN'S BOOK
COUNCIL, 1945

Commenced in 1938 as the Association of Children's Book Editors and assumed its present title in 1945. Consists of publishers of children's books and functions as an information centre. Has sponsored a Vacation Reading Programme since 1964 compiled by a panel of librarians, and issues the booklist *Reading on Vacation* as a guide to participants.

Collaborates with librarians in compiling bibliographies of recommended booklists, books about children's reading which contain sources of review information. Addenda sheets are issued to keep the bibliographies up to date.

A quarterly newsletter is published, entitled *Calendar*, in which appropriate holidays and anniversaries are listed for display purposes, information on award-winning books, articles on special subjects, and news of the world of children's books. Each year a separate *Children's Books: awards and prizes* is prepared in co-operation with the Westchester Public Library.

Sponsors book fairs in large cities and encourages schools and other communities to organize their own.

The Children's Book Council jointly awards with the National Book Committee the National Book Award for Children's Literature. This is awarded annually to an author for creative excellence in children's literature:

1968	MEINDERT DEJONG	*Journey from Peppermint Street*
1969	ISAAC B. SINGER	*A Day of Pleasure: stories of a boy growing up in Warsaw*
1970	LLOYD ALEXANDER	*The Marvellous Misadventures of Sebastian*
1971	DONALD BARTHELME	*The Slightly Irregular Fire Engine, or the Hithering, Thithering Djinn*

CHAPTER 4

Guidance from
General Keys to Book Selection

EARLY CHILDREN'S BOOKS

Reference was made in Chapter 2 to the Catalogues of early children's books which have been issued by the public libraries of Glasgow (1965), Hammersmith (1965), and Preston (1967); to the handlist to the University of Leicester, School of Education collection (1960); and to the catalogue of the Hockliffe Collection at Bedford College of Education (1969). In Chapter 3 the Catalogue of the world-famous Osborne Collection at Toronto (1958) is described. Another catalogue related to the Osborne Collection is the publication *From Morality and Instruction to Beatrix Potter: an exhibition of tales for children* (1949), which was compiled for an exhibition held by the corporation of Eastbourne at the Library Association Conference of 1949, shortly before the Osborne Collection was sent to Toronto.

An outstanding work is the superbly illustrated French catalogue of more than 6000 early children's books in two volumes: K. A. Gumuchian's *Les Livres de l'Enfance du XVe au XIXe Siècle* (1930). A one volume edition was published by the Holland Press, London, in 1967.

The collection of Dr. A. S. W. Rosenbach is listed in *Early American Children's Books*, which was first published in 1933 by the Southwark Press of Portland, Maine, and was reprinted in 1966 by the Kraus Reprint Corporation of New York. This is a well-produced bibliography of over 800 items in a chronological sequence published between 1748 and 1836. A fascinating foreword is provided by Dr. Rosenbach and various facsimiles are included.

In 1946 the National Book League exhibited a selection of more than 1000 items most of which had originally formed the collection of F. R. Bussell. The catalogue, *Children's Books of Yesterday*, was compiled by Percy Muir and arranged in sections which include: Instructional, Nursery Rhymes and Other Verses, Story Books, Illustrated Books, Periodicals, American Juveniles. The entries are annotated. Other catalogues worthy of mention are the Pierpont Morgan Library, New York, *Children's Literature: books and manuscripts* (1954), which is illustrated and annotated; and the Boston Public Library catalogue of an exhibition of the Wilbur M. Stone Collection, *Four Centuries of Children's Books* (1928).

Dr. C. W. Higson's *Sources for the History of Education* (Library Association, 1967) is a union list of material in the libraries of 15 Institutes and Schools of Education. It includes more than 1500 children's and school books dated 1801 to 1870 as well as earlier material.

A reliable bibliographical guide to the study of chapbooks is Victor E. Neuburg's *Chapbooks: a bibliography of references to English and American chapbook literature of the eighteenth and nineteenth centuries* (Vine Press, 1964). More than half of the volume is devoted to an informative account of the sources and categories of chapbooks, the development of their bibliography, and outstanding collectors and collections. The bibliography contains approximately 170 references and ten plates are included. In 1966 Dawsons of Pall Mall issued *Newbery–Carnan–Power: a provisional check-list of books ... issued under the imprints of John Newbery and his family in the period 1742–1802.*

As yet there are very few bibliographies of individual writers of books for young people, but an authoritative example is Eric Quayle's *R. M. Ballantyne: a bibliography of first editions* which was published by Dawsons of Pall Mall in 1968. It is arranged annalistically, the descriptions are full, and there is an index. A similarly detailed work, also published by Dawsons, is S. H. Williams's *The Lewis Carroll Handbook* which was revised by Roger Lancelyn Green in 1970.

STANDARD GUIDES TO MODERN BOOK SELECTION

Unfortunately there has never been an up-to-date standard bibliography of children's books in this country, and the lists which are available are not a satisfactory substitute.

In 1968 the Library Association Youth Libraries Group's *First Choice: a basic book list for children* (Fig. 2) was published which was edited by Eileen Colwell, Esme Green, and Phyllis Parrott. There are 665 books listed in this widely criticized publication with mainly evaluative annotations. The principal division is into fiction (45 per cent) and non-fiction (55 per cent), the former being subdivided into picture books, books for younger readers, books for older readers; the latter by the main classes of the Dewey Classification. There are three indexes: fiction by author and title; and non-fiction by author and title; and also by subject. Index references are to item numbers and not to pages. This is not, of, course, intended to be a standard bibliography but a list of books of high quality which would be recommended as the basic stock of any children's library. Only children's books are included so that the list does not cater for teenagers. It can only be commended with reservation.

A Library Association production which deals only with fiction is Mrs. M. F. Thwaite's *Children's Books of This Century* (1958), the contents of which are based on the Association's collection now located at the Manchester Polytechnic Department of Librarianship. The books listed date from 1899 to 1956 in an annotated chronological sequence. Notes on editions are included together with references to children's periodicals represented in the collection. Another Library Association publication is the County Libraries Group Readers' Guide *Attitudes and Adventure: a selection of books for young adults* (1965, 3rd edn., 1971) (Fig. 3), which was compiled by Colin and Sheila Ray. Books on attitudes to sex, work, the family, other people, society and religion, and various categories of stories are included.

Kathleen Lines produced an outstanding work for the National Book League in 1950 entitled *Four to Fourteen: a library of books for children* (Cambridge U.P.). A second edition of approximately 1000

363   GRIMM, Jacob Ludwig Carl, *and* GRIMM, Wilhelm Carl
      Tales from Grimm; freely translated and illustrated by Wanda Gag. London,
      Faber, 21/–. 1959. 247 p. col. front., illus. 22½ cm. Originally pub-
      lished, 1937.   398·2
      Vigorous and stylish versions of 16 well-known and lesser known tales: the black and
      white illustrations reflect the spirit of the stories.

364   HAVILAND, Virginia, *compiler*
      Favourite fairy tales told in Poland; retold by Virginia Haviland; illustrated
      by Felix Hoffman. London, Bodley Head, 16/–. [d Sep] 1966. [4], 90 p.
      col. front., illus. (some col.). 24½ cm. (Favourite fairy tales series).
      Originally published, Boston (Mass.), Little, Brown, 1963.   398·2
      A delightfully illustrated collection of folktales which will be enjoyed by younger
      readers. Other titles in the series cover the tales of Scotland, Spain and Italy.

365   LANG, Andrew, *editor*
      The blue fairy book; illustrated by Ben Kutcher. London, Longmans
      Green, 18/–. [1949]. 372 p. illus. 21 cm.   398·2
      Originally published in 1889, this is a reprint which has been reset and illustrated.
      The first in a series which contains fine retellings of traditional tales from varied
      sources.

366   MANNING-SANDERS, Ruth
      Damian and the dragon: modern Greek folk-tales; illustrated by William
      Papas. London, Oxford U.P., 21/–. Sep 1965. [5], 190 p. illus., 8 col.
      plates. 22½ cm.   398·2
      The style in which this traditional material is retold makes lively and delightful
      reading.

367   MANNING-SANDERS, Ruth, *compiler*
      The red king and the witch: gipsy folk and fairy tales; illustrated by Victor
      G. Ambrus. London, Oxford U.P., 17/6. Sep 1964. [7], 175 p. col.
      front., illus., 7 col. plates. 22½ cm.   398·2
      Traditional tales told by the gypsies of many countries for countless generations; an
      ideal book for the storyteller.

368   PERRAULT, Charles
      [Contes de ma Mère l'Oye]. Complete fairy tales; translated from the
      French by A. E. Johnson and others; with illustrations by W. Heath Robinson.
      London, Constable. 16/–. Jul 1962. viii, 184 p. front., illus. 24 cm.
                                                                      398·2

FIG. 2. Specimen entries from *First Choice: a basic book list for
Children.*
(By courtesy of the Library Association.)

People

The books in this section describe the gradual developments in personal relationships and the tragedies and comedies of daily life in a family or other coherent group. This approach may appeal to some readers' demand for continuity and relegates history, where it appears, to the role of a more general back-cloth to foreground events.

ARMSTRONG, T. *The Crowthers of Bankdam.* Collins, 25/-; Fontana, 6/-.
Yorkshire woollen trade dynasty in the nineteenth and early twentieth centuries.

BENNETT, A. *The old wives' tale.* Hodder & Stoughton, 25/-; Pan, 6/-.
Lives of three women in the Potteries, late nineteenth century.

BENTLEY, P. *Inheritance.* Gollancz, 30/-.
Yorkshire family in the late nineteenth century.

COLLINS, N. *Bond Street story.* Collins, 25/-.
The private lives of the staff in a big departmental store.

COOKSON, C. *Life and Mary Ann.* Macdonald, 15/-.
One of a series about a girl growing up on Tyneside.

DE LA ROCHE, M. *The building of Jalna.* Macmillan, 21/-.
Set in Canada in 1850, the first of a long series about the Whiteoak family.

DELDERFIELD, R. F. *The green gauntlet.* Hodder & Stoughton, 35/-.
A sequel to *A horseman riding by* (42/-), this story, based in Devon, covers the period from the 1940s to 1960s.

GOUDGE, E. *Green dolphin country.* Hodder & Stoughton, 21/- and 6/-.
An emigrant and his bride in nineteenth century New Zealand.

"MISS READ". *Village school.* Joseph, 25/-; Penguin, 3/6.
One of a series of diaries of the daily life of a rural teacher.

PRIESTLEY, J. B. *Angel Pavement.* Heinemann, 35/-; Penguin, 6/-.
A City office in the 1930s.

STEVENSON, A. *Ralph Dacre.* Collins, 21/-.
North-west England during the Industrial Revolution.

YOUNG, F. B. *My brother Jonathan.* Heinemann, 35/-.
Two brothers, one the father s favourite, are in love with the same girl.

FIG. 3. Specimen page from *Attitudes and Adventure: a selection of books for young adults.*
(By courtesy of the Library Association.)

entries was issued in 1956. The sections include *The First Bookshelf*, *Saints and the Bible*, *Poetry*, *Fairy Tales and Fables*, *Gods and Heroes*, *Famous People*, and various groupings of non-fiction. There are also books suitable for reading aloud. With each entry there is a brief evaluative annotation and some indication of the ages for which books have been written. Full indexes of authors and titles are included.

A more recent useful booklist is the National Book League's *British Children's Books* (1963, new edn., 1967). It is based on a League exhibition of representative British authors in print. The arrangement is in four chronological sections: pre-1914; 1914–39; 1940–60; and 1961–7, which subdivides into fiction and non-fiction. More than 550 books are listed with brief annotations. In co-operation with the Commonwealth Office, the National Book League's *Children's Books on the Commonwealth* appeared in 1968, and lists almost 250 books. Each section includes both fiction and non-fiction and is in author order with descriptive annotations.

In 1970 lists entitled *Reading for Enjoyment* were issued by Children's Booknews Ltd. for the age groups 2–5, 6–8, 9–11, and 12+. These lists were edited by Elaine Moss, Brian Alderson, Jessica Jenkins, and Aidan Chambers respectively. A very useful, less formally arranged guide to children's books is *What Shall I Read?* which is published annually by Book Promotion Services. Reading and interest ages are indicated.

Useful lists of books for younger children include Eileen Colwell's *To Begin With ... A Guide to Reading for the Under-Fives* (Mason, 1964) and Hazel Bell's *Situation Books for Under-Sixes* (Mason, 1970). The former contains lists of picture books, nursery rhymes, stories for adults to read to children, and notes on Bible stories and informative series, whilst the latter is a guide to over 250 books for reading to children at such times as the arrival of siblings, birthdays, starting school, and journeys.

The Havering Public Library *Biographies for Children* (4th edn., 1967) includes over 3000 entries arranged under biographee. This was compiled by Keith Golland. Dates of publication are omitted but the author index includes publishers' names with each entry. More initiative should be encouraged on the part of public libraries and other bodies in the compilation of such booklists for sale on a national basis.

Junior Fiction Index (2nd edn., 1971) is published by the Association of Assistant Librarians and has been compiled by Patricia Frend in co-operation with the Youth Libraries Group of the Library Association together with a number of public libraries. It is a selective list arranged by subjects and excludes picture books and out of print material. The first edition of *Junior Fiction Index* was widely criticized for its lack of system, but the present edition is greatly improved and of real value.

The guides already listed are either obtainable from bookshops or from public and school libraries. There is in addition a wealth of guidance from the book trade. Whitaker's *Children's Books in Print: a reference catalogue* (1969) lists over 14,000 children's books in ninety-nine classified sections consisting of picture books, first reading books, fiction, and non-fiction subjects. An indication of reading and interest ages is given with each item, and an author and title index is included.

Woodfield and Stanley's *Books for Young Readers* (3rd edn., 1969) is in two volumes. Volume 1 is devoted to fiction in three alphabetically arranged groups: picture books, folk tales and legends, and junior fiction. Reading and interest ages are indicated, and descriptive and evaluative annotations provided. Volume 2 covers non-fiction and is arranged by broad classes. The omission of indexes is a weakness which could have been avoided. Other Woodfield & Stanley lists include: *Stories for the Very Young, Stories for Younger Children, Junior Fiction* (for children over 10), and *Junior Non-Fiction*. Various other library suppliers publish stock lists, such as Dunn & Wilson's *Pre-Bound Children's Books for Junior Libraries*, W. and R. Holmes' *In Stock Juvenile Catalogue*, and the Holt-Jackson *Stock Juvenile List*.

Most publishers issue catalogues of their children's books which are usually very attractive in appearance. Although some of the publishers maintain high standards, it would be unwise to assume that all books handled by one house are beyond reproach. Only perusal of a book can show its suitability for a particular purpose.

Having examined the various standard and selective guides which are available for the selection of material, the next step is to refer to the current reviewing periodicals.

GUIDES TO NEW BOOKS

The most frequent publication which lists new children's books is the *British National Bibliography* which appears weekly. The main disadvantages of *BNB* are the lack of selection and the fact that, apart from fiction, the children's material is scattered throughout the classified sequence. A note is appended to an entry, however, if a book is intended for children. The weekly index cumulates monthly and the issues of each quarter cumulate and are eventually amalgamated into an annual volume. Cumulated indexes are available for 1950–4, 1955–9, 1960–4 and 1965–7. Also, there are subject cumulations which provide lengthy but non-selective lists of fiction for children. It would be salutary if the Council of *BNB* should agree to produce a separate, frequently issued bibliography of new children's books.

The Bookseller is also published weekly and has been in circulation since 1909. Lists are in author and title order and are cumulated in *Whitaker's Books of the Month and Books to Come*. Children's books and School books are indicated. Each spring and autumn, special reviews of forthcoming publications are made in which separate sections are devoted to books for children.

Complementary to *The Bookseller* is Whitaker's *Cumulative Book List* (1924–date) which appears quarterly and cumulates annually. It is in alphabetical order and cumulates for periods of years from 1939. It should be stressed that the *Cumulative Book List* and *The Bookseller* do not have separate sections of children's books and are only useful if the inquirer already knows which particular book he is looking for.

British Book News (1940–date) is issued monthly by the British Council and includes reviews of *Books for Young Readers*.

The first independent periodical in this country devoted to the criticism and study of children's literature was *The Junior Bookshelf* or in the fields. The endpapers are particularly attractive with their wholesome loaf, plum jam, apples and jug of milk, and of course the flowers in which this artist throughout has taken an obvious if unbotanical delight.   SBN 233 96235 2   C.M.

FATIO, L. *The Happy Lion's Treasure*. Illus. by
R. Duvoisin. 32 pp. $10\frac{1}{4} \times 8\frac{1}{4}$.   .   Bodley Head   £1·05
KEATS, E. J. *Hi, Cat*! Illus. by the author. 32 pp.
$8\frac{1}{4} \times 9\frac{1}{4}$.   .   .   .   .   .   Bodley Head   £1·05
  Among all the exciting experiments in colour and form with which we are bombarded on both sides of the Atlantic, two artists working safely and confidently within their characteristic manners send out joyful and welcome beams of light. The Happy Lion seems to have been with us for ever; Peter and Archie, and Willie the dachshund, have not been around for so long, but we love them almost as much.
  Ezra Jack Keats is a master of the contemporary scene, as much at ease in the back streets of New York as Charles Keeping is in Joseph's Yard. What is more, he sees fun as well as beauty among the dustbins. *Hi, Cat*! shows what happens to Archie and his friends when "someone new" moves into the street. The little black and white cat is explosive. The tiny scrap of story is handled with great dexterity, in vivid and hilarious pictures and with a thread of unobtrusively perfect narrative.
  Louise Fatio's text for the Happy Lion stories is not as good as this. She labours her points and underlines the sentimentality more than is necessary. But before Roger Duvoisin's drawings criticism is dumb. He has a marvellous directness, and his fun is always in harness with zoological naturalism. The new story is nothing much, but the pictures are as good as any in this happily interminable series.
                    SBNs 370 01123 6 : 370 01546 0   M.C.

GOODALL, J. (Il.) *Shrewbettina's Birthday*. 32 pp. $5\frac{1}{4} \times 7$
                                Macmillan   75p
  Shrewbettina -- could you have guessed it ? — is a shrew. She nearly has her handbag pinched on her birthday morning, but a manly rat catches the sneak-thief and is allowed to escort her home. Later he makes a big hit at her party.
  This little book has the same form and mannerisms as Mr. Goodall's *Paddy Pork* stories ; that is, it is wordless, and each pair of pages is separated by a half-page in which the action is come

FIG. 4. Specimen review from *The Junior Bookshelf*.
(By courtesy of *The Junior Bookshelf*.)

(Fig. 4) which appeared for the first time in 1936. It is edited by Diana Morrell, who in this respect has the difficult task of continuing the work of H. J. B. Woodfield, the founder of the periodical. *Junior Bookshelf* is issued six times each year, contains interesting articles, but is mainly devoted to usually responsible reviews which are initialled. The reviews are in sections: For Librarians, Picture Books, For Children Under Ten, For Children From Ten to Fourteen, For the Intermediate Library, Series, and Foreign Books. Sometimes a section entitled The Bridge is included which consists of adults' books which have been judged suitable for young people aged 15–19. A separate index of authors and titles is issued annually. From 1967 issues of this periodical have been copied on microfilm by the American University Microfilm Inc.

Margery Fisher's *Growing Point* (Fig. 5) began in 1962 and is issued nine times each year. The reviews are mainly by Mrs. Fisher herself and the publication serves to keep up to date her much valued survey *Intent Upon Reading* (q.v.). Books are often grouped together under topics in contrast to the individual treatment which is usual in *Junior Bookshelf*. The subject groupings of *Growing Point* present a completely different approach to the age divisions in *The Junior Bookshelf*, and the two periodicals are therefore complementary in character.

Children's Book Review (Fig. 6) commenced publication in 1971 and appears six times annually. The editor is Valerie Alderson, and reviews are by well-known children's librarians, teachers, and other specialists, and all contributions are initialled. The individual reviews are grouped into broad subject divisions, and non-fiction is well represented.

On four occasions in each year *The Times Literary Supplement* contains an insert on children's books. Material is reviewed in blanket articles which bring kinds of books together, such as picture books or fantasy or suggestions for particular age groups. These special supplements are usually issued in May or November, but their appearance may vary by a few weeks. Most newspapers review children's books occasionally but their value varies with the newspapers.

*Why, when others are throwing away armfuls of shining ducats and thalers, you,
I suppose, have little more than a sixpence or two to spend. 'Tis a sorry life you
lead, truly!'*
The awkwardness of this story (try reading it aloud to a child) does not extend
absolutely to the other tales. *Little Mook*, for instance, moves along rather more
freely, but it is still sticky to read aloud, where Anthea Bell's prose shapes itself
consistently if unobtrusively to the story-teller's voice. The Cape edition has
much to commend it but I do not feel persuaded to trade in my old lamp.

ADVENTURES IN TIME AND SPACE

RICHARD CARPENTER *Catweazle and the magic Zodiac* Penguin, Puffin Original,
20p Ill. George Adamson. 175 pages. 7 x 4¼.
Once more the ruefully dotty face of Catweazle looks out from various chaotic
scenes which he has involuntarily created. His journey from Norman times to the
present is this time caused by an untimely fall into the moat of Farthing Castle,
where he has been imprisoned; he finds himself on the estate of the present-day
Lord Collingford and seizes upon young Cedric, son of the house, as ally,
interpreter and scapegoat. Determined to learn how to fly, Catweazle seeks the
signs of the zodiac to complete a spell. Each of his blundering actions brings him
some equivalent modern object (two plastic dolls for Gemini, an inn sign for the
Bull, an inkwell shaped like a Crab, and so on) and the end of the book sees the
magician soaring away in a stolen balloon, leaving confusion and laughter
behind him. The scrapes he gets himself and Cedric into are reminiscent of
Worzel Gummidge's adventures of a generation back (for example, Lady
Collingford unveils a statue of Justice to find Catweazle lurking behind the
canvas). Here is the typical material of farce—absurdity justified by the author's
pace and ingenuity of detail and the rousing mock-medieval tones of a boldly
conceived comic hero.

PETER DICKINSON *Emma Tupper's diary* Gollancz £1·00 191 pages. 8 x 5½.
Extracts from Emma's diary serve as the author's version of Victorian chapter-
headings; with their hints of mysterious adventure they whet the appetite for the
flashbacks in which the course of the past day or days is traced. This cunning
narrative scheme and the peculiarly subtle divulging of the central surprise bring
this new book closer to Peter Dickinson's detective stories than to the "Changes"
books. Here, it is true, is the same concern for the state of Britain, the same
obsession about machines, that have informed all his children's books; man's

FIG. 5. Specimen review from *Growing Point*.
(By courtesy of Margery Fisher.)

BROWN, ROY
The Battle of Saint Street. Il. James Hunt
Abelard-Schuman, 156 pp., 8¾" × 5½"   £1.25
Set securely against a background of building works,
backstreets and homes where money has to be carefully counted, the story shows how Roly's animal-loving
friend Jigger causes a head-on clash with the Tolley
mob when he steals the enemy's ill-treated dog. As usual,
Roy Brown peoples his book with a rich array of characters, ranging from the scraggy gran, with her deaf aid
running the newspaper shop next to the jeweller's upon
which two ne'er-do-wells feast covetous eyes, to the
exuberant Mrs. Popolas defending her washing against
all attackers, and the music-loving nightwatchman who
prefers the children to be playing on his site rather than
on the busy streets. The Parsleys come over less well
(the boy with his unspecified illness, the mother with her
seances and insipid invalid snacks) and an environment
that strives so hard to be authentic suffers a little from
the euphemistic 'blindings' and 'buckets' but there is
much to please and the end, where the dog is sur-
rendered, is just right. Ten up.
ISBN 0 200 71731 6   D.L.R.

CLEAVER, VERA & BILL
Grover
Hamish Hamilton, 128 pp., 8¾" × 5"   £1.10
Grover is another successful story by the authors of
Where the Lilies Bloom. Some of the same qualities
appear, in particular the sympathetic, realistic and un-
sentimental portrayal of children's concerns and conversations, their bafflement and occasional cool contempt of
adult's behaviour. There is the same deft mingling of
humour, seriousness and sadness and the ability to convey
more to the reader than Grover, from whose viewpoint the

FIG. 6. Specimen review from *Children's Book Review.*
(By courtesy of Five Owls Press.)

Robert Maxwell and Woodfield & Stanley are engaged in the dissemination of useful information relating to new books. Maxwell's sponsor a free bibliographical card service giving advance details of publications and audio-visual materials with an indication of interest levels. Information on material for young people is grouped as follows: All Ages; 5–7; 7–11; 11–14; and 14–17. Each card contains full bibliographical details and an annotation. Woodfield & Stanley issue a monthly supplement to their standard stock lists, *About Children's Books*, and have produced lists of new books to be published in the near future.

Publishers issue seasonal catalogues of their new books which are sometimes devoted entirely to children's books and sometimes have a wider coverage.

The disadvantage from the selector's point of view is that the reputable reviews are published too long after the books are available. There is probably not the same urgency for new children's books to appear on library shelves as quickly as adult books. If the selector has difficulty in visiting booksellers or has no system of obtaining new books on approval, it may be profitable for him to make his preliminary selection from the independent reviews, and in any case it is helpful to compare one's view of a book with that of an expert.

STANDARD AND CURRENT GUIDES TO AMERICAN LITERATURE

The H. W. Wilson Co. *Children's Catalog* (Fig. 7) went into a twelfth edition in 1971, and is supplemented annually. It was first published in 1909, and is a classified catalogue of almost 5100 books with an author, title, and subject index. Annual supplements are selected from material which first appears in the monthly *Wilson Library Bulletin*. This is a general periodical which includes children's books with critical annotations.

Mary Eakin's *Good Books for Children: a selection, 1950–1965* was published by the University of Chicago Press in 1966. 1400 titles are listed and annotated, and represent a selection from *The Bulletin of*

383.2   Postage stamps

Lewis, Roger
Stamp collecting; written and illus. by
Roger Lewis. Knopf 1952 44p illus $1.75
(4-6)   383.2
  1 Postage stamps
    "A family activity book"
    "Treats briefly but adequately for the
  beginner the history of stamps, how to
  start a collection, preparing and sorting
  stamps, identification, how to use a stamp
  catalog, watermarks, perforations, stamp
  albums, special stamps, first-day covers,
  topical collections. There are tables of
  stamp identification and terms used in
  stamp collecting. Illustrated with line
  drawings and photographs." Booklist

Petersham, Maud
America's stamps; the story of one hundred years of U.S. postage stamps [by]
Maud and Miska Petersham. Macmillan
(N Y) 1947 144p illus maps $5.50   383.2
  1 Postage stamps   2 U.S.—History
    "This picture album, which is not a
  stamp catalogue, contains reproductions
  of the stamps used during the hundred
  years since the founding of the Federal
  postal system. Stampless covers are
  shown, together with the early issues,
  cancellation marks and special stamps of
  many kinds. Interspersed among the reproductions, the Petershams have scattered pictures which indicate the period
  when certain stamps were in use, and
  brief pertinent text. History and romance
  lie behind these profusely illustrated
  pages which hold interest for philatelists
  of any age." Horn Bk

Scott Publications, inc.
* Scott's Standard postage stamp catalogue.
The Company 2v in 1 illus $13.50   383.2
  1 Postage stamps
    Contents: v 1 The Americas and the
  British Commonwealth of Nations; v2 Nations of Europe, Africa, Asia and colonies
    Known as the American "Stamp Col-
  lector's Bible", this encyclopedic annual
  publication gives date of issue, color,
  shape, design, surcharge or overprint, per-
  foration, watermark, and value of all
  stamps ever issued by any government.
  Stamps are either illustrated or described,
  with space for insertion of the collector's
  stamps

Zarchy, Harry
Stamp collector's guide, written and illus.
by Harry Zarchy. Knopf 1956 178p illus
lib. bdg. $3.49   383.2
  1 Postage stamps
    "The author begins with a brief history
  of postal systems, and then discusses kinds

(5-7)
  1 Telecommunication
    Here are "photos of ol
  phones, modern teletypes,
  signal flags, blinkers, s
  communications vans, al
  pigeons and ship-to-shor
  transatlantic cables and tl
  them, communications ba
  lites rocketing around th
  lisher's note
    An "interesting glimpse
  munications built around
  ity photographs." Librar

384.9   Visual s

Coggins, Jack
Flashes and flags; the sto
written and illus. by Jack
1963 88p illus $3.25 (5-7
  1 Signals and signaling
    An "account of the sig
  used for sending prearrar
  the days before advanced
  munication and of thos
  Hand signals, flag system
  of the Morse code, semap
  phore arms, traffic signa
  land, and in the air and
  in sports are described
  tured. Illustrated in color
  grams and drawings." F
    "Much reference inform
  but the organization of tl
  make it easy to use as a
  Library J

385   Railroad tran

Buehr, Walter
Railroads today and yester
illus. by Walter Buehr. 1
illus map lib. bdg. $2.86
  1 Railroads
    "A technological history
  of the United States unite
  tion of modern operatin
  form an effective study o
  roading. Operation of mc
  tems, hump yards, car
  distribution systems, an
  locomotives is detailed."
  ence Book List for Childr
    "A short section on t
  railroad adds zest to th
  lustrations in black and
  thor add much to the t
  book." Library J

FIG. 7. Specimen entries from *The Children's Catalog.*
(By courtesy of H. W. Wilson Co., New York, United States.)

Gawain and the Green Knight, The Knight of the Lion, and *The Knight of the Cart.* While some details differ from those in the *Arthurian Romances* of Chrétien de Troyes as translated by Comfort, the retelling is a concise version of the prodigious tale and is true to the spirit of the original. Erec's honor and Enid's love stand firm throughout encounters with robbers, giants, would-be wifestealers, and the constraining sorcery of a woman's devotion. But along with high adventure and chivalric standards, the reteller has injected touches of humor, using the traditional figure of Sir Kay as a foil. Attractive black-and-white illustrations by a Kate Greenaway medal winner add another facet to a distinguished piece of storytelling. s. b. a.

ALEXANDER MEHDEVI, Reteller   *Bungling Pedro & other Majorcan Tales*   120 pp. Knopf 1970 4.50
Illustrated by Isabel Bodor. The author, an Iranian who summers in Majorca, has gathered from Mallorquin lore ten tales of town and countryside and retold them with smoothness and flavor. From the fireside *rondaies* come droll rustic tales of pigs and farmhands (one simpleton tale has much the same plot line as "Epanimondas" or "Lazy Jack"); from the tavern-sung rhymes of *glossadors* (troubadours) derive extraordinary events surrounding princesses and counts. In addition, the reteller also relied upon an old granny called Sa Padrina as a source of his material. Each selection opens with the Majorcan expression: "Long before the snow fell on the Rock" (the Rock being Majorca) and closes with the concept that the main characters of the tale "are still alive if they're not dead." Lively drawings of varying sizes amply suggest the atmosphere and character of the folklore v. h.

RONALD MELZACK, Reteller   *Raven, Creator of the World: Eskimo Legends*   95 pp. Little 1970 4.95
Illustrated by Laszlo Gal. Sometimes drawn out by description ("The soft, white snow-hills sparkled in the pale, silvery light"), these stories will tempt the storyteller less perhaps than one who reads aloud to children. Younger readers may be put off by the packed pages of text. However, the stories, identified by derivation from such basic sources as museum expedition and other anthropological and ethnological reports and the *Journal of American Folklore,* are important for the folklorist. Beginning with "How Raven Created the World," these

FIG. 8. Specimen reviews from *The Horn Book Magazine.*
(By courtesy of Horn Book Inc., Boston, United States.)

the Center for Children's Books, which is sponsored by the Graduate Library School of Chicago University. This is not intended to be a list of potential classics and no attempt has been made to establish a balance in terms of subject coverage or levels of appeal. The arrangement is alphabetical by authors with some indication of age ranges. There is also a subject and title index.

Outstanding recent guides have been produced by the American Library Association. *Notable Children's Books, 1940–1959* (1966) lists almost 300 titles of enduring value and good quality arranged in an author sequence with descriptive annotations and a title index. *Books for Children, 1960–1965* (1966) lists 4000 children's books in Dewey order with evaluative annotations. This is a 5-year compilation of titles listed in the children's books section of *The Booklist,* and is supplemented. Entries are indexed by author, title, and subject.

R. R. Bowker issue an annual *Best Books for Children.* This is an annotated catalogue containing books for children from pre-school to high school. It is arranged by subjects, and there is an author and title index. In the 1967 edition there were 4000 entries.

Current material is reviewed in the A.L.A. *Booklist* (1905–date) to which reference has been made; *Top of the News,* the quarterly periodical of the Children's and Young Adults' Services Divisions of the A.L.A. since 1942; and *The Bulletin of the Center for Children's Books* (1948–date) which appears monthly.

The most celebrated reviewing journal of children's books in the world is the pioneering *The Horn Book Magazine* of Boston (Fig. 8). It has appeared six times yearly since 1924 and was the model for the British periodical *The Junior Bookshelf* (1936). *The Horn Book* contains regular articles on aspects of children's literature and presents a very high standard in book reviews.

A final title which is particularly helpful because of its frequency of publication is the fortnightly *Library Journal* which includes a *School Library Journal* each month. The section consists of articles, news, graded reviews, and lengthy lists of new books.

CHAPTER 5

Guidance from Keys
to Book Selection for Schools

IN SCHOOLS the librarian relies on his colleagues and the pupils for suggesting additions to the library. Very often committees are appointed consisting of representative members of staff and pupils who advise on selection as well as in other matters concerning the library.

The wise school librarian will also maintain friendly contact with the local public library. In the county areas it is frequently the duty of a schools' organizer to supply the schools with their collections, but if the best selections are to be made, the teachers should be consulted as they know what work is being undertaken. Naturally this demands a teaching profession aware of the value of books in their work, and unfortunately this is sometimes more an ideal than a reality. Whatever the system of organization there should be close liaison between school and public library. Demonstration collections, booklists, personal conversations are all means to the end of good book selection.

Booksellers may be willing to order new books for inspection and publishers will send them on request. Teachers can take the opportunity to visit book exhibitions whenever possible, and particularly the Tann Collection, which is often displayed at courses.

The guides to book selection described in the last chapter are of value to school librarians, but the following material is of more specific interest.

A tremendous help in book selection is provided by the School Library Association, which issues booklists and guides to both specific kinds of books as well as to those of a more general coverage.

Peter Platt's *A Guide to Book Lists and Bibliographies for the Use of Schools* (1969) is a very useful if not sufficiently critical introduction to bibliographical material. It includes two kinds of lists: those which are solely bibliographies and those to be found as parts of other works. Over 500 items are listed in broad subject groups and there is also a specific subject index.

Books for Primary Children: an annotated list (Fig. 9) is compiled by the Primary Schools Subcommittee of the Association and edited by Berna Clark. It was published in 1969, consisting of over 1000 entries. The basic groupings are fiction, non-fiction, series, and some adult books enjoyed by children. Indexes are of subjects, authors, and fiction titles.

For secondary schools there are three main lists. The first is Peggy Heeks's *Eleven to Fifteen: a booklist of non-fiction for secondary school libraries* (new edn., 1963); and the second, *Modern Adult Fiction for School and College Libraries* (new edn., 1960). The latter was compiled by Norman Culpan and lists with annotations almost 300 books published since 1918. Norman Culpan also co-operated with W. J. Messer in *Contemporary Adult Fiction, 1945–1965: for school and college libraries* (1967). Approximately 300 annotated titles are included.

Peggy Heeks edited a guide to quick reference books entitled *Books of Reference for School Libraries: an annotated list* (2nd edn., 1968). This is arranged in Dewey order and consists of approximately 300 examples of quick reference books in the main subject fields in addition to general reference material. There is an index of authors and titles.

Some guides are produced on particular subjects such as *French from Five to Fifteen* (1962) compiled by Hugh Shelley; *Books and the Sea: a list of modern books on the sea and shipping* (1964) which was compiled in co-operation with the National Maritime Museum; and *Social Studies: an annotated list of recent books on politics, economics, international relations and world affairs* (1965, supplemented 1966) compiled by Catherine Adler. Approximately half of this latter list of 244 books is devoted to world affairs and was prepared for teachers, students in higher education and sixth forms.

and 11 line drawings. Phoenix House, 12s. 6d. 1962.

The author built his stone age house—according to the methods used in pre-historic days—when he was nineteen.

535 HOLSAERT, EUNICE. Dinosaurs; illustrated by Robert Gartland. Chatto, Boyd & Oliver, 8s. 6d. 1967. (Open Gate Library.)

Short, simple sentences make up the very easy text which is made very attractive by the illustrations on every page.

536 NAPIER, JOHN. The origin of man; illustrated by Maurice Wilson. Bodley Head, 13s. 6d. 1968. (Natural Science Picture Book.)

An impressive illustration accompanies each page of text, traces man's history from his closest relatives to modern times. Showing how man occupied himself down the ages.

537 POSIN, DANIEL Q. What is a dinosaur?; illustrated by Maidi Wiebe. Collins, 6s. 1963.

Coloured illustrations enhance the simple, but informative text.

538 SELLMAN, R. R. Prehistoric Britain; illustrated by the author and. Alan Sorrell. Methuen, 12s. 6d. 1958.

For the older junior, the text covers the most interesting known prehistoric features of this country.

539 SWINTON, W. E. Digging for dinosaurs; illustrated by Barrie Driscoll. Bodley Head, 12s. 6d. 1962. (Natural Science Picture Books.)

Excellent series with very imaginative drawings and short but significant text.

Natural History

540 CLEGG, JOHN (editor). Private lives of animals: Book 1. House and garden; Book 2. Field and farm. Warne, 22s. 6d. each. 1967.

Carefully coloured illustrations to nearly thirty different species; to each is devoted a double page of information, and drawings.

541 GAGG, J. C. The countryside; illustrated by K. Gell. Oxford, Blackwell, 7s. 6d. 1962.

Encourages children to observe and record. Suggestions of work to follow, and accompanied by very good coloured drawings.

FIG. 9. Specimen entries from *Books for Primary Children*.
(By courtesy of the School Library Association.)

The National Book League has done a great deal to increase the use of books in school libraries. In 1969 a briefly annotated catalogue of *School Library Books: non-fiction* was issued (Fig. 10). It consists of over 2000 selected books arranged by subjects. There are indexes of authors, editors, compilers, and series. The League's *Classical Studies: background reading for secondary schools, an annotated booklist* (1968), includes fiction, mythology, social life, and architecture in the ancient world.

Complementary to the guide to non-fiction, six *School Library Fiction Booklists* appeared in 1966. The lists are in author order and deal with the following topics: *Historical Fiction*; *Children and Adults* (Fig. 11); *Mystery and Adventure*; *Children of Other Lands*; *Animal Stories*; and *Fantasy*. Each list, which contains material for children aged 7–13, includes between 160 and 220 annotated titles which have been selected by a panel of teachers and librarians. A seventh list was issued in 1967 containing books especially selected for teenagers and is entitled *Have You Read This?*

Various professional associations interested in special fields of study issue booklists to their members. Typical examples of these are lists published by John Murray for the Association for Science Education entitled *Science Books for a School Library* (5th edn., 1968) and *Science for Primary Schools: list of books* (1966). The former, which is annotated, is arranged by broad groupings, each subdivided alphabetically by authors, but there is no index, whilst the latter consists of books for teachers and children in separate sequences. More than 1200 books for children are listed and are arranged by topics. Indications of age ranges are given and there is a subject index. Another useful guide in this category is *School Library Mathematics List* (1966) which was compiled by A. P. Rollett for the Mathematical Association.

Many local authorities prepare catalogues of recommended books. Particularly notable in this respect is the Kent Education Committee which issues numerous separate subject catalogues of recommended books and publications for both primary and secondary schools. These catalogues are only intended to advise teachers, and there is no

736   Zim, Herbert S. OUR SENSES AND HOW THEY WORK. *World's*
o.p.   *Work (Science Books)* 1965, 13s 6d. 64 pp. Illus. by Herschel
      Wartik. SBN 437 89916 0.   (612.84/8)
      One of a series of simple introductions. First published in
      the USA. 3BCD.

ENGINEERING (620)

737   Adams, H. CYCLES AND CYCLING. *Blackwell (Learning Library)*
      1965, 9s. 63 pp. Col. frontis., illus. (some in col.) by F. T.
      W. Cook. SBN 631 06640 3.   (624.22)
      Outlines the development of the first Stone Age wheels to
      today's modern bicycle, including sections on road safety,
      looking after your bicycle and how the various different parts
      work. 3BCD.

738   Adamson, Gareth. MR BUDGE BUYS A CAR. *Brockhampton Press*
      (Picture Science Books) 1965, 15s. 32 pp. Illus. (some in
      col.). $9\frac{3}{4} \times 8$ in. SBN 340 03662 1.   (629.222)
      An account of earlier forms of transport, which concludes
      with a practical description of how a present-day motor-car
      engine works. 3BCD.

739   Baxter, Eric. THE STUDY BOOK OF COAL. *Bodley Head (Study*
      Books) 1959, 13s. 48 pp. Col. illus. by Donald Green.
      SBN 370 00815 4.   (622.33)
      One of a series of simple reference books which combine a
      historical approach to the subject with practical information.
      3CD.

740   Baxter, Eric. THE STUDY BOOK OF WATER SUPPLY. *Bodley Head*
      (Study Books) 1959, 13s. 48 pp. Col. illus. by Jack Townend.
      SBN 370 00816 2.   (628.1)

FIG. 10. Specimen entries from *School Library Books: non-fiction.*
(By courtesy of the National Book League.)

CHILDREN AND ADULTS

town glimpse adult problems and face some of their own when they become involved in the doings of the criminal Flick Williams and his gang.

169 *Townsend, John Rowe. HELL'S EDGE. *Hutchinson* 1963, 15s. 223 pp.

Amaryllis moves from London to a West Riding town nicknamed 'Hell's Edge'. The story deals in a mature way with the working-out of suspicion and touchiness between the girl and her northern kindred, spicing this with a pleasant and uncommon mystery.

170 ‡Travis, Falcon. GRAND HOWL. *Brockhampton Press* 1965, 8s 6d. 120 pp. Frontis., illus. by Gareth Floyd, diags. by Donald Green.

A Wolf Cub story in which the details of enrolment and badge winning are cleverly interwoven with the amusing antics of Ginger, the new member, who thought he was good and, in fact, was.

171 *Trease, Geoffrey. THE MAYTHORN STORY. *Heinemann* 1960, 15s. vi, 217 pp. Frontis., illus. by Robert Hodgson.

Relationships between young people of different backgrounds are still rarely tackled with any conviction in English children's books. In this exception the friendship of Sandra and Mike creditably survives all hazards.

172 Trevor, Meriol. THE ROSE ROUND. *Hamish Hamilton* 1963, 15s. 176 pp.

Sound sense of values, interesting plot and characters who develop convincingly. These include a crabbed old woman, reconciled to the crippled and clumsy son she despised, and the girl who marries the son.

FIG. 11. Specimen entries from *School Library Fiction: children and adults.*
(By courtesy of the National Book League.)

suggestion of schools in Kent being expected to conform. The example of Kent in this work could well be followed by other local authorities.

Guides to teaching particular subjects are also a useful source for standard lists of books. *The Handbook for Geography Teachers* (5th edn., 1964) is of exceptional value. It was edited by M. Long and published by the University of London Institute of Education. This includes annotated lists for the primary stage, the secondary stage, and for teachers and sixth forms. Geography is considered in its widest sense, and sections are included on map reading, transport, exploration, as well as detailed lists for individual countries, and different branches of geography. Textbooks, information books, and series are included.

A similar volume from the same publisher is *The Handbook for History Teachers* (1962), edited by W. H. Burston and C. W. Green. There are approximately 200 pages of recommended books divided into a wide range of topics. This too is annotated.

Other examples of teaching handbooks with booklists are G. H. Gopsill's *The Teaching of Geography* (3rd edn., 1966) published by Macmillan; and N. F. Newbury's *The Teaching of Chemistry* (3rd edn., 1965) published by Heinemann.

Publishers produce lists especially for schools. A check of current catalogues reveals *Batsford Books for Schools*, *Cambridge Books for School Libraries*, *Nelson's School Books*, and many others. More specific lists cater for different educational grades, such as *Basil Blackwell Secondary Books*, *Macmillan Books for Infant and Junior Schools*. The Oxford University Press goes even further and has subject lists for particular grades, such as *Oxford Music Books* and *Books on Music for Infant and Junior Schools*.

In addition to the general and subject booklists there are also specially prepared reviews of current material.

The School Librarian (1937) is issued quarterly by the School Library Association (Fig. 12). Apart from articles on school libraries and books for children, there is a substantial section devoted to reviews of new books. The reviews are graded: From 16 to Upper Sixth, 11–15, 7–11, and For the Younger Readers. Each review is signed and most of them are detailed and evaluative.

BAILEY, P. C., HOLLAND, D., QUARLES, T. and WAITS, E. *Laboratory guide for an introduction to modern biology.* International Textbook, £2·00. 1970. pp. × 310. Diagrs. SBN 7002 2297 9.

OBVIOUSLY THE PLACE for a book with this title should be on the laboratory bench and not the library shelf. However, this American work contains a good deal of material different from that included in both earlier 'traditional' British syllabuses and the newer sort, and this may limit its laboratory use. There may be a justification for its inclusion in the reference section of a library, both as a demonstration of alternative approaches to a subject, and as a source for students engaged in a range of projects.   H. M. THOMAS

Applied Science

HOGG, GARRY. *The hovercraft story.* Abelard-Schuman, £1·25. 1970. pp. 175 Photogrs. SBN 200 71625 5.

THE HOVERCRAFT has not, of course, escaped the attention of the 'popular' writers and there are now a number of books to choose from, most quite suitable for school use. Garry Hogg is a prolific but competent writer who is concerned to get his facts right and obviously sets himself a high standard. This particular book is valuable because it gives interesting details of early experiments and later developments and a full account of the extended trials recently carried out under desert and arctic conditions. It is well up to date at the time of publication and has many good photographs.   W. ASHWORTH

TAYLOR, JOHN W. R. *Rockets and spacecraft—how they work;* illustrated by John W. Wood & William Hobson. Dent, £1·25. 1971 pp. 94. SBN 460 06417 7.

IT IS INEVITABLE that there should be a spate of books on rocketry and spacecraft with the resultant difficulty of choosing between them. The present one is a revised and expanded version of an earlier book in the same series called *Rockets and Satellites Work Like This.* Its illustrations, all black-and-white and mostly diagrammatic in style, compare unfavourably with the highly-coloured photographic reproductions of many competing books, especially those of American origin, but the price is low for the present day and the text explains principles in an easy-to-understand manner. Rocket weapons and missiles as well as space rocketry are covered and, where money is short, this unusual feature gives the booklet an additional advantage.   W. ASHWORTH

LARSEN, EGON. *Hovercraft and hydrofoils work like this;* illustrated by Charles

FIG. 12. Specimen reviews from *The School Librarian.*
(By courtesy of the School Library Association.)

The Times Educational Supplement, which is issued weekly, includes reviews of books for use in schools. Special sections containing books for particular age groups or individual subjects are sometimes produced. Some of the reviews are blanket in treatment while others deal with single items. Various other educational periodicals such as *The Teacher*, a weekly, include reviews.

Subject periodicals often have reviews related to books in their fields. Among these are *Education in Chemistry* (quarterly), *Geography* (quarterly), *History Today* (monthly), *Physics Education* (quarterly), *School Science Review* (three times yearly), *Teaching Arithmetic* (three times yearly), and *Use of English* (quarterly).

Some local education authorities issue lists of new books for the benefit of teachers in their areas. These are often produced by the County Library which was placed under the control of the education authority in 1919, but that legislation was repealed by the Public Libraries Act of 1964. Many county libraries have now become completely independent of the education committee and one must hope that the separation will not impede the close liaison which has existed for so long. Teachers in Cheshire have been helped by the well-produced termly *School Library Review*; in Staffordshire by *The School Bookshelf*; and in the West Riding of Yorkshire by *The School Library*. Such lists should not be the province of county authorities alone, but would do much to forward public-school library co-operation in the boroughs too.

Increasing interest is being shown in books for backward boys and girls. Books are being planned with the abilities of these children in mind, and some attempt is being made to minimize the failure of the estimated 20 per cent of our children who suffer from reading disability, although normal in other respects.

Books for backward children have particular features. They do not have many words to the page and the illustrations are accompanied by appropriate captions selected from the text. There is a textual stress on repetition which is increased for duller children. The vocabulary is chosen to equate with the reading age of the children but the content is designed to suit their interests. It is important to remember that a child of 12 may have a reading age of 6, but his interests will normally be the same as those of other children of 12. It would be totally unsuitable to provide a story about a toy engine with human characteristics for such a child as the stimulant of an interesting plot would be absent. It is, generally speaking, better for backward children to read easier books than those of their own level of ability rather than books which are too difficult for them. This is particularly so where recreational literature is involved. Difficulties will frustrate and lack of interest may well result. On the other hand, non-fiction can be more difficult because if the child is really interested in finding out a piece of information he will persist until he succeeds.

The important thing is to stimulate interest, and this is more easily accomplished if the child feels he is achieving some success. It is believed that many backward children have suffered from an unsuitable teaching approach. Apart from other undesirable results, continuous failure in school can eventually lead to delinquency. Sir Cyril Burt has suggested that properly organized classes for backward children would catch 70 per cent of incipient criminals.

Therefore, we are not solely concerned with the teaching of reading as an exercise in some academic vacuum, nor as a means of opening the way to the treasures of literature, but are using it in the building of a community in which the members feel they have a positive place, and do not regard themselves as outcasts. Obviously, suitable books will play an important part, and there is an increasing flow from the publishers, as well as guides to its availability.

A First Survey of Books for Backward Readers, compiled by the Bristol University, Institute of Education, and published by the London University Press in 1956, is a most thorough guide to material available for children who have reading difficulty. A supplement was added in 1962. The main schemes of reading, graded series, supplementary readers, are all included, together with books for use in English and other subjects. For each series of readers the interest age and the reading age are given, as well as information regarding vocabulary, contents, method of reading, and notes of the style of covers, size of type, and illustrations. An appendix lists and gives details of

JETS   Various authors   (Jonathan Cape)

BOYS AND GIRLS	pp.	RA	IA	Price
Twelve titles	112–128	8–9	12–18	50p library
				25–30p p/back

Covers   Illustrated and brightly coloured card; rather insecure binding which will not stand up to rough handling.

Printing   Good; clear 12pt. type; some pages rather over-crowded.

Vocabulary   Restricted; very simple sentence structure and uncomplicated style.

Appraisal   This is a series of gay, easy stories intended as leisure reading for teenagers. It should be good bait to attract those pupils in their last years at school who still regard reading as an arduous duty rather than a relaxation. These stories are lively and up-to-date; the characters are mainly young people just starting to learn their first jobs; the plots are concerned with the problems they have to face. Mixed up with the story-telling is a surprising amount of palatably presented common-sense! All-in-all, the mixture is ideal and cannot help but be popular with most youngsters without academic leanings.

Titles include:

Sally of St. Patrick's	Skid Pan
Half-Day Thursday	The Four Aces

ENGLISH PICTURE CLASSICS   Various editors   (Oxford University Press)

BOYS AND GIRLS	pp.	RA	IA	Price
Eleven titles	128	9–10	12–16	18p–25p

Covers   Stiff linson, printed with coloured illustrations.

Printing   Good; clear 10pt. type; excellent page layout.

Illustrations   Black and white sketches by a team of versatile artists with distinctive styles. Eight full-page plates and smaller illustrations on nearly every page. Attractive end-plates introduce the characters in the stories.

Vocabulary   Slightly restricted; glossaries of difficult words at the end of each book. Simplified sentence structure.

Appraisal   These abridged versions of well-known novels are excellent of their type and are popular with older backward readers. The abridging has been skilfully

FIG. 13. Specimen entry from Hart and Richardson's *Books for the Retarded Reader.*
(By courtesy of Ernest Benn Ltd.)

interested organizations. The principal drawback of these volumes is that they are no longer up to date.

A more recent guide in this category is *Books for the Retarded Reader* (1971) (Fig. 13) which was compiled by J. A. Hart and J. A. Richardson and published by Benn. It begins with a chapter on general principles of helping children who have reading difficulties which is followed by information on specially produced series for retarded readers in similar detail to the Bristol surveys. The contents include introductory and supplementary schemes for both younger and older children and fiction and non-fiction to be found in a school library.

The Library Association County Libraries Group prepared *The Reluctant Reader*, the third edition of which appeared in 1969. It includes annotated series of books for use with slow and reluctant readers and series of books to be found on library shelves which include titles suitable for the needs of this group of children.

A similar slight publication is the National Book League *Help in Reading* (Fig. 14) which is revised frequently. The material is selected and annotated by J. C. Daniels and S. S. Segal, and is arranged in two sections: Books for the Teacher and Books for Pupils. The League's *Fiction for the Slow Reader* (1970) is also of value, and is compiled by Audrey M. Sprague.

Alan Pullen's *Words of Persuasion: reference books for retarded readers* was published by Combridge in 1962. It contains over 150 books. Details are given of type, binding, illustrations, and sentence length, with good annotations. The arrangement is based on the Dewey Decimal Classification.

Some local authority library and education departments produce special lists of books for backward readers. Kent Education Committee produces one, as do the Lindsey and Holland and West Riding County Libraries.

In addition may be cited the special publishers' catalogues such as Macmillan *Books for Slow Learners*, and the Oxford University Press *Books for Backward Children*. Many publishers include books for slow learners in their catalogues for school libraries.

GRADED SUPPLEMENTARY READERS

62 Chandler, Edna Walker.
    Cowboy Sam.
    E. J. Arnold, 7s 6d to 8s 6d each.
    Reading age: 6–7   Interest age: 9–11
    Nine graded readers.

63 Clarke, Mollie.
    Looking at Words.
    Hart-Davis, 3s each.
    Reading age: 5½–7   Interest age: 5–9
    A set of twelve graded readers. Books 7–12 also available in
    i.t.a. Also useful for the partially sighted.

64 Hobley, L. F. and Leyden, P. H.
    The Story Path to Reading.
    Blackie.
    Reading age: 8–9   Interest age: 9–13
    Twelve graded readers, 3s 3d to 6s 3d each, plus two textbooks
    of exercises, games and puzzles, 8s 3d.

65 Jones, W. R.
    Step Up and Read Stories.
    University of London Press, 2s to 2s 6d each.
    Reading age: 8   Interest age: 13+

66 Kennett, John.
    Kennett Library.
    Blackie, 5s 6d to 6s 6d each.
    Reading age: 7–13.   Interest age: 10–16
    This is a graded series of classics retold for schools. Examples
    of the classics are: Stevenson's *Kidnapped,* Emily Brontë's
    Wuthering Heights and Dickens' *Oliver Twist.* In all there are
    twenty-six titles in four grades.

67 Kirby, Douglas J.
    Tim's Gang. Books 1–4.
    Hamish Hamilton, 4s 3d each.

FIG. 14. Specimen entries from *Help in Reading.*
(By courtesy of the National Book League.)

The firm of Dunn & Wilson Ltd. issues a stock list of *Supplementary Readers for Backward Children*, which is arranged by publishers. Reading ages and interest ages for which the books have been written are indicated.

Some periodicals include references to books for slow learners. The Guild of Teachers of Backward Children has issued *Forward Trends* since 1957, and the National Association of Remedial Teachers has issued *Remedial Education* since 1966. Both are published quarterly and include articles and book reviews.

The Slow Learning Child is produced by the University of Queensland and appears three times a year. The reviews of backward readers are similar in format and content to those in *The Bristol Survey*, and books shown are usually available in British editions.

Chatto & Windus, the publishers, issue *Use of English* every quarter-year, and some of the reviews are on books for slow learners. Special articles are sometimes included, as, for example, in the autumn issue of 1966, which contained an article and a reading list on "Literature for Backward Readers" by Michael Tucker.

A large body of opinion in this country tends to think of libraries as being depositories only for books and periodicals which they will conserve or utilize depending on their policy. This concept of the function of libraries is outdated. The Public Libraries and Museums Act, 1964, stipulates that facilities in public libraries are made "available for the borrowing of, or reference to, books and other printed matter, and pictures, gramophone records, films and other materials, sufficient in number, range and quality to meet the general requirements and any special requirements both of adults and children".

In the United States a recent development has been the establishment of district materials centres. Progressive opinion regards these as essential if a full programme of instructional materials is to be provided in schools. The use of the word "materials" is deliberate and is intended to include not only books but also other auditory and visual materials. It is envisaged that there should be such a centre in every borough and one in every county region, which would provide a professional library for teachers and librarians, and make available materials for long- or short-term loans to schools. It is an idea which could be well examined more widely in Britain.

There is a growing interest in Britain, at both national and local levels, in the provision of audio-visual materials in schools. Each week in *The Times Educational Supplement* there is a section, which consists of news and views on these increasingly important media.

The Educational Foundation for Visual Aids publishes a catalogue, *Visual Aids, Films and Filmstrips*. It is in eight parts and is revised bi-annually, while each January a supplement is included in the monthly periodical *Visual Education*. This catalogue covers most subjects. For example, Part One deals with Scripture, English, Modern Languages; Part Five and Six with Science; and Part Eight with Art, Domestic Science and Sport. Each part is divided into two categories: teaching material, each item of which includes details of title, type of film or filmstrip, running time, producer, date of production, hiring fee or price, an annotation, and age range; and a list of background material.

VENISS (Visual Education National Information Service for Schools) provides information to its members on all aspects of visual education. It is organized by the National Committee for Audio-Visual Aids in Education and the Educational Foundation for Visual Aids. Members receive EFVA catalogues and all current pamphlets, the monthly *Visual Education*, and all special lists.

A number of organizations produce and distribute films and filmstrips and issue their own catalogues. Among these are Common Ground Filmstrips Ltd. which supplies films on sale only, and Visual Publications which forwards material on approval. Other organizations include specializing bodies such as the British Film Institute, the Central Film Library; government departments, such as the Central Office of Information, the Department of Education and Science; nationalized bodies, such as the Gas Council, the National Coal Board; public and private companies; trade associations; local education authorities; and various professional and other bodies. Sometimes the films and filmstrips are for hire and sometimes for sale.

Guides to the teaching of subjects sometimes list audio-visual materials. *The Handbook for History Teachers* by W. H. Burston and C. W. Green (1962) contains a 70-page section on illustrations, films, wall charts, wall maps, and each entry is annotated. Visual aids are listed in G. H. Gopsill's *The Teaching of Geography* (3rd edn., 1966).

Subject periodicals are often a useful source of information for these materials. *Education in Chemistry* includes films; *School Science Review* reviews filmstrips; and *Use of English* films and records.

It will be an exciting experience for all concerned with education in the next few decades to participate in not only the increased use of books in schools, but also that of many other media of the written and spoken word. The opportunities for such a dynamic programme are becoming available, but it rests with enthusiastic and informed individuals to exploit them.

CHAPTER 6

Guidance from Histories and Criticisms of Children's Literature

THE present chapter is divided according to the different varieties of history and criticism, both general and specific, and the relevant works are evaluated. Before embarking on a survey of material one very useful but slim work must be mentioned. This is the booklist prepared by the Committee of the Youth Libraries Group of the Library Association, edited by Marcus Crouch. Its title is *Books About Children's Literature* and it was first published in 1963. A second edition was issued in 1966 (Fig. 15).

It is based on the H. J. B. Woodfield Collection, items from which are indicated with an asterisk, and briefly lists "the principal books which are reasonably accessible in this country". The sections consist of lists of books on the history of children's literature, criticism and bibliography, illustration, authorship, periodicals, and biography Almost 200 items out of approximately 350 fall into the latter category. Inclusion of a title in this list does not imply that it has won the unqualified approval of the Youth Libraries Group, and as the brief annotations are descriptive rather than evaluative, it is impossible for the layman to distinguish the outstanding from the mediocre.

The Library Association list compares badly with two American publications. In 1966 the Library of Congress published *Children's Literature: a guide to reference sources* (Fig. 16). This is an illustrated study of over 1000 items compiled under the direction of Virginia Haviland, head of the Children's Book Section of the Library of Congress. Sections are included on history and criticism, authorship, illustration, bibliography, the library and children's books, and

History of Children's Literature

ANDREWS, Siri, *ed.*
The Hewins lectures, 1947–62.   1963.   Boston, Horn Book.
Lectures on aspects of American children's books.

ASHTON, John.
*Chap books of the eighteenth century, with facsimiles, notes and introduction. 1882.   Chatto & Windus.

AVERY, Gillian, with Angela Bull.
Nineteenth century children: heroes and heroines in English children's stories, 1780–1900.   1965.   Hodder & Stoughton.

BARRY, Florence V.
A century of children's books.   1922.   Methuen.
Contains a chronological list, 1700–1825.

BLANCK, Jacob.
Peter Parley to Penrod: a bibliographical description of the best-loved American juvenile books (1827–1929).   1938.   New York, Bowker.

CROUCH, Marcus.
Treasure seekers and borrowers: children's books in Britain, 1900–1960.   1962. Library Association.

DARTON, F. J. Harvey.
*Children's books in England: five centuries of social life.   1932.   Second edition, 1958.   Cambridge University Press.
An authoritative and scholarly history of the development of children's literature, viewed against the social history of the times. Each chapter has detailed bibliographies. The second edition is edited by Kathleen Lines.

—Children's books—in Cambridge history of English literature, Volume XI, Chapter 16.   1914.   Cambridge University Press.

DE VRIES, Leonard.
Flowers of delight . . . from the Osborne collection of early children's books. 1965.   Dennis Dobson.

ENGLISH CHILDREN'S BOOKS, 1563–1900: an exhibition.   1960.   Times Bookshop.

EYRE, Frank.
Twentieth century children's books.   1952.   Longmans (for the British

FIG. 15. Specimen entries from *Books About Children's Literature*.
(By courtesy of the Library Association and Marcus Crouch.)

327 Swinnerton, Frank A. R. L. STEVENSON, A CRITICAL STUDY. New York, M. Kennerley, 1915. 215 p. PR5496.S8

The first, biographical, chapter emphasizes the influence of storytelling and reading aloud by Stevenson's nurse on his sense of style, and of her strict Covenanting religious principles on the development of his mind and outlook. The following chapters critically evaluate his writings, treating them by type: essays, poems, plays, short stories, novels, and romances. Swinnerton concludes with generalizations on his strengths ("Stevenson deserves praise for most admirable clarity . . . apt phrases are as common with Stevenson as leaves on a tree") and shortcomings (lack of depth, of true emotion). A bibliography is included (p. 213–216).

Stockton, Frank R. (1834–1902)

328 Griffin, Martin I. J. FRANK R. STOCKTON; A CRITICAL BIOGRAPHY. Philadelphia, University of Pennsylvania Press; London, H. Milford: Oxford University Press, 1939. 178 p. PS2928.G7 1939

A chronological treatment of Stockton's life as represented in his work. It discusses Stockton's association with the great illustrators of the day who contributed their work to his books. Synopses and many quotations from his stories and novels are included in the latter part of the study. He contributed an extensive series of travel papers, "Personally Conducted," to *St. Nicholas* and reviewed children's books for *Scribner's Monthly.* A bibliography is included (p. 149–173).

Streatfeild, Noel

329 Wilson, Barbara K. NOEL STREATFEILD. New York, Walck, 1964. 63 p. (A Walck monograph) PR6037.T77Z9 1964

FIG. 16. Specimen entries from Virginia Haviland's *Children's Literature: a guide to reference sources.* (By courtesy of the Library of Congress.)

Smith, L. H. The unreluctant years: a critical approach to children's literature. Chicago 1953.
Meigs, C. et al. A critical history of children's literature. New York 1953.
Hürlimann, B. Europäische Kinderbücher in drei Jahrhunderten. Zürich 1959, 1963 (rev); tr Oxford 1967.
Ford, B. (ed). Young writers, young readers. 1960. Articles by various authors from Jnl of Education, etc.
Fisher, M. Intent upon reading. Leicester 1961, 1964 (rev).

—— Growing point. Northampto
Crouch, M. Treasure seekers an
Thwaite, M. F. From primer to p
in England to 1900. 1963.
Avery, G. and A. Bull. Ninet
1965.
De Vries, L. (ed). Flowers of de:
Ellis, A. How to find out abo
Oxford 1966; 1968 (rev).

(2) PRINCIPAL WRITERS

Edgeworth, Maria (1767-1849). The parent's assistant: or stories for children. 3 vols 1795.
—— [Early lessons] Harry and Lucy part 1. 1801 etc.
—— Moral tales for young people. 5 vols 1801. For full bibliography see col 665, above.
Taylor, Isaac ('of Ongar') (1759-1829). Scenes in Europe. 1819.
—— Bunyan explained to a child. 2 pts 1824, 1825.
—— The biography of a brown loaf. 1829.
—— The ship. 1830.
Taylor, Ann, neé Martin (1757-1830). The family mansion: a tale. 1819.
Taylor, Ann (neé Martin), and Jane. Correspondence between a mother and her daughter at school. 1817.
Taylor, Ann, afterwards Gilbert (1782-1866). The wedding among the flowers. 1808.
For Ann Taylor see Autobiography and other memorials of Mrs Gilbert ed J. Gilbert 2 vols 1874.
Taylor, Jane (1783-1824). Display: a tale for young people. 1815.
—— Contributions of Q. Q. 2 vols 1824.
For Jane Taylor see Memoirs and poetical remains, with extracts from correspondence, ed I. Taylor 2 vols 1825; Mrs. H. C. Knight, Jane Taylor: her life and letters, 1880; L. B. Walford, Four biographies from Blackwood, 1888.
Taylor, Ann, afterwards Gilbert, and Jane. Original poems for infant minds, by several young persons [i.e. Ann and Jane Taylor, Isaac Taylor their father, Isaac Taylor their brother, Bernard Barton, and Adelaide O'Keeffe (see below)]. 2 vols 1804-5, 1875 (complete edn finally rev Mrs Gilbert); ed E. V. Lucas [1903] with Rhymes for the nursery etc. Many selections under various titles, e.g. Little Ann and other poems, illustr Kate Greenaway [1883]; Meddlesome Mattie and other

The butterfly's ball produced 1
those by Mrs Dorset, such as
W.B., 1807; The lion's parliam:
breakfast, 1808; The horse's '
grand gala by Mrs Cockle, 180&
Samuel James Arnold (1774-1:
1808; The feast of the fishes b:
The ape's concert by 'A. Tabb'
dogs, 1808; The wedding am(
Taylor, 1808; The lobster's vo;
rose by B. Hoole, Mrs Hoflar
Tuer, Pages and pictures fr(
books, 1898-9.
Turner, Elizabeth (d. 1846). The d:
in verse, adapted to the ideas (
eight years old. 1806; ed C. W
—— The cowslip. 1811; ed C. W
—— The pink. 1811; ed M. How
—— The crocus. [c. 1820?].
—— The rose. nd.
—— The blue-bell: or tales and f:
—— Short poems for young childr(
Selections are Mrs Turner'
E. V. Lucas 1897; Gr
rhymes, ed G. K. Chester
by her and other nineteer
see The book of verse
Green 1962.
Hofland, Mrs, née Wreaks (1770-,
1812.
—— Adelaide: or the massacr(
1822.
—— The young Crusoe. 1828.
See col 733, above.
Lamb, Charles (1775-1834). T

FIG. 17. Specimen entries from *The Cambridge Bibliography of English Literature*, Vol. III. (By courtesy of the Cambridge University Press.)

international and national studies. There is an index of authors, titles, and subjects. In 1968 R. R. Bowker published *The World of Children's Literature* which is edited by Anne Pellowski. It is a bibliography of 4500 items representative of the development of children's literature and libraries in 106 countries. Full descriptions, useful annotations, and an exhaustive index are provided. The arrangement is in broad geographical groupings subdivided by countries, and the publications of each country are arranged alphabetically by authors.

The Cambridge Bibliography of English Literature, edited by F. W. Bateson, is also useful in a search for material relating to children's literature. It was published in four volumes (the last being an index) in 1940, and, in a chronological sequence subdivided by periods and forms, covers literature and criticisms related to the years 600 to 1900. A supplement was issued in 1957. In Volume I school and textbooks are listed (on pp. 374–7); in Volume II chapbooks and children's books (p. 105), school and textbooks (pp. 125–30), and children's books (pp. 553–6); in Volume III texts and criticisms of school and children's books (pp. 135–6). Material in the Supplement is to be found on pp. 455 and 649. In addition the works of particular authors are found with their criticisms in the sections devoted to the individuals. A new edition is in process of compilation by George Watson, of which Volume III (1800–1900) was published in 1969 (Fig. 17) and Volume II (1660–1800) in 1971.

In the following survey, an attempt has been made to be selective although the exclusion of a particular work should not be taken to mean that it has been censored. A number of books which were useful when published are now so out of date as to present a snare to the student and the general reader.

HISTORIES

ADAMS, BESS PORTER. *About Books and Children: a historical survey of children's literature.* New York, Henry Holt. 1953.
"This is a book about children, their schools, and their books" and is designed "to give parents, teachers, and their friends a quickened

appreciation of the world in which children spend many of their waking hours."

Appendices list Newbery and Caldecott Medals with brief annotations, books about children and their books, and graded lists of books ranging from those for the youngest through to adolescence.

AVERY, GILLIAN. *Nineteenth Century Children: heroes and heroines in English children's stories, 1780–1900*. Hodder & Stoughton. 1965.
Surveys the attitudes of writers to their readers, the changing nature of children in fiction, and adult standards of good behaviour in the young. The author has devoted a high proportion of her book to earlier material, and an appendix contains over 120 very helpful biographical references. Sixteen representative illustrations are included which add to the value of the work.

DARTON, F. J. HARVEY. *Children's Books in England: five centuries of social life*. Cambridge U.P. 1932. 2nd edn., 1958.
This is *the* major work on the history of children's books and relates the books of each age to the contemporary educational and social ideas. It includes bibliographical and commercial details. No attempt has been made to deal with aesthetic merit and it is a clear-cut survey of the historical struggle between amusement and instruction in literature for children.

The treatment is chronological and Darton refers only to material he has actually seen. Where he has not seen a first edition he admits as much. The chief works are listed at the ends of the appropriate chapters.

It is a scholarly work and has lost none of its original authoritative qualities in the second edition by Kathleen Lines, with its separate list of books published since 1932 and the supplement to the chapter bibliographies.

DOUGLAS, ALISON. *The Scottish Contribution to Children's Literature*. Library Review. 1966.
An instructive survey of Scottish authors of children's books based on articles which appeared originally in *The Library Review*.

ELLIS, ALEC. *A History of Children's Reading and Literature.* Pergamon Press. 1968.
Discusses the educational and literary factors which have assisted or hindered the growth of working-class literacy in England and Wales from the nineteenth century to the present decade. The factors considered include educational provision, the use of books in schools, the availability of school and public libraries, and the evolution of recreational literature of all kinds.

GREEN, ROGER LANCELYN. *Tellers of Tales: children's books and their authors from 1800 to 1968.* Kaye and Ward. 1946. New edn., 1969.
The first edition was written for young readers, but the new one is directed towards an adult audience and includes more writers than the original work. Particular authors are used as centres of interest and the stress is on the period prior to 1930. No American or foreign authors are included.
Good bibliographical notes on the dates of editions from 1800 to 1964 are given, together with lists of books under the names of their authors, and lists of medal winners.
In all, it is a popular and very readable book and is especially useful to the interested parent who wishes to help his children to find good literature.

HÜRLIMANN, BETTINA. *Three Centuries of Children's Books in Europe.* Oxford U.P. 1967.
An extensive and readable survey of European literature for children, originally published in 1959 by Atlantis of Zurich. Translated from the German and edited by Brian Alderson.
This book includes chapters on fairy tales, fantasy, Robinsonnades, and other adventure stories, school books, and illustration. Hans Andersen, Heinrich Hoffmann, Antoine de Saint-Exupéry, and Jean de Brunhoff are considered in separate chapters, as is the development of children's literature in Switzerland. Particularly useful is the bibliography compiled by the editor and the explanatory notes which appear throughout the book.

KIEFER, MONICA. *American Children Through Their Books, 1700–1835.* University of Pennsylvania Press. 1948.
A picture of "the book-diet of those long-ago children" and "a glimpse of the psychological pressures put upon them". A full fourteen-page bibliography is appended on various aspects of the subject.

MEIGS, CORNELIA, and others. *A Critical History of Children's Literature: a survey.* . . . New York, Macmillan. 1969.
A book with a strong American bias, but useful in showing the early common development of English and American literature, and the interesting comparisons of the two literatures.
It is in four parts: Roots in the Past up to 1840; Widening Horizons 1840–90; Rightful Heritage 1890–1920; and The Golden Age, 1920–1967.
In its nostalgic and sentimental treatment of childhood it may irritate many readers, but this should not be allowed to obstruct the historical message of the book.

MEIGS, CORNELIA. *Louisa M. Alcott and the American Family Story.* Bodley Head. 1970.
Mainly devoted to Louisa M. Alcott followed by a brief factual survey of the family story. The omission of such writers as Elizabeth Wetherell, Martha Finley, and numerous other contributors to the *genre* detracts from the value of this volume. An index would have been useful.

MUIR, PERCY. *English Children's Books, 1600 to 1900.* Batsford. 1954.
The author has paid tribute to the influence on his work of Harvey Darton. This book is not as exhaustive as Darton and the author differs further in that he approached his task from the angle of the book collector. The text is compiled around checklists. A good chapter is included on *The Importance of Pictures.* Well illustrated and produced in the manner one expects from Batsford.

TARG, WILLIAM (ed.). *Bibliophile in the Nursery: a bookman's treasury of collectors' lore on old and rare children's books.* Cleveland, World Publishing Co. 1957.

Contributions from the work of a number of authorities including Paul Hazard, F. J. Harvey Darton, Iona and Peter Opie, Frederic Melcher, and many others, mainly from the United States.

The absence of an index is a serious defect and limits the value of a very interesting book.

THWAITE, M. F. *From Primer to Pleasure: an introduction to the history of children's books in England from the invention of printing to 1900.* Library Association. 1963.

Mrs. Thwaite's book is a full and useful contribution to the selection of works dealing with the history of children's literature.

It is intended to be an introduction to more scholarly and detailed histories, as, for example, Harvey Darton's work. The author had in mind the needs of public and school librarians, although in readability she makes a far wider appeal. There is a helpful chapter on children's books abroad in the period under review, which rather conflicts with the coverage as shown in the title.

Appendices list books advertised by John Newbery in the third edition of *Goody Two-Shoes*, 1766; a chronological table, 1479–1800; and a seventeen-page bibliography in classified order.

TOWNSEND, JOHN ROWE. *Written for Children: an outline of English children's literature.* Garnet Miller. 1965.

A history of English children's fiction for the general reader. Excludes picture books and poetry. Mr. Townsend is more concerned with highlights than presenting a detailed survey, which ensures the readability of his book but presents snares to the student.

SURVEYS OF TWENTIETH-CENTURY LITERATURE

CROUCH, MARCUS. *Treasure Seekers and Borrowers: children's books in Britain, 1900–1960.* Library Association. 1962. Amended 1970.

This book is complementary to Mrs. M. F. Thwaite's *From Primer to Pleasure*, and with it presents a history of children's literature from the earliest times to the beginning of the present decade.

Mr. Crouch is one of the leading authorities on children's books of the twentieth century. The narrative is presented in a chronological sequence which includes some passing references to the social background.

EGOFF, SHEILA. *The Republic of Childhood: a critical guide to Canadian children's literature in English.* Oxford U.P. 1967.
A survey of outstanding Canadian children's books in commemoration of Canada's centennial year. Although a chapter is devoted to Indian legends and early children's books, most of this volume is concerned with material issued between 1950 and 1965. Categories of children's books are dealt with, and each chapter is followed by reading lists with evaluative annotations.

ELLIS, ANNE W. *The Family Story in the 1960s.* Clive Bingley. 1970.
The historical development of the family story is traced and the treatment analysed of relationships, everyday life, and problems encountered by children in the 1960's. The author reveals the contrast between family life and its portrayal in children's books. Useful lists are appended of sources of information and family stories.

EYRE, FRANK. *British Children's Books in the Twentieth Century.* Longmans. 1971.
A revised and enlarged edition of a book published for the British Council in 1952. It is concerned principally with original work by British writers and illustrators, but a section is also included which deals with books either set in or written by authors from Australia, Canada, New Zealand, and South Africa. Trends are examined and outstanding examples provided.

FISHER, MARGERY. *Intent Upon Reading: a critical appraisal of modern fiction for children.* Brockhampton. 1961. Rev. edn., 1964. (Fig. 18).
Margery Fisher is recognized by many as the leading commentator on current literature for children and her *Intent Upon Reading* has become a much-valued publication.
The arrangement is by topics such as Pictures in the Nursery Fire, Magic Carpets, Good Chaps and Bad Chaps, and other phrases obscure to all but the initiated. So much is covered that inevitably

TRAVELLERS IN TIME   131

*Nesbit, E. THE STORY OF THE AMULET (1906) 1957, FIVE CHILDREN AND IT
(1902) 1957, illustrated by H. R. Millar. THE HOUSE OF ARDEN (1908)
1949, HARDING'S LUCK (1903) 1949, illustrated by Desmond Walduck.
Benn.

Pardoe, M. ARGLE'S MIST 1956, ARGLE'S CAUSEWAY 1958, ARGLE'S ORACLE
1959. *Routledge.* Illustrated by Audrey Fawley. Three children and a schoolmaster mysteriously visit Britain in the time of Cymbeline, Hampshire in the
twelfth century, and Greece at the time of Alcibiades and Socrates.

*Pearce, A. Philippa. TOM'S MIDNIGHT GARDEN. *O.U.P.* 1958. Illustrated by
Susan Einzig.

Sauer, Julia. FOG MAGIC. *Viking,* New York 1943. Illustrated by Lynd Ward.
Girl in Novia Scotia joins life of village of long ago, now lost; a beautiful
and impressive story.

Severn, David. THE FUTURE TOOK US. *Bodley Head* 1958. Illustrated by Jillian
Richards. Two schoolboys go forward to Kent and London in 3,000 A.D.

Severn, David. DREAM GOLD. *Bodley Head* 1949. Illustrated by A. K. Lee. Two
schoolboys in Cornwall follow in dream an ancient adventure of pirates and
treasure.

Severn, David. DRUM-BEATS! *Bodley Head* 1953. Illustrated by Richard
Kennedy. Children in co-educational boarding school see into Africa and the
fate of an expedition lost years before.

*Streatfeild, Noel. THE FEARLESS TREASURE. *Michael Joseph* 1953. Illustrated
by Dorothy Braby.

*Strong, L. A. G. THE FIFTH OF NOVEMBER. *Dent* (King's Treasuries of Literature Series) (1937) 1940. Illustrated by Jack Matthew.

*Trevor, Meriol. SUN SLOWER, SUN FASTER 1955, illustrated by Edward
Ardizzone. THE OTHER SIDE OF THE MOON 1956, illustrated by Martin
Thomas. *Collins.*

*Uttley, Alison. A TRAVELLER IN TIME. *Faber* 1939. Illustrated by Phyllis
Bray.

Wallace, Kathleen. THE PRIZE ESSAY. *Heinemann* 1953. Illustrated by Richard
Kennedy. Mature story for girls of fourteen and over. Two schoolgirls
begin to see and talk to the Brontës, while studying their lives and work.
Very moving and done with masterly tact.

*Welch, Ronald. THE GAUNTLET. *O.U.P.* 1951. Illustrated by Terence Freeman.

FIG. 18. Specimen reading list from Margery Fisher's *Intent Upon
Reading*.
(By courtesy of the Brockhampton Press.)

at times this work is little more than booklists. It must be stressed, however, that there is such a flood of children's books available that it is difficult to visualize anyone improving upon Mrs. Fisher's book. She has produced a very comprehensive critical survey with numerous helpful extracts from the material under discussion. At the end of each chapter are classified reading lists of both children's books referred to in the text and other suggestions for further reading.

In the 1964 edition two additional chapters have been included on Realism and Reality, and Standards and Achievements 1961–64.

LOCK, MURIEL, and others. *Reference Material for Young People*. Clive Bingley. 1967. 2nd edn., 1971.

Surveys a large selection of reference and other information books, periodicals, and audio-visual materials. The contents are not confined to children's books, but include standard and bibliographical works. Publishers and dates are given, and there is an exhaustive index of almost 150 pages.

RAY, SHEILA G. *Children's Fiction: a handbook for librarians*. Brockhampton. 1970. 2nd edn., 1972.

A useful handbook to current fiction, intended primarily for students of librarianship and other librarians who are not conversant with children's books. The chapters are mainly by categories of fiction but some deal with books for special groups of readers including backward children, immigrants, and teenagers; and one is concerned with the publishing aspects of children's literature. List for further reading are appended to each chapter and there is a detailed index.

ESSAYS AND CRITICISMS

ANDREWS, SIRI (ed.). *The Hewins Lectures, 1947–1962*. Boston, Horn Book Inc. 1963.

Texts of the annual lectures in memory of Caroline M. Hewins, presented to either the New England Library Association or to the

Massachusetts Library Association on aspects of writing for children. Contributors include Alice M. Jordan, Virginia Haviland, Elinor Whitney Field, Bertha Mahony Miller, Ruth Hill Viguers, and Margaret Lane. Among the variety of topics dealt with are From Rollo to Tom Sawyer, Jacob Abbott, The American Sunday School Movement, Susan Coolidge, Authors Who Began in St. Nicholas, The Folklore of New England, and Rachel Field. Biographies of the lecturers and extensive bibliographies are appended.

BECHTEL, LOUISE SEAMAN. *Books in Search of Children: speeches and essays*. Hamish Hamilton. 1970.
A collection of essays and speeches selected and introduced by Virginia Haviland. Various topics relating to American children's literature are treated, including such individual authors as Elizabeth Coatsworth and Padraic Colum.

CARLSEN, G. ROBERT. *Books and the Teen-age Reader: a guide for teachers, librarians, and parents*. Harper & Row. 1967. 2nd edn., 1971.
Includes chapters followed by reading lists on the psychological development of the teenager, books written for and adopted by teenagers, classics, poetry, and non-fiction. Much of the material discussed is of British origin, but the absence of an index is unfortunate.

CASS, JOAN E. *Literature and the Young Child*. Longmans. 1967.
A guide to suitable books for children aged 2–8. Chapters are included on picture books and their illustrations, fantasy stories, poetry, and storytelling and its techniques. Four stories are retold and lists of picture story and poetry books are given.

CHAMBERS, AIDAN. *The Reluctant Reader*. Pergamon. 1969.
An enthusiastic appraisal of the kind of literature likely to appeal to the majority of teenagers, and the responsiblity of publishers, librarians, and teachers to ensure its accessibility. An index would have been useful.

COOK, ELIZABETH. *The Ordinary and the Fabulous: an introduction to myths, legends and fairytales for teachers and storytellers*. Cambridge U.P. 1969.

An interpretation of the well-known legends and fairy tales with suggestions how they can best be told to children. An annotated list of books is an additional guide to the availability of material.

FENWICK, SARA INNIS (ed.). *A Critical Approach to Children's Literature*. Chicago U.P. 1967.

A series of papers delivered at the 1966 annual conference of the Graduate Library School at Chicago. Topics include children's reading and adult values, social values, and machine animism in children's literature.

FORD, BORIS (ed.). *Young Writers, Young Readers: an anthology of children's reading and writing*. Hutchinson. 1960. Rev. edn., 1963.

A collection of essays originally published in *Journal of Education* on children's literature by experts including James Britton, Janice Dohm, David Holbrook, and James Reeves. Topics include Enid Blyton, Walter de la Mare, W. E. Johns, and Robert Louis Stevenson.

HAZARD, PAUL. *Books, Children and Men*. Boston, Horn Book Inc. 1944.

A translation from the French by Marguerite Mitchell in extremely poetic language.

It is divided into broad groupings in many of which Hazard has advanced original ideas: Men Have Always Oppressed Children (Instruction), Children Have Defended Themselves (Adoption of adult literature), Superiority of the North Over the South, National Traits, and The Soul of Man.

There is a short bibliography which includes numerous foreign histories and criticisms.

HILDICK, WALLACE. *Children and Fiction: a critical study in depth of the artistic and psychological factors involved in writing fiction for and about children*. Evans Brothers. 1970.

This book crystallizes the author's wide experience as a writer and teacher. He compares the approach and style of a variety of writers and suggests means of relating fiction to the developmental needs of young people. One of four appendices consists of notes on the editing of British and American English in children's books.

THE HORN BOOK. *A "Horn Book" Sampler on Children's Books and Reading*, edited by Norma R. Fryatt. Boston, Horn Book Inc. 1959.
A series of essays, both historical and critical, originally published in *The Horn Book Magazine* between its inception in 1924 and 1948. Subjects chosen include Eleanor Farjeon, Wanda Gág, Arthur Rackham, and Beatrix Potter. The articles contain a good deal which would not usually be found in more general criticisms.

MOORE, ANNE CARROLL. *My Roads to Childhood: views and reviews of children's books*. Boston, Horn Book Inc. 1961.
The contents of this were first published separately in the 1920's and brought up to date in 1939. While the content is mainly American, references are made to the important British publications.
Selected lists of books for various age groups are included as well as a representative list of books published between 1926 and 1938.

SMITH, JAMES STEEL. *A Critical Approach to Children's Literature*. McGraw-Hill. 1967.
A study primarily of the literary values of children's books. Covers various categories of fiction, adult books used by children, poetry, non-fiction, classics, illustrations, and the importance of television. Appropriate books, mainly American, are listed at the ends of chapters. A stimulating and challenging book.

SMITH, LILLIAN H. *The Unreluctant Years: a critical approach to children's literature*. American Library Association. 1953.
Lillian H. Smith served for 40 years in the children's work of the Toronto Public Library, and in her book drew on her wide experience in examining the principles involved in the selection of books for the young.
It is not an exhaustive guide but sets out to justify children's literature, to show its historical development. Individual types of book are considered: The Fairy Tale, Myths and Legends, Poetry, Picture Books, Stories of Fantasy, and Historical Fiction.

TREASE, GEOFFREY. *Tales Out of School*. Heinemann. 1948. 2nd edn., 1964.

A readable survey of children's recreational literature with such fanciful chapter headings as The Comic and the Blood, Cloak and Sword, Midnight in the Dorm, The Family in Fiction.

In the first edition Geoffrey Trease campaigned for better standards of writing for children: "Every time a glossy oblong of trash is rejected with due contempt, a blow has been struck in the fight for better children's fiction".

The second edition shows how the situation has improved since those immediate post-war years, but omits to tell in all modesty of the great influence of Trease himself in the change.

VIGUERS, RUTH HILL. *Margin for Surprise: about books, children, and librarians.* Longman. 1966.

A collection of essays by an editor of *The Horn Book Magazine* in which are considered the criticism, sources and development of children's literature. As a children's librarian, Mrs. Viguers expresses her views on school and public library work with children and gives particular attention to the origins and importance of storytelling, and the reading needs of adolescence. This is an outstanding book.

WHITE, DOROTHY NEAL. *About Books for Children.* Oxford U.P. 1949.

Discusses the main types of books such as Picture Books, Fairy Tales, Realistic Stories in historical and contemporary settings; and various categories of non-fiction, including Social Studies, Arts and Crafts, and Science. Chapters on Poetry, Plays, Periodicals, and Encyclopaedias are also included. Collections of myths and legends, and longer plays for children are listed in appendices.

WILLIAMS, GLADYS. *Children and Their Books.* Duckworth. 1970.

A guide for parents to the uses of children's books at different stages of development, and the sources from which information may be obtained. Suggested titles are listed in an appendix. No index.

ILLUSTRATION

MAHONY, BERTHA E., and others (eds.). *Illustrators of Children's Books, 1744–1945*. Boston, Horn Book Inc. 1947.
A scholarly survey followed by bibliographies and biographical sketches. Prolifically illustrated in black and white. International scope. This book was supplemented by

VIGUERS, RUTH HILL, and others (eds.). *Illustrators of Children's Books, 1946–1956*. 1958.

KINGMAN, LEE, and others (eds.). *Illustrators of Children's Books, 1957–1966*. 1968.
This latter book does not maintain the standards of the earlier volumes but is still very useful.

HÜRLIMANN, BETTINA. *Picture Book World*. Oxford U.P. 1968.
A sequel to the author's *Three Centuries of Children's Books in Europe* in which she discusses modern picture books from twenty-two countries. First published by Atlantis Verlag, Zurich, in 1965, and edited and translated by Brian Alderson. It is unfortunate that very few of the illustrations have been reproduced in colour and that they are not printed alongside the relevant text. A useful bio-bibliographical supplement is included.

MORRIS, CHARLES H. *The Illustration of Children's Books*. Library Association. 1957.
A Library Association pamphlet dealing with the history of children's book illustration from the days of John Newbery to the mid-twentieth century. A section is included on the kind of pictures which appeal to children followed by a select bibliography.
Mr. Morris was engaged on a more exhaustive work, but unfortunately died before he was able to complete it. This is a serious gap in the history and criticism of children's literature.

RYDER, JOHN. *Artists of a Certain Line: a selection of illustrators for children's books*. Bodley Head. 1960.
Includes a historical introduction followed by notes on modern illustrators with examples of their work. Approximately forty

illustrators are included, for example, Edward Ardizzone, Susan Einzig, Peggy Fortnum, Charles Keeping, and William Stobbs.

SMITH, JANET ADAM. *Children's Illustrated Books*. Collins. 1947.
One of the Collins series of *Britain in Pictures*. It treats the subject from the chapbooks to the twentieth century, and includes a number of representative illustrations, some of them in colour. A useful but slim volume.

AWARDS

International

INTERNATIONAL YOUTH LIBRARY. *Children's Prize Books*. Verlag Dokumentation. 1969.
Offers information on the history and purpose of awards given for children's books in twenty-four countries and also international prizes.

Britain

LIBRARY ASSOCIATION. *Chosen for Children: an account of the books which have been awarded the Library Association Carnegie Medal, 1936–1965*. Library Association. 1967.
This volume brings up to date the original edition which was published in 1957, and has been compiled once more by Marcus Crouch. Descriptions of each book are followed by brief quotations and personal notes usually written by the authors themselves. Line drawings from the books and photographs of the authors are included. It is regrettable that the brief biographical sketches of the 1957 edition have been omitted.
Supplementary information on Carnegie Medals can be found in the May or June issue of the *Library Association Record*.

United States

MILLER, BERTHA MAHONY and FIELD, ELINOR W., eds. *Newbery Medal Books, 1922–1955*. Boston, Horn Book Inc. 1955.

A reprint of articles first published in *The Horn Book Magazine* together with speeches made by successful authors.

The same editors produced a similar volume entitled *Caldecott Medal Books, 1938–1957*, also published by Horn Book Inc. in 1957. The first date corresponds with the year in which the Medal was awarded and not that in which the books were published. In the present survey the dates of publication are used rather than the date the award was made.

KINGMAN, LEE (ed.). *Newbery and Caldecott Medal Books, 1956–1965.* Boston, Horn Book Inc. 1965.

Contains acceptance papers, biographies of authors and illustrators, and excerpts from books. Examples are included in black and white of illustrations from Caldecott winners and also an interesting survey of *Picture Books Today* by Norma R. Fryatt. Complete lists of Medal winners and runners-up are appended.

SMITH, IRENE. *A History of the Newbery and Caldecott Medals.* New York, Viking Press. 1957.

A study of the development, processes of selection, scope and influence of the Newbery and Caldecott Medals from their inception in 1922 and 1938, to 1957 and 1956, respectively.

Appendices list Newbery and Caldecott winners and runners-up.

LITERATURE IN SCHOOLS: HISTORY

Britain

ELLIS, ALEC. *Books in Victorian Elementary Schools.* Library Association. 1971.

A Library Association pamphlet which surveys the availability and use of books in elementary schools in England and Wales during the Victorian period. Appendices show what reading standards were expected of the children and the extent to which they were successful in the reading examination.

CHANCELLOR, V. E. *History for Their Masters: opinion in the English history text-book, 1800–1914.* Adams & Dart. 1970.

United States

CARPENTER, CHARLES. *History of American Schoolbooks.* Pennsylvania U.P. 1963.
Discusses the early New England primers as well as other types of primers, readers, literary texts, and histories. Based on sources in the Library of Congress and the New York Public Library. A chapter is included on the development of school book publishing followed by a bibliography of more than one hundred items.

ELSON, RUTH MILLER. *Guardians of Tradition: American School Books of the nineteenth century.* Nebraska U.P. 1964.
A study based on more than 1000 of the most popular text-books. It shows how school books so often fail to reflect accurately the world as it really is, and predispose children to certain distorted opinions which they grow up believing to be the truth. The content of such books is discussed as regards their treatment of God and Nature, The Nature of Man, Social Experience, and other matters. A bibliography of the textbooks which have been used is given in particular groupings: Readers, Spellers, Geographies, Histories, Arithmetics. Within each group the books are arranged chronologically.

JOHNSON, CLIFTON. *Old-time Schools and School-books.* New York, Dover Publications. 1963.
An unaltered publication of a work first published in 1904 by the Macmillan Company. The new Dover edition is in paperback form, and has a well-written introduction by Carl Withers. This book is concerned with the educational history of Massachusetts, a State which was noted for its pioneering work in education. The chapters deal with Spellers, Readers, Arithmetics, Geographies, and Histories. A number of poor reproductions from old school books are included.

LITERATURE IN SCHOOLS: PRESENT DAY

HUCK, CHARLOTTE S. and KUHN, DORIS Y. *Children's Literature in the Elementary School*. New York, Holt, Rinehart & Winston. 1961. 2nd edn., 1968.

Not entirely a history and criticism of children's literature but considers book selection related to child development, and has a detailed coverage of American books both fiction and non-fiction. The second edition includes an additional chapter on the teaching of literature.

Appendices list children's book awards, including the Newbery and Caldecott Medals, together with other less well known ones available in an award-conscious country. The awards of other countries besides the United States are also listed with brief descriptions of their intention. Other appendices list aids to book selection and publishers of children's books in the United States.

KAMM, ANTONY and TAYLOR, BOSWELL. *Books and the Teacher*. London U.P. 1966. 2nd edn., 1968.

Probably the most useful guide for teachers in existence on the subject of books in schools. A wide range of topics includes the use of books by teachers, the encouragement of pupils in the use of books, institutions, bibliographies and reviews from which guidance may be obtained and criteria for the selection of the material. A helpful reference section includes lists of books for various purposes, book clubs, educational publishers, and other interesting information.

LARRICK, NANCY. *A Teacher's Guide to Children's Books*. Columbus, Ohio, Merrill. 1960.

Dr. Larrick has divided her subject into four sections: the first deals with the kinds of books read in each grade of school, the second suggests ways of arousing interest in good literature, the third tells how classroom reading activities may be evaluated, and the fourth gives lists of books in title order for use by children and teachers, and consists of approximately one-quarter of the whole work.

BIOGRAPHIES

A major part of the Library Association's *Books About Children's Literature* is devoted to biographical material, there being approximately 200 such entries arranged by biographees.

Two useful publications which contain biographical sketches are:

KUNITZ, STANLEY J. and HAYCRAFT, HOWARD, eds. *The Junior Book of Authors*. H. W. Wilson Co. 1934. 2nd edn., 1951.

There are 289 autobiographical sketches of authors and illustrators. With few exceptions classical authors are excluded, and those represented are mainly American. Non-American authors include Helen Bannerman, Jean de Brunhoff, Walter de la Mare, Eleanor Farjeon, Johanna Spyri, and Jules Verne.

FULLER, MURIEL, ed. *More Junior Authors*. H. W. Wilson Co. 1963. (Fig. 19).

A companion volume to Kunitz and Haycraft of 268 authors and illustrators. Includes some British writers such as Edward Ardizzone, C. S. Lewis, E. Nesbit, Rosemary Sutcliff, J. R. R. Tolkien, Geoffrey Trease and Henry Treece; and from Europe, Laurent de Brunhoff, René Guillot, and Astrid Lindgren.

The multi-volume *Dictionary of National Biography* can be consulted for the more important earlier writers for children, but a more handy source is Gillian Avery's *Nineteenth Century Children*, the appendix of which contains over 120 biographical references to authors writing prior to 1900.

Brian Doyle compiled *The Who's Who of Children's Literature* (Hugh Evelyn, 1968), which records a selection of approximately 300 authors and illustrators for whom biographical and bibliographical information is given. International coverage is claimed from 1800 to date, but many outstanding European writers are omitted. This is a fascinating and useful work as is his duplicated *Who's Who of Boys' Writers and Illustrators* which was privately published in 1964.

was produced in the Cleve-

s of whom I have written in
years are all deeply rooted
:ground. Frederick Douglass
ace a Slave—used to visit my
:'s farm in Indiana. This
if the underground railway
away slaves. When I was
South, Dr. George Washing-
nis green-black alpaca coat,
sight. I have walked with
woods near Tuskegee. The
Wheatley was a tale first
y father when I was a little
have wanted to tell the In-
ir American heritage. I had
y in The Story of Poca-

a little girl movies were not
hd television was unheard
oks. As I write now, I try to
readers as the books which
out and held me. And I
: people in the books which
precious. The great city of
:s something very personal
n one knows Jean Baptiste
its founder. It is my hope
about dark-skinned Ameri-
d understanding and appre-
ier more and to hold very
for which so many have
and died.

* * *

received both her bachelor
er of arts degrees at Oberlin

ble Servant as the best creative work published the previous year in the field of race
relations, and the National Institute of Arts
and Letters Award for "contributions to
American literature."

René Guillot
1900-
AUTHOR OF
The Wind of Chance; Grishka and the Bear;
Sama; Sirga: Queen of the African Bush; Etc.

Autobiographical sketch of René Guillot:

I WAS born in the district of Saintonge,
between La Rochelle, France, and Royan,
in a small marshland village of the Seugne.
At the beginning of World War I, I was
fourteen years old; I spent my time working
the vines and gathering the wheat and corn
with the help of my grandfather's two oxen.
The name of my village was Courcoury. It
means "running, running streams," because
the community is surrounded on all sides
by water—from the Charente, the Seugne,
and the marshes.

After completing my studies at the Col-
lège (i.e. high school) des Saintes and at the
University of Bordeaux, where I took my
degree in mathematics, I married and went
to Senegal in Africa. There, at the beginning, I was the only professor at the lycée
(public high school) of Dakar, which I had
just established. There I taught mathematics for twenty-five years, until World
War II. I was a volunteer in that war, and
became a lieutenant in a battery of Ameri-

FIG. 19. Specimen entry from Muriel Fuller's More Junior Authors.
(By courtesy of the H. W. Wilson Co., New York, United States.)

Most of the outstanding figures have been the subject of biographies of varying authority and readability. It ought to be fairly easy to obtain such lives, of which the following are readable examples:

BATTISCOMBE, GEORGINA and LASKI, MARGHANITA, eds. *A Chaplet for Charlotte Yonge*. Cresset Press. 1965.

GREEN, ROGER LANCELYN. *Kipling and the Children*. Elek Books. 1965.

HUDSON, DEREK. *Lewis Carroll*. Macmillan. 1954.

LANE, MARGARET. *The Tale of Beatrix Potter*. Warne. 1946. New edn· 1968.

MACKAIL, DENIS. *The Story of J. M. B.: a biography*. Davies. 1941.

MARTIN, ROBERT B. *The Dust of Combat: a life of Charles Kingsley*. Faber. 1959.

MAXWELL, CHRISTABEL. *Mrs. Gatty and Mrs. Ewing*. Bell. 1949.

MOORE, DORIS LANGLEY. *E. Nesbit: a biography*. Benn. 1933. New edn. 1967.

NOAKES, VIVIEN. *Edward Lear: the life of a wanderer*. Collins. 1968.

QUAYLE, ERIC. *Ballantyne the Brave*. Hart-Davis. 1967.

STIRLING, MONICA. *The Wild Swan: the life and times of Hans Christian Andersen*. Collins. 1965.

WARNER, OLIVER. *Captain Marryat: a rediscovery*. Constable. 1953.

Outstanding autobiographical works of three outstanding contributors to children's books have been published in recent years:

ARDIZZONE, EDWARD. *The Young Ardizzone: an autobiographical Fragment*. Studio Vista. 1970.
Half-forgotten memories of the author's boyhood to the time he began his career as an artist. Evocative illustrations decorate each page.

NESBIT, E. *Long Ago When I Was Young*. Whiting & Wheaton. 1966.
A personal reminiscence of the author's childhood with an introductory preface by Noel Streatfeild, and illustrated by Edward Ardizzone.

POTTER, BEATRIX. *The Journal of Beatrix Potter from 1881 to 1897.* Warne. 1966.
This was written in a code which was deciphered by Leslie Linder. It contains views held by the author on social questions and public figures as well as more personal details.

A series which has contributed to the biography and criticism of children's literature is the Bodley Head *Monographs* which is under the general editorship of Kathleen Lines. It is particularly valuable for its volumes on such recent writers as Lucy Boston, Rosemary Sutcliff, and Geoffrey Trease. Initially, authors were considered in small individual volumes, but revised editions have been issued in which each volume contains three monographs, such as Arthur Ransome, Rudyard Kipling, and Walter de la Mare. The revised editions include authors not previously studied, such as Hugh Lofting and Henry Treece. The authors brought together in the omnibus volumes do not appear to have anything in common except that they have written for children.

John Rowe Townsend's *A Sense of Story: essays on contemporary writers for children* (Longman, 1971) is an additional guide to the life and work of current British, Commonwealth, and United States authors. The book contains essays on nineteen writers, including Joan Aiken, Leon Garfield, Madeleine L'Engle, Philippa Pearce, and Ivan Southall.

A pointer to the growing importance of children's books can be seen, not only in the vast development in children's literature since the Second World War, but also in the increasing flow of biographical, critical, and historical material. There is still much ground to be covered. Up-to-date biographies in detail, of G. A. Henty, James Janeway, A. A. Milne, Mrs. Molesworth, to mention a few, would be a desirable addition to the literature available.

PUBLISHING HISTORY

Information on the development of children's literature can be acquired from the histories of individual publishers. The following are examples which include material which is relevant to a study of children's writers and publishing trends:

BLACKIE, AGNES C. *Blackie & Son, 1809–1959*. Blackie. 1959.

CLARKE, W. K. LOWTHER. *A History of the S.P.C.K.* S.P.C.K. 1959.

HEWITT, GORDON. *Let the People Read: a short history of the United Society for Christian Literature*. U.S.C.L. 1949.

KEIR, DAVID. *The House of Collins*. Collins. 1952.

KING, ARTHUR and STUART, A. F. *The House of Warne: one hundred years of publishing*. Warne. 1965.

MORGAN, CHARLES. *The House of Macmillan, 1843–1943*. Macmillan. 1943.

MUMBY, F. A. *The House of Routledge, 1834–1934*. Routledge. 1934.

NOWELL-SMITH, SIMON. *The House of Cassell, 1848–1958*. Cassell. 1958.

So much work has been undertaken since the Second World War in the recording of events, ideas, and opinions relating to literature for children, and the next 20 years will no doubt witness a great deal more. There is a general acknowledgement of the importance of children's books, but it is necessary to remember that the attention is only increasing and will probably not achieve its fullest development for many years to come.

SURVEYS OF CHILDREN'S READING

BATEMAN, ROBIN. "Adult books for 13–15-year olds: a report on the use by secondary grammar school children of a collection of adult books", *Use of English*. Winter 1964.
Based on a list of 224 fiction and 114 non-fiction volumes compiled from longer lists by branch librarians of the Leeds Public Library.

BUTTS, DENNIS. "What do some boys and girls read and why", *Use of English*. Winter 1963.
A survey of the reading tastes of 486 A-stream children aged 11–15 in attendance at fourteen secondary modern schools in Yorkshire.

CARSLEY, J. D. "The interest of children (aged 10–11) in books", *British Journal of Educational Psychology*. February 1957.
Based on 2040 replies to a questionnaire distributed to boys and girls aged 10+ in thirty junior schools in the Merseyside area.

JENKINS, PENELOPE. "Children's reading and children's television: a survey of 6- and 7-year-old children in Leeds", *Journal of Librarianship*. April 1971.
Carried out in 1968/9 among 677 infant school children in Leeds. Includes information on the reading patterns of young people.

JENKINSON, A. J. *What Do Boys and Girls Read?* Methuen. 1940.
Based on approximately 3000 replies to a questionnaire sent to young people at seventeen senior schools (11–14 age group) and eleven secondary (grammar) schools.

LANE, M. J. and FURNESS-LANE, K. A. *Books Girls Read: a survey of reading habits carried out in a comprehensive school for girls.* Society of Young Publishers. 1967.
Conducted by questionnaire through a comprehensive school of 1600 girls. Conflicts with most surveys of the secondary school age group in its conclusion that the quantity of books read does not change significantly after age 11.

LENG, I. J. *Children in the Library: a study of children's leisure reading tastes and habits.* University of Wales. 1968.
Conducted through examination of systematically maintained records at a public library. Sample of 555 boys and girls aged 6–13. Compares findings with other surveys.

SMITH, W. H., and HARRAP, GEORGE G. *Survey of Boys' and Girls' Reading Habits.* Smith/Harrap. 1957.
Survey of the reading tastes of 8000 young people aged 11–18 at schools in England and Wales. Only a pamphlet, but findings based on exceptionally large sample.

WHITE, DOROTHY NEAL. *Books Before Five.* New Zealand Council for Educational Research. 1954.
A diary kept by the author of her young daughter's reading, and

both her own and the child's reactions to the books. There are six chapters, each of which deals with a period of 6 months. A list of books is appended in the order in which they were mentioned in the text.

YARLOTT, G., and HARPIN, W. S. "1000 Responses to English literature", *Educational Research.* February 1971.
Based on an inquiry circulated in 1968 to eighteen selective secondary schools in Derbyshire, Lincolnshire, and Nottinghamshire. The survey was compiled from a sample of 1000 pupils, the majority of them O-level candidates. Boys and girls are represented in equal proportions.

CHAPTER 7

Guidance from Periodical Articles

No INDEX exists which is devoted entirely to the recording of periodical articles about literature for children. In spite of this such articles are recorded on quite a wide scale in reputable indexes of more general coverage on both sides of the Atlantic.

Poole's *Index to Periodical Literature* is one of the earliest and most comprehensive of indexes. It is contained in two volumes which cover the period 1802–81, together with supplements from 1882 to 1906. Only American and English periodicals are dealt with. This is the only index covering so long a period.

The H. W. Wilson Company publication *Library Literature: an author and subject index to selected material on library science and librarianship* has been in circulation since 1921, and is now supplemented by bi-monthly indexes which cumulate into annual and then biennial volumes (Fig. 20). This publication was preceded by H. G. T. Cannon's *Bibliography of Library Economy*, in two volumes, which indexed material published between 1876 and 1920. More than 180 periodicals are indexed in *Library Literature*, including *The Horn Book Magazine*, *The Junior Bookshelf*, *The School Librarian*, *Top of the News*, and various European journals.

Two other H. W. Wilson indexes include references to articles on children's literature. *The Social Sciences and Humanities Index* (1965–date) is issued quarterly with annual cumulations which are to be further cumulated. There is an author and subject coverage of approximately 200 periodicals, mainly of United States origin. Originally the title of this index was *The International Index to Periodicals* (1907–29; 1930–65). The second is *The Reader's Guide to Periodical Literature*

CHILDREN'S literature—Authors and illustra-
tors—*Continued*
Harman, E. P. Ronald Rood. North Country
Lib 9:182-3 N '66
Haugaard. E. C. Thank you note [for the
first Boston Globe-Horn book award for
excellence in text] and a credo. Horn Bk
44:14 F '68
Higgins. J. E. Kate Seredy: storyteller. Horn
Bk 44:162-8 Ap '68
Hightower. F. From reading to writing. Horn
Bk 44:24-9 F '68
Hodges, C. W. On writing about King Alfred.
Jr Bkshelf 31:159-63 Je '67
Hodges, E. J. Magic of serendipity. Horn Bk
43:370-4 Je '67
Howell, D. B. Portraits of Mississippi authors:
Rose Elliott Hutchins. bibliog Miss Lib
News 31:236 D '67
Hunter, K. Soul brothers: background of a
juvenile. Pub Wkly 193:30-1 My 27 '68
Jacob. H. M. Elizabeth Coatsworth. bibliog
North Country Lib 11:118-19 Jl '68
Jones. M. E. Connecticut's Puddleby-on-the-
marsh: Hugh Lofting. Horn Bk 44:463+
Ag '68
Karl, J. Elaine L. Konigsburg. Lib J 93:
1285-6 Mr 15: Sch Lib J 15:111-12 Mr '68
Klemin, D. Art of art for children's books:
a contemporary survey. Potter, C.N. '66 128p
il
Krumgold, J. Archetypes of the twentieth
century. mythic roots of an initiation trilogy. Lib J 93:3926-9 O 15; Sch Lib J 15:
112-15 O '68
Kunze, H. Schatzbehalter: von besten aus
älteren deutschen kinderliteratur (Treasure
chest: from the best of older German children's literature). Berlin, Kinderbuchverlag
'64 437p il
Lauderbach, J. Pied piper festival: bringing
authors and children together. Calif Sch Lib
39:160-4 My '68
Lien. B. Den 2. nordiske ungdomsforfattar-
kongress i Stockholm (2d Scandinavian
Congress of authors for young people in
Stockholm]. Bok og Bibl 33:215-17 Jl '66
Lindgren-Fridell, M. Att illustrera H. C.
Andersen (To illustrate H. C. Andersen).
Skolbiblioteket 12 no2-3:74-6+ '66
Mary Oliver. Sister. Everyman for small-
fry, a portrait of Munro Leaf. Cath Lib W
39:425-6 F '68
Mould, G. H. Weirdstone of Brisingamen: a
four-way experience with the novel by Alan
Garner. Sch Libn 15:146-50 Jl '67
Pearce, P. Writing a book. Horn Bk 43:317-
22 Je '67
Peterson, H. Barnboksförfattaren författare
(Is the author of children's books an au-
thor)? Biblioteksbladet 51 no 10:729-30 '66
Polland, M. A. On the writing of ghost
stories. Horn Bk 44:147-50 Ap '68
Prieto, M. I said it two ways (and I still
do). Horn Bk 44:209-10 Ap '68
Reading for recreation: report on the conference organized by the Bristol branch of
the School library association, 11th March,
1967. Sch Libn 15:271-6 D '67

Wood, J. P. Honest audience. Horn
612-16 O '67
Yates, E. Why did you end your st
way? Horn Bk 43:709-14 D '67
Zemach, H. and Zemach, M. I liked
the mother fell in the mud. Pu
193:131-2 F 26 '68
See also
Book illustration
Fairy tales
Folk literature
Ghost stories

Awards, citations and prizes

Awards. Horn Bk 44:463 Ag '68
Barnebokprisene for 1965 (Prizes
dren's books 1965). Bok og Bibl
My '66
Book World awards prizes for a
book festival. Pub Wkly 193:28 My
Books of international interest: prize
children's books. See issues of B
Child study association awards. Lib
Ap 15: Sch Lib J 15:49 Ap '68
Children's book award for 1968. A
Lib J 17:198 Jl '68
Children's spring book festival awar
Bk 44:351 Je '68
Clark, M. T. On accepting the A
children's book of the year award
5 no1:29-30 '67
'68
Eleanor Farjeon award. Sch Libn
'68
Eleanor Farjeon award, 1966. Sch Li
Jl '67
Eleanor Farjeon award to Mr Brian .
Liaison p52 Jl '68
Fourth Canadian children's book aw
ner. Canad Lib Assn Feliciter 13:3(
Ag '68
Fowler. V. E. An editor recalls: f
man to English to the Batchelde
Top News 24:395-8 Je '68
Golden eagle of CINE [Council on
tional nontheatrical events] to The
is mutual. Lib J 93:506 F t '68
Hawaii state children's book award.
44:367 Je '68
Honors have been accorded to The
is mutual. Horn Bk 43:526 Ag '68
International biennial for childre
illustration prizes. Bkbird 5 no1:31
Ivan Southall is winner of the 1968 a
the Australian children's book of
Pub Wkly 94:8 O 28 '68
Juvenile book awards: 1967. Lib
Mr 15: Sch Lib J 15:115 Mr '68
Lewis Carroll shelf awards, 1967.
Bul 62:447 N '67
Ness, E. Caldecott acceptance spee
Bk 43:434-8 Ag '67
Pleasure is mutual wins award at
American film festival in New Y
mark 26:342 Jl '67
Pleasure is mutual wins two new
Bkmark 27:4 O '67
Sonn, H. Fehlt dem jugendbuch
agement? Deutscher jugendbuchpi

FIG. 20. Specimen entries from *Library Literature.*
(By courtesy of the H. W. Wilson Co., New York, United States.)

n. Val Arnold-Forster. Guard-

·en on holiday without their
n. Times, (29 May 68) p.13

n. Claire Rayner. Times, (3

mond Fanning. Town and
(Oct-Nov 68) p.440-2. il.

W.M. Hatchett. Town and
(Oct-Nov 68) p.486-8. il.
ons
yground. Observer, (12 May 68)

lity. Anne Bavin. Guardian,

parisienne. Peter Lennon.
8) p.6

W.D. Abernethy. Town and
(Oct-Nov 68) p.471-5. il.
Gillian Figures. Guardian,

ection
bara Kahan. New Society,

ildren a year. Kay Evans.
p.6
ection

·en

with children's home background.
·itish J. of Criminology, 8

Children in Trouble attacked. R.F. Sparks. New
Society, (26 Sep 68) p.449
Children in trouble defended. Terence Morris. New
Society, (17 Oct 68) p.566-7
Children in Vietnam
Children of Vietnam. Barbara Evans. Sunday Times
Mag., (7 Jan 68) p.14 + il.
Children's Books and Reading
Chairman Mao's thoughts for children. John Scott.
Sunday Times Mag., (4 Aug 68) p.36-7 il.
A child is not a mini-adult: the great revolution in
young readers gathers talent and strength. Sheila
More. Times, (6 Jan 68) p.19
Children, books and teachers in training. Robert
Hoare. Bookseller, (27 Jul 68) p.250-1
Children's books. Times Literary Suppt., (3 Oct 68)
p.1105-28
Children's books supplement. 1. A bit more practice.
Alan Garner. 2. Looking for a winner. Peggy Heeks.
3. Anti-Superman. Nicholas Tucker. Times Literary
Suppt., (6 Jun 68) p.577-96
The gadfly and the spy. [Russian children's books].
Tibor Szamuely. Spectator, (17 May 68) p.665
Greyfriars, USA. Denis Brogan. Spectator, (31 May
68) p.740-1
How school libraries select and buy their books.
Bookseller, (12 Oct 68) p.1252+
Modern painters for modern youth. Robert Hughes.
Spectator, (8 Nov 68) p.661-2
A national centre for children's literature. Peggy Heeks.
Bookseller, (9 Nov 68) p.1596
Parents are people, too. Katharine Whitehorn. Obser-
ver, (5 May 68) p.25
Parkinson for children. Marcus Crouch. Times Literary
Suppt., (5 Dec 68) p.1370-1
Reformed nursery rhymes. Nicholas Tucker. Times
Literary Suppt., (5 Dec 68) p.1365-6
Children's Books and Reading
Related Headings :
'Boy's Own Paper'
Children and Libraries
Comics
Garner, Alan
Harris, Mary K.
Henty, G.A.

FIG. 21. Specimen entries from *British Humanities Index*.
(By courtesy of the Library Association.)

(1900–date), which appears fortnightly except in July and August, when it appears monthly. It indexes over 150 popular periodicals and the volumes cumulate. *The Social Sciences and Humanities Index* is concerned generally speaking with more scholarly material than *The Reader's Guide*. A *19th Century Reader's Guide to Periodical Literature*, in two volumes, indexes material published between 1890 and 1899.

The principal British indexes which contain articles on children's literature are published by the Library Association. *British Humanities Index* began in 1962, and is issued quarterly with annual cumulations (Fig. 21). It was previously known as *The Subject Index to Periodicals* (1915–22; 1926–61).

British Education Index is published three times each year by the B.N.B. for the librarians of the University Institutes of Education. The first volume in 1961 indexes articles from 1954 to 1958, and four further volumes and supplements bring it up to date. In the main, educational periodicals are indexed, many of which have occasional articles on children's literature.

There is a number of journals in Britain which have regular articles on children's literature. An outstanding periodical for parents and others interested in the subject is *Books for Your Children*, which since late 1965 has been issued quarterly with a special December supplement. The founder and editor is Anne Wood, a teacher, and this is the first venture of its kind. It includes helpful suggestions for children's reading and items of topical interest. None of the articles is lengthy but they cover a wide range.

Numerous periodicals in Britain and elsewhere have regular or occasional articles on literature for children, and the following list is a selection of work of more than ephemeral interest published since 1955.

GENERAL

"Book reading and book owning as part of education" by J. Duff. *School Librarian*. March 1955.

"Choosing for children" by Margery Fisher. *School Librarian*. March 1963,

"Fear and evil in Children's books" by Catherine Storr. *Children's Literature in Education*. March 1970.

"Reading and child development in the junior years" by Colin Field. *School Librarian*. July 1968.

"Realism and escapism in children's literature" by James Guthrie. *Junior Bookshelf*. January 1958.

"Social values in children's literature" by Emily Neville. *Library Quarterly*. January 1967.

ADOLESCENTS

"Books for adolescents" by Peggy Heeks. *School Librarian*. July 1966.

"Choosing fiction for adolescents" by Norman Culpan. *School Librarian*. July 1961.

"A study in adolescent reading", by Joan W. Butler. *Library Association Record*. October 1956.

ADVENTURE STORIES

"Life without adults" by Alec Ellis. *Junior Bookshelf*. December 1969.

See also under individual writers: R. M. Ballantyne, Nina Bawden, Erich Kästner, Arthur Ransome, R. L. Stevenson, A. Rutgers van der Loeff.

ANIMAL STORIES

"Animals and dressed animals" by M. J. P. Laurence. *Junior Bookshelf*. December 1957.

"Man and beast" by Alec Ellis. *Junior Bookshelf*. October 1968.

"Masses of bears" by Geraldine Procter. *Junior Bookshelf*. March 1961.

"Sing ho! for the life of a Bear" by R. L. Green. *Junior Bookshelf*. October 1961.

See also under Individual Writers: Kenneth Grahame, René Guillot, A. A. Milne, Beatrix Potter, Alison Uttley.

ASIA

"Children's books in the East" by Bettina Hürlimann and others. *Library Association Record.* March 1964.
"Children's literature, the South Asian picture" by Antony Kamm. *International Library Review.* April 1969.
See also Malaysia, Pakistan.

AUSTRALIA

"An indigenous children's literature" by Barbara Buick. *Library Journal.* 15th November 1967.
See also under Individual Writers: H. F. Brinsmead, Ivan Southall, Patricia Wrightson.

AWARDS

"Prize-winning books for children" by H. K. Evans. *School Librarian.* July 1966.
See also under Carnegie Medal, Hans Christian Andersen Award, Newbery Medal.

BACKWARDNESS

"Literature for backward readers" by Michael Tucker. *Use of English.* Autumn 1966.
"Low stream books" by David Holbrook. *Use of English.* Summer 1964.

CARNEGIE MEDAL

"A clutch of Carnegie's" by M. Hutton. *School Librarian.* July 1963.
"Newbery and Carnegie awards" by Janice Dohm. *Junior Bookshelf.* January 1957.
See also under Individual Writers: Kitty Barne, L. M. Boston, Hester Burton, Pauline Clarke, I. W. Cornwall, Walter de la Mare, Eleanor

Farjeon, Leon Garfield, Alan Garner, Eve Garnett, Cynthia Harnett, C. S. Lewis, William Mayne, Mary Norton, Philippa Pearce, K. M. Peyton, Arthur Ransome, Rosemary Sutcliff, Philip Turner, D. J. Watkins-Pitchford.

CHILE

"The history of juvenile literature in Chile" by C. B. Villasante. *Bookbird.* September 1967.
"Work with children's literature in Chile" by Pepita Turina. *Bookbird.* December 1969.

COLLECTIONS. See ORGANIZATIONS AND COLLECTIONS

CZECHOSLOVAKIA

"Children's books in Czechoslovakia" by Mary Ørvig. *International Library Review.* July 1970.

FAIRY TALES

"The dragon's grandmother" by C. Duff-Stewart. *Junior Bookshelf.* March 1958.
"The educational and moral value of folk and fairy tales" by J. Langfeldt. *Junior Bookshelf.* January 1961.
"Facts and fairies" by B. J. Moore. *School Librarian.* December 1962.
See also under Individual Writers: Andrew Lang.

FAMILY STORIES

"The family in fiction" by Anne Ellis. *School Librarian.* December 1968.
"The family story as a reflection of reality" by Alec and Anne Ellis. *Junior Bookshelf.* October 1967.
"The social background of children's fiction" by J. K. G. Taylor. *School Librarian.* December 1962.

"To survive or not to survive?" by Anne Ellis. *Library Review.* Summer 1968.

See also under Individual Writers: Kitty Barne, Nan Chauncy, Mrs. Ewing, Eve Garnett, Eleanor Graham, Astrid Lindgren, William Mayne, E. Nesbit, Philip Turner, Barbara Willard, Patricia Wrightson.

FANTASY STORIES

"The fantastic tale for children" by Göte Klingberg. *Bookbird.* September 1967.

"Little folk and young people" by Alec Ellis. *Junior Bookshelf.* April 1966.

"Machine animism in modern children's literature" by H. J. Schwarcz. *Library Quarterly.* January 1967.

"On the elvish craft" by Jane Curry. *Signal.* May 1970.

"To seek and to find: quest literature for children" by June S. Terry. *School Librarian.* December 1970.

See also under Individual Writers: W. Awdry, J. M. Barrie, Lewis Carroll, Pauline Clarke, Helen Cresswell, Walter de la Mare, Eleanor Farjeon, Alan Garner, Tove Jansson, Edward Lear, C. S. Lewis, Hugh Lofting, George MacDonald, Mrs. Molesworth, E. Nesbit, Mary Norton, J. R. R. Tolkien, Ursula Moray Williams.

FRANCE

"No time for childhood" by Herbert Lottman. *Library Journal.* 15th November 1966.

See also under Individual Writers: René Guillot.

GERMANY

"Children's and young people's literature in the German Federal Republic" by W. Overwien. *International Library Review.* October 1969.

"The children's book in the post-war period in Germany" by Klaus Doderer. *Bookbird.* September 1965.
"Twenty years later" by Horst Kunneman. *Library Journal.* 15th November 1966.
See also under Individual Writers: Hans Baumann, Heinrich Hoffmann, Erich Kästner.

HANS CHRISTIAN ANDERSEN AWARD

"The first award of the Hans Andersen medal" by Philippa Pearce. *Junior Bookshelf.* November 1956.
"The Hans Andersen award" by Eileen Colwell. *Junior Bookshelf.* July 1958.
See also under Individual Writers: Eleanor Farjeon, Tove Jansson, Erich Kästner, Astrid Lindgren, Gianni Rodari, Maurice Sendak.

HISTORICAL FICTION

"Problems of historical juvenile books" by Richard Bamberger. *Bookbird.* December 1964.
"War in books for young people" by Mary Ørvig. *Bookbird.* June 1967.
See also under Individual Writers: Hans Baumann, Hester Burton, Leon Garfield, Cynthia Harnett, G. A. Henty, Rudyard Kipling, K. M. Peyton, Rosemary Sutcliff, Geoffrey Trease.

HUMOROUS LITERATURE

"Children and humorous literature" by Robin Bateman. *School Librarian.* July 1967.
"A developmental analysis of children's responses to humour" by K. H. Kappas. *Library Quarterly.* January 1967.
"Humour in children's literature" by Lucia Binder. *Bookbird.* December 1970, March 1971, June 1971.

HUNGARY

"Contemporary children's book illustration in Hungary" by I. P. Brestyánszky. *Bookbird*. June 1971.

ILLUSTRATION

Victor G. Ambrus. "Introducing illustrators: Victor Ambrus" by M. R. Hodgkin. *Junior Bookshelf*. March 1964. "Victor Ambrus" by Victor Ambrus. *Junior Bookshelf*. June 1966.

Edward Ardizzone. "Creation of a picture book" by Edward Ardizzone. *Junior Bookshelf*. December 1961. "Edward Ardizzone" by Nicholas Tucker. *Children's Literature in Education*. November 1970.

John Burningham. "Drawing for children" by John Burningham. *Junior Bookshelf*. July 1964.

Walter Crane. "Walter Crane: first, second or third?" by J. E. Vaughan. *Junior Bookshelf*. April 1968.

Richard Doyle. "Remembering Richard Doyle" by Alan Morley. *Signal*. May 1971.

Margery Gill. "Introducing illustrators: Margery Gill" by Judy Taylor. *Junior Bookshelf*. October 1966.

Helen Oxenbury. "Drawing for children" by Helen Oxenbury. *Junior Bookshelf*. August 1970.

Mervyn Peake. "Mervyn Peake, 1911–1968" by Marcus Crouch. *Junior Bookshelf*. December 1968.

Arthur Rackham. "Arthur Rackham, 1867–1939" by Marcus Crouch. *Junior Bookshelf*. October 1967.

Gerald Rose. "Illustrating for children" by Gerald Rose. *Junior Bookshelf*. July 1961.

Maurice Sendak. "20th century illustrators: Maurice Sendak" by Janice Dohm. *Junior Bookshelf*. April 1966.

E. H. Shepard. "... and gives to Pooh a local habitation and a name". *Junior Bookshelf*. March 1959.

William Stobbs. "On illustrating books" by William Stobbs. *Junior Bookshelf*. July 1960.

Brian Wildsmith. "Brian Wildsmith: medallist" by Marcus Crouch. *Junior Bookshelf.* July 1963.
"Children's tastes in book illustration" by F. R. Witty. *School Librarian.* March 1955.
"The function of illustrations in children's books" by Frantisek Holesovsky. *Bookbird.* March 1966.
"Illustration and the emotional world of the child" by Bettina Hürlimann. *Bookbird.* September 1969.
"Illustration in children's books" by Charles Keeping. *Children's Literature in Education.* March 1970.
"The influence of illustrations on the emotional world of children" by F. Rudaš. *Bookbird.* June 1969.
"Research work in the field of picture books" by Hans Bödecker. *Bookbird.* March 1966.
"Trends of European picture book production since 1945" by Bettina Hürlimann. *International Library Review.* January 1971.
"The visual language of the picture book" by Olga Richard. *Wilson Library Bulletin.* December 1969.

INDIVIDUAL WRITERS

Joan Aiken. "Joan Aiken" by Alec Ellis. *School Librarian.* June 1970. "A thread of mystery" by Joan Aiken. *Children's Literature in Education.* July 1970. "Joan Aiken" by Lesley Aers. *Use of English.* Summer 1971. "Joan Aiken" by J. R. Townsend. *Signal.* May 1971.
Gillian Avery. "Gillian Avery" by Dennis Butts. *School Librarian.* July 1968.
Rev. W. Awdry. "The reverend's railways" by Dennis Butts. *Books.* March–April 1965.
R. M. Ballantyne. "R. M. Ballantyne" by Dennis Butts. *School Librarian.* December 1966.
Nina Bawden. "Nina Bawden: an author for today" by Elaine Moss. *Signal.* January 1971.
Kitty Barne. "Kitty Barne: an appreciation" by Eileen Colwell. *Junior Bookshelf.* October 1961.

J. M. Barrie. "Barrie and 'Peter Pan' " by R. L. Green. *Junior Bookshelf*. October 1960.

Hans Baumann. "Hans Baumann" by Richard Bamberger. *Bookbird*. September 1965.

Enid Blyton. "Who's Afraid of Enid Blyton?" by Edward Blishen. *Where*. July 1967. "Phenomenon or South Sea Bubble?" by George Greenfield and Constance Martin. *Books*. Winter 1970.

L. M. Boston. "The place that is Green Knowe" by L. M. Boston. *Junior Bookshelf*. December 1962.

H. F. Brinsmead. "How and why I write for young people" by H. F. Brinsmead. *Bookbird*. December 1969.

John Bunyan. "John Bunyan" by R. C. Stephens. *School Librarian*. July 1959.

Hester Burton. "How I came to write 'A Time of Trial' " by Hester Burton. *Junior Bookshelf*. July 1964.

Lewis Carroll. "The Carroll–Tenniel partnership" by Frances Collingwood. *Books*. November–December 1964. "Picnic in Wonderland" by R. L. Green. *Junior Bookshelf*. July 1962. "Alice in America" by Janice Dohm. *Junior Bookshelf*. October 1965.

Nan Chauncy. "Half a world away" by Marcus Crouch. *Junior Bookshelf*. June 1965.

John Christopher. "John Christopher: allegorical historian" by Jay Williams. *Signal*. January 1971.

Pauline Clarke. "Chief genii Branwell" by Pauline Clarke. *Junior Bookshelf*. July 1963.

I. W. Cornwall. "On getting a medal" by I. W. Cornwall. *Junior Bookshelf*. July 1961.

Helen Cresswell. "Helen Cresswell–craftsman" by Marcus Crouch. *Junior Bookshelf*. June 1970. "If it's someone from Porlock, don't answer the door" by Helen Cresswell. *Children's Literature in Education*. March 1971. "Warm sun, cold wind" by Margaret Greaves. *Children's Literature in Education*. July 1971.

Walter de la Mare. "Farewell to Walter de la Mare" by Marcus Crouch. *Junior Bookshelf*. October 1956.

Mrs. Ewing. "Juliana Horatia Ewing and her books" by Jean Kenward. *Books*. September–October 1966.

Eleanor Farjeon. "Eleanor Farjeon" by Margery Fisher. *Bookbird*. December 1965. "Eleanor Farjeon" by Helen Thomas and others. *Junior Bookshelf*. August 1965. "In search of Elsie Piddock" by Denys Blakelock. *Junior Bookshelf*. February 1968.

F. W. Farrar. "F. W. Farrar and novels of the public schools" by A. Jamieson. *British Journal of Educational Studies*. October 1968. "The school novels of Dean Farrar" by P. G. Scott. *British Journal of Educational Studies*. June 1971.

Wanda Gág. "Through peasant eyes" by Marcus Crouch. *Junior Bookshelf*. March 1962.

Leon Garfield. "Leon Garfield: a remarkable children's writer" by Edward Blishen. *Where*. September 1968. "Writing for childhood" by Leon Garfield. *Children's Literature in Education*. July 1970. "Garfield's golden net" by Richard Camp. *Signal*. May 1971.

Alan Garner. "The weirdstone of Brisingamen: a four-way experience" by G. H. Mould. *School Librarian*. July 1967. "Young writer with a new dimension" by Pamela Cooley. *Times Educational Supplement*. 6 October 1967. "The owl service: a study" by Eleanor Cameron. *Wilson Library Bulletin*. December 1969. "Coming to terms" by Alan Garner. *Children's Literature in Education*. July 1970. "Alan Garner: an opinion" by Lesley Aers. *Use of English*. Winter 1970.

Eve Garnett. "Rally round the Ruggles" by Sandra Paxford. *Junior Bookshelf*. April 1970.

Rummer Godden. "Rumer Godden" by Norman Culpan. *School Librarian*. July 1956.

Eleanor Graham. "Eleanor Graham" by Cynthia Harnett and others. *Junior Bookshelf*. July 1962.

Kenneth Grahame. "The children's Falstaff" by Nicholas Tucker. *Times Literary Supplement*. 26 June 1969. "The magic of Kenneth Grahame" by R. L. Green. *Junior Bookshelf*. March 1959.

René Guillot. "René Guillot" by Raoul Dubois. *Bookbird*. December 1964.

Cynthia Harnett. "Cynthia Harnett" by Eileen Colwell. *Junior Book-shelf.* March 1957.

G. A. Henty. "Rise and fall of Henty's empire" by John Springhall. *Times Literary Supplement.* 3 October 1968.

Heinrich Hoffmann. "Struwwelpeter: yes or no?" by L. Mosheim. *Junior Bookshelf.* December 1963.

Tove Jansson. "Moomin-sagas" by Marcus Crouch. *Junior Book-shelf.* December 1966.

Erich Kästner. "Did 'Emil' start something?" by James Reeves. *School Librarian.* July 1959. " 'Emil's' father celebrates his 70th birthday" by Lucia Binder. *Bookbird.* March 1969.

Rudyard Kipling. "Rudyard Kipling" by R. L. Green. *Junior Book-shelf.* December 1956. "Puck country" by Marcus Crouch. *Junior Bookshelf.* March 1960. "Rudyard Kipling" by Timothy Rogers. *School Librarian.* December 1961.

Andrew Lang. "Andrew Lang in fairyland" by R. L. Green. *Junior Bookshelf.* October 1962.

Edward Lear. "Just nonsense?" by Jean Kenward. *Books.* January–February 1966.

C. S. Lewis. "Chronicles of Narnia" by Marcus Crouch. *Junior Bookshelf.* November 1956. "C. S. Lewis" by M. Hutton. *School Librarian.* July 1964. "The wrath of God: an opinion of the Narnia Books" by Penelope Lively. *Use of English.* Winter 1968.

Astrid Lindgren. "Astrid Lindgren and a new kind of books for children" by Richard Bamberger. *Bookbird.* September 1967. "Astrid Lindgren: Swedish writer of children's books" by S. Hagliden. *Junior Bookshelf.* July 1959.

Hugh Lofting. "From fairy tale to children's novel" by Wolfgang Schlegelmilch. *Bookbird.* December 1970.

George MacDonald. "George MacDonald" by M. Hutton. *School Librarian.* December 1964.

William Mayne. "The art of William Mayne" by H. Fotheringham. *Junior Bookshelf.* October 1959. "William Mayne" by Edward Blishen. *Use of English.* Winter 1968.

A. A. Milne. "A. A. Milne" by Eleanor Farjeon. *Junior Bookshelf*. March 1956.

Mrs. Molesworth. "Mrs. Molesworth" by R. L. Green. *Junior Bookshelf*. July 1957.

E. Nesbit. "E. Nesbit" by R. L. Green and others. *Junior Bookshelf*. October 1958. "E. Nesbit in Kent" by Marcus Crouch. *Junior Bookshelf*. January 1955.

André Norton. "André Norton" by Margery Fisher. *School Librarian*. July 1967.

Mary Norton. "Mary Norton" by Colin Field. *School Librarian*. July 1963.

Elsie Oxenham. "Fifty Years of the Hamlet Club" by L. Muir. *Junior Bookshelf*. February 1966.

Philippa Pearce. "Philippa Pearce" by Brian Jackson. *Use of English*. Spring 1970. "The novels of Philippa Pearce" by David Rees. *Children's Literature in Education*. March 1971.

K. M. Peyton. "Streets ahead in experience" by Marcus Crouch. *Junior Bookshelf*. June 1969.

Beatrix Potter. "The art of Beatrix Potter" by Janice Dohm. *Junior Bookshelf*. October 1955. "Beatrix Potter, 1866–1943". *Books*. July/August 1966. "My Beatrix Potter" by Janice Dohm. *Junior Bookshelf*. August 1966. "The stories of Beatrix Potter" by A. K. D. Campbell. *Children's Literature in Education*. July 1971.

Arthur Ransome. "Arthur Ransome" by G. Bott. *School Librarian*. December 1960. "Arthur Ransome" by G. Bott and others. *Junior Bookshelf*. January 1964. "Dr. Arthur Ransome, C.B.E." by Marcus Crouch. *Junior Bookshelf*. August 1967. "From swallow to sea bear" by Pamela Whitlock. *Junior Bookshelf*. August 1967. "In search of Swallowdale" by S. Simsova. *Children's Book News*. July–August 1970.

James Reeves. "The truthful poet" by Dennis Butts. *Junior Bookshelf*. December 1966.

Gianni Rodari. "Gianni Rodari" by Carla Poesio. *Bookbird*. September 1968.

Malcolm Saville. "A book is a book is a book" by Rosemary Manning. *Signal*. September 1970.

Ian Serraillier. "The poetry of Ian Serraillier" by Marcus Crouch. *Junior Bookshelf*. December 1958.

Mrs. Sherwood. "On Little Henry" by C. Parrish. *Junior Bookshelf*. October 1964.

Ivan Southall. "From Simon Black to Ash Road and beyond" by Juliana Bayfield. *Bookbird*. December 1968. "Ivan Southall" by Alix Pirani. *Use of English*. Spring 1971.

Elizabeth G. Speare. "Elizabeth George Speare" by Muriel Hutton. *School Librarian*. September 1970.

R. L. Stevenson. "The child's voice" by Dennis Butts. *Junior Bookshelf*. December 1965. "R. L. Stevenson: a lifetime of hero worship" by Barbara Brill. *Library Review*. Winter 1969.

Hesba Stretton. "Pathetic simplicity: an introduction to Hesba Stretton and her books for children" by Lance Salway. *Signal*. January 1970.

Rosemary Sutcliff. "Combined ops" by Rosemary Sutcliff. *Junior Bookshelf*. July 1960. "The historical novels of Rosemary Sutcliff" by J. V. Marder. *Use of English*. Autumn 1968. "More songs tomorrow" by C. Duff-Stewart. *Junior Bookshelf*. November 1964. "Rosemary Sutcliff's 'Dawn Wind' " by Roger Gard. *Use of English*. Summer 1970. "Scarlet on the loom" by C. Duff-Stewart. *Junior Bookshelf*. November 1959.

J. R. R. Tolkien. "The Lord of the Rings" by W. D. Emrys Evans. *School Librarian*. December 1968.

Geoffrey Trease. "Geoffrey Trease" by Margaret Meek. *School Librarian*. July 1965. "Why write for Children?" by Geoffrey Trease. *School Librarian*. July 1960.

Philip Turner. "Philip Turner" by Philip Turner. *Junior Bookshelf*. June 1966.

Alison Uttley. "Dreams and memories" by Eileen Colwell. *Junior Bookshelf*. February 1970.

A. Rutgers van der Loeff. "Other people's lives" by A. Rutgers van der Loeff. *Children's Literature in Education*. July 1971.

D. J. Watkins-Pitchford. " 'B. B.' as a writer for young people" by Margery Fisher. *Bookbird.* September 1967.

Laura Ingalls Wilder. "Laura Ingalls Wilder" by Isabel Wilner. *Bookbird.* September 1967.

Barbara Willard. "Barbara Willard" by Margery Fisher. *School Librarian.* December 1969.

Ursula Moray Williams. "Ursula Moray Williams" by Elaine Moss. *Signal.* May 1971.

Patricia Wrightson. "Patricia Wrightson" by Margery Fisher. *School Librarian.* March 1969.

INFORMATION BOOKS

"Catechetical methods in the 18th and 19th centuries" by Margaret Maison. *Times Educational Supplement.* 17 June 1966.

"Choosing non-fiction for children, 7–11 years" by Eric Linfield. *School Librarian.* December 1961.

"Educational publishing". *Times Educational Supplement.* 18 November–9 December 1966.

"Factual books for young children" by J. C. Gagg. *School Librarian.* December 1970.

"Has the text book had its day?" by J. R. C. Yglesias. *Books.* September–October 1966.

"Information books: further criteria" by Eric Linfield. *School Librarian.* July 1965.

"Non-fiction for juniors" by S. W. Allen. *School Librarian.* December 1966.

"The questions" (Richmal Mangnall) by H. A. Beaton. *Books.* July–August 1966.

"Writing about science for children" by Millicent E. Selsam. *Library Quarterly.* January 1967.

IRAN

"The progress of children's literature in Iran during the past decade" by Lily Ayman. *International Library Review.* April 1969.

ISRAEL

"Books of a pioneer culture" by Uriel Ofek. *Library Journal*. 15 November 1966. "The juvenile book in Israel" by Hans Lebrecht. *Bookbird*. December 1965.

ITALY

"The situation and problems of juvenile literature in Italy in the post-war period" by G. F. D'Arcais and A. M. Bernardinis. *Bookbird*. June 1965.
See also under Individual Writers: Gianni Rodari.

MALAYSIA

"School libraries and children's literature in Malaysia" by Dennis Gunton. *Library World*. April 1967.

NEWBERY MEDAL

"Newbery and Carnegie awards" by Janice Dohm. *Junior Bookshelf*. January 1957.
See also under Individual Writers: Hugh Lofting, Elizabeth G. Speare.

NORWAY

"Children's books in Norway" by Jo Giaver Tenfjord. *Junior Bookshelf*. January 1962.

ORGANIZATIONS AND COLLECTIONS

Britain. "Children's books at the Victoria and Albert Museum" by J. I. Whalley. *Children's Book News*. May–June 1970.
Britain. "Children's literature: a plea for parity" by M. F. Thwaite. *Times Literary Supplement*. 26 June 1969.

Britain. "A national centre for children's literature—a symposium" by J. A. B. Townsend and B. W. Alderson. *Library Association Public Libraries Conference Proceedings*, 1968.

Canada. "Toronto Public Library Lillian H. Smith Collection". *Canadian Library*. September–October 1968.

Germany. "Twenty years of the International Youth Library" by Stephen Churchward. *Library Association Record*. November 1968.

Germany. "The Section for Children's and Young Adults' Books, Deutsche Staatsbibliothek, Berlin" by Heinz Wegehaupt. *UNESCO Bulletin for Libraries*. November–December 1968.

Netherlands. "Bureau Boek en Jeugd" by A. J. Moerkercken van der Meulin. *Bookbird*. March 1969.

Sweden. "Swedish Institute for Children's Books" by Mary Ørvig. *Bookbird*. March 1969.

United States. "The Information Center on Children's Cultures" by Anne Pellowski. *International Library Review*. October 1969.

PAKISTAN

"Children's literature in Pakistan" by A. Waheed. *Bookbird*. September 1969.

POETRY

"On poetry and children" by Alan Tucker. *Signal*. January 1970.

"Using poetry with children" by C. Duff-Stewart. *Junior Bookshelf*. July 1957.

See also under Individual Writers: Walter de la Mare, James Reeves, Ian Serraillier.

POLAND

"Children and juvenile books in Poland" by Irmela Brender. *Bookbird*. June 1967.

RUSSIA

"The house at 43 Gorky Street" by Ivan Dyomin. *Library Journal.* 15 November 1966.
"Russian children's literature on the contemporary stage" by N. Medvedeva. *International Library Review.* April 1971.

SCHOOL STORIES

"Tom Brown started it" by Brian Doyle. *Books.* May–June 1966.
"Yesterday's schoolgirls" by C. S. Tatham. *Junior Bookshelf.* December 1969.
See also under Individual Writers: F. W. Farrar, Elsie Oxenham.

SCIENCE AND SPACE FICTION

"Expanding horizons" by L. Jordan. *Junior Bookshelf.* March 1960.
See also under Individual Writers: John Christopher, André Norton.

SWEDEN

"A short survey of children's books in Sweden, 1945–1965" by Mary Ørvig. *Books.* Spring 1967.
"Swedish Institute of children's books" by Mary Ørvig. *Bookbird.* March 1969.
See also under Individual Writers: Astrid Lindgren.

TRANSLATIONS

"Children's books in translation" by Mildred L. Batchelder. *Bookbird.* June and September 1971.
"The critique of translations" by I. M. Artl. *Bookbird.* September 1969.
"Torments of translation" by H. H. Watts and S. C. Gross. *Junior Bookshelf.* November 1960.

UNITED STATES

"Modern American books for modern English Children" by Alice B. McGuire. *Junior Bookshelf.* December 1959.

"Negro life in current American children's literature" by L. B. Hopkins. *Bookbird.* March 1968.

See also under Illustration: Maurice Sendak.

See also under Individual Writers: Wanda Gág, Hugh Lofting, André Norton, Elizabeth G. Speare, Laura Ingalls Wilder.

See also under Newbery Medal.

IT is inevitable that the lengthier surveys of literature for children are too detailed for all except the specialist. Roger Lancelyn Green's *Tellers of Tales* is probably the most useful introduction to the subject from 1800, but even in the latest edition (1969), Mr. Green does not discuss very many post-Second World War authors. Current literature is dealt with in a most satisfactory manner in Margery Fisher's *Intent Upon Reading* (1964) and Sheila Ray's *Children's Fiction* (1972), but all the books discussed are not claimed to be of the highest quality.

The next eight chapters are designed to guide the reader to an understanding of the development of children's literature in this country and abroad, to indicate the most outstanding writers and some of the editions in which their work can be obtained, and the principal groupings into which children's books may be divided. In her review of the first edition of this book in *Library World*, M. C. Waite remarked that anyone who follows up the reading lists will "be well on the way to a detailed knowledge of children's literature". If this is accomplished, the author will be well satisfied.

CHAPTER 8

A History of Children's Literature to 1900

THE development of children's literature can be dated from 1744 when John Newbery published *A Little Pretty Pocket Book*. This was the first book especially designed for children's entertainment and for no other specific moral or educational purpose.

From Anglo-Saxon times until the eighteenth century, children's books were inseparably linked with education, but after Newbery, children's books as such became distinct from school books. Before the seventeenth century children had no real books of their own and it was at that time that schoolbooks, chapbooks, moral and fairy tales developed.

There are many well-known books which were adopted by children although they were not written for them. John Bunyan's *The Pilgrim's Progress* (1678) was not written for children but very quickly became popular with them. When Bunyan consciously set out to write a children's book in his *Divine Emblems* (1701) the result was a failure. Captain Marryat's *Mr. Midshipman Easy* (1836) was not written with an audience of boys in mind but was an immediate success, while his deliberate attempt to cater for them in *Masterman Ready* (1841) was not such a winner. Other adult works which have been adopted by children include Aesop's *Fables*, Daniel Defoe's *Robinson Crusoe* (1719), and Jonathan Swift's *Gulliver's Travels* (1726). Many of these books were filled with morals and satire which the young people carefully ignored while extracting the delightful stories which have retained their favour to the present day.

Chapbooks flourished between 1700 and 1840. They were very popular and presented four centuries of oral tradition in a degenerate literary form. They contained stories of Guy of Warwick, Reynard the Fox, Tom Hickathrift, Robin Hood, and other legendary heroes, and nursery stories. In time the number was increased by versions of *Gulliver's Travels, Robinson Crusoe*, and the fairy tales of Charles Perrault. These publications were not originally intended for children but specially written series appeared in the late seventeenth century, for example, nursery rhymes, *Red Riding Hood*, and *Cinderella*.

The chapbooks were poorly written and comprised a few badly chosen words. The stories were devoid of any style or grammar. There was a great deal of action and imagination but the dramatic incidents were spoiled by the small vocabulary and poor writing. Many of the phrases were repeated frequently, which was incidentally a feature which appealed to children. Eventually the market was captured by John Newbery who contributed greatly to an improved social status for the chapbook.

In Puritan England the literature was related to the religious attitude of the Puritans and their singleness of purpose was reflected in chilpren's books, as they took yet another opportunity to evangelize. The Puritans were opposed to all forms of recreational literature, and made unsuccessful attempts to destroy it.

One of the classic examples of Puritan literature for children was James Janeway's *A Token for Children* (1671). It was the most quoted of any book to eighteenth-century children, with the exception of the Bible, and contained stories of pious children who died young, often as young as 2 years. Another example is Thomas White's *A Little Book for Little Children* (12th edn., 1703), in which are recounted similar tales of small children "divers whereof are those who are lately deceased", and also includes gory accounts of Christian martyrs.

In contrast, Newbery's *A Little Pretty Pocket Book* was sold with a ball for boys and a pincushion for girls, and consists of picture games. Newbery issued many other books which were equally successful. The formats were specially designed with decorative title-pages, the text in good English, and with strong bindings. Newbery took advantage of material which had often accumulated unused for generations, and catered for the new urban society which was beginning to evolve from the Industrial Revolution.

A direct descendant of the Puritan literature was the Moral Tale of the late eighteenth and nineteenth centuries. The principal exponents of this form were Thomas Day, Mrs. Sarah Kirby Trimmer, Maria Edgeworth, and Mrs. Martha Sherwood.

Day achieved fame with *Sandford and Merton* (1783–9), which was designed to present Rousseau's educational ideas in the guise of fiction for English boys. It was regularly reprinted until 1887, and was the best and most complete example of the highly moral tale provided at that time. It was not universally approved as it made no allusions to orthodox religion but implied that practical goodness was sufficient: quite the contrary to the Puritan tenet of salvation by faith. This book gave a distorted picture of a vicious rich and a virtuous poor, and it is of interest to contrast it with the contemporary *Beggar's Opera* by John Gay and the cartoons of Hogarth.

Mrs. Trimmer's *The History of the Robins: for the instruction of children in their treatment of animals*, appeared in 1786. It was written for children but not always in a language they would appreciate. Children were invited to consider the stories as a series of fables to convey moral instruction to themselves and to excite in them compassion for birds. This lady had strong views on what was bad for children rather than what was good.

Maria Edgeworth was the daughter of Richard Edgeworth, the educationist, and most of her tales were written in the pattern of his ideas. Her father's influence was bad as it caused her to preach and moralize too much, but not to the extent of many of her contemporaries. Among her books are *The Parent's Assistant* (1796) and *Moral Tales* (1801). She often pictured the world as a schoolroom, from which the teacher was absent but returned in time to teach bad children the error of their ways. Themes of honesty, industry, and thrift are frequently dealt with, and the rich are reminded of their duty to their poorer neighbours.

Mrs. Sherwood spent a number of years in India, where she was influenced by the Calvinistic ideas of Henry Martyn, and these are reflected in her work. She is remembered for *The History of the Fairchild Family* (1818–47), which consists of a series of stories centring around the Fairchild parents and their children. She stressed the importance of a religious education in stilted artificial language, and each chapter consists of a story, a prayer, and a hymn. One horrific incident which was included in earlier editions was when Mr. Fairchild took the children to see a corpse on a gibbet to impress upon them the results of quarrelling.

It is highly unlikely that children today would wish to read any of these moral tales with the exception of some of Maria Edgeworth's stories, for example *Lazy Lawrence* and *The Birthday Present*. At the same time it must be said that most children's books draw morals, and indeed most young people would not have it otherwise. In the early moral tales, however, the moral predominated, whereas in modern literature it is usually subsidiary to the plot. The transition began in such works as Catherine Sinclair's *Holiday House* (1839).

Stories of fantasy, the offspring of fairy tales, became very popular in the nineteenth century, and most of them have their devotees in the twentieth century. Many of them were written for particular children. Lewis Carroll wrote *Alice in Wonderland* for Dean Liddell's daughter; Edward Lear wrote some of his limericks and other nonsense poems for the grandchildren of the Earl of Derby; and Charles Kingsley wrote *The Water Babies* for his son.

The earliest exponent was William Roscoe, a prominent Liverpool lawyer, historian, botanist, and poet, who wrote *The Butterfly's Ball* (1807) purely to amuse his own children. This was the second great book in the Newbery tradition. It had no educative purpose, was the most popular children's book of its day, and is now almost forgotten. It was not very good poetry but the rhyme was full of fun and fancy.

Edward Lear's *A Book of Nonsense* (1846) marked an important advance in the development of children's books, but his limericks now appear rather primitive. His main aim was to amuse and in this he succeeded.

In the 1850's came John Ruskin's *The King of the Golden River*

(1851), W. M. Thackeray's *The Rose and the Ring* (1855), and Frances Browne's *Granny's Wonderful Chair* (1857).

The Water Babies, Charles Kingsley's morally larded fairy tale, appeared in 1863. The story shows Kingsley's hatred of social injustice and exposed the plight of chimney boys. The story of Tom, a normal little boy who became a water baby, is much loved by younger children, who wisely ignore the author's homilies.

The great date of the nineteenth century in children's literature was 1865. It was in that year that Lewis Carroll's *Alice in Wonderland* was published. It was completely original and stands out beside smaller writings of the time like Robert Southey's *The Three Bears* and John Ruskin's *The King of the Golden River*. The characters often seem more real than many historical personages: the White Rabbit, the Mad Hatter, the Queen of Hearts, and the King she dominated. *Alice* was followed in 1872 with *Through the Looking-Glass*, which is one of the few sequels which maintains the standards of the original. In it chessmen replaced playing cards, and a second group of unforgettable characters were introduced.

Charles Dickens' *The Magic Fishbone* appeared in 1868. It was first published in the periodical *All the Year Round*. Many children's stories in the nineteenth century followed this practice before their publication in book form.

George MacDonald, like Kingsley, was conscious of a duty to preach. He wrote numerous books among which are *At the Back of the North Wind* (1871), *The Princess and the Goblin* (1872), and its sequel *The Princess and Curdie* (1883). The first tells of a boy's travels with the North Wind, while the others are pure fairy stories.

Two women writers who deserve mention are Mrs. Margaret Gatty, whose *Parables from Nature* (first series, 1855) have always been a success; and her daughter, Mrs. Juliana Horatia Ewing, whose *Brownies and Other Tales* (1870) have also remained popular. Some of Mrs. Ewing's stories moralize rather a lot but are still enjoyable to read.

The last great writer of fantasy in the nineteenth century was Mrs. Mary Louisa Molesworth. She wrote prolifically for children, and over 100 stories are listed in Roger Lancelyn Green's monograph. Among her stories two of the best are *The Cuckoo Clock* (1877) which uses a clock as the route to fairyland just as Carroll used a rabbit hole and a looking-glass; and *The Carved Lions* (1895) which some think one of the greatest stories of all children's literature. Mrs. Molesworth wrote other kinds of stories but it is her fairy tales which are most read today.

Another writer of note was Charlotte M. Yonge who wrote family stories such as *The Heir of Redclyffe* (1853) and *The Daisy Chain* (1856); and historical novels like *Unknown to History* (1882). Miss Yonge had strong Anglo-Catholic beliefs which greatly influenced the content of her work. She made a major contribution to literature for adolescent girls who were so often left to read poorer literature due to the absence of anything better.

Another popular brand of writing which developed and which has found many imitators since is the boys' adventure story. This attracted numerous pens but the most popular have been Captain Marryat, R. M. Ballantyne, G. A. Henty, W. H. G. Kingston, and Robert Louis Stevenson.

The formula was discovered by accident in Marryat's sea stories. He wrote his first book for children in 1841 with the title *Masterman Ready* in which he tried to improve on Johann Wyss' *The Swiss Family Robinson* (1812–13). Marryat was critical of the navigational and topographical details in Wyss' story, but having corrected these in his own work, he proceeded to preach, and almost made didacticism more important than his plot. Marryat was more successful with *The Children of the New Forest* (1847), one of the few pro-Royalist stories of the Civil War in which the Roundhead cause was depicted without prejudice. The theme of children living in primitive conditions in the forest was really an extension of being shipwrecked on an island.

Kingston wrote 171 books, but only *Peter the Whaler* (1851) is read today. The characters are rather flat, and although less than half the book concerns whaling, it is an exciting story.

Ballantyne took great pains with local background in most of his books after making á blunder in a description of coconuts in *Coral*

Island (1858). He spent a fortnight at the Bell Rock for *The Lighthouse* (1865), and for a period of 6 years was a clerk with the Hudson Bay Company when he gathered material which he used years later in *The Dog Crusoe* (1861). Other well-told tales by this author include *The Young Fur Traders* (1856), his first book for boys; and *The Gorilla Hunters* (1861), his sequel to *Coral Island*. The latter has been reinterpreted by William Golding in his novel *The Lord of the Flies*.

G. A. Henty put military history into boys' stories and set out to give his readers a sense of Empire at a time when Jingoism was at a premium. He wrote over eighty tales, all of which have a good historical background, but his heroes are stereotyped, and to read one is to have read all. His work includes *With Clive in India* (1884), *By Right of Conquest; or, with Cortez in Mexico* (1891), and *With Kitchener in the Soudan* (1903).

Perhaps the greatest of the adventure stories in this period are *Treasure Island* (1883) and *Kidnapped* (1886) by Robert Louis Stevenson. The first has given some giant-size characters to the world like Long John Silver, and events are dominated by the boy hero, Jim Hawkins. *Kidnapped* has a Jacobite background and describes the thrilling adventures of David Balfour after his attempt to claim his inheritance.

The plots of most of the boys' stories were highly improbable, but a herald of a more realistic family/adventure story appeared in 1882 from the pen of Richard Jefferies. *Bevis: the story of a boy*, describes the exploits of the hero and his friend Mark on a country estate in Wiltshire, and it was in this setting that they explored the unknown jungles, faced savages, fished, sailed, swam, and went shooting. This book differed from former "Robinsonnades" such as *Robinson Crusoe*, *Masterman Ready*, and *Coral Island*, in that imaginative adventures were enacted in familar surroundings.

A further development of the second half of the nineteenth century was that of the picture book for younger children, in the work of Walter Crane, Randolph Caldecott, and Kate Greenaway. In this kind of book it is not usually necessary for a child to be able to read as the pictures interpret the story. Much of the work of these three illustrators was published by Routledge. Editions are still available, published by Warne, for example Crane's *The Baby's Opera* (1876); Caldecott's *Picture Books* with their splendid portrayals of John Gilpin, the Queen of Hearts, and various fascinating details of country life; and Greenaway's *Marigold Garden* (1885).

Most of the nineteenth-century books which are still likely to interest children have been included in the Dent series of *Children's Illustrated Classics*. Authors represented include R. M. Ballantyne, Frances Browne, Lewis Carroll, Charles Dickens, Mrs. Ewing, Charles Kingsley, George MacDonald, Captain Marryat, Mrs. Molesworth, Robert Louis Stevenson, W. M. Thackeray, and Charlotte M. Yonge. Earlier work in this series includes John Bunyan's *The Pilgrim's Progress*, Daniel Defoe's *Robinson Crusoe*, and Jonathan Swift's *Gulliver's Travels*. Many of these authors are also available in the Puffin series of paperbacks.

Since 1960 an interest from various quarters in early children's books has resulted in the production of an interesting amount of material relating to the period prior to 1900. The editions, many of which are reprints from old plates, have not necessarily been produced with children in mind but to satisfy an adult audience. In 1965 Dobson's published an attractive book entitled *Flowers of Delight* which was compiled by Leonard de Vries. It contains selections from pre-Victorian children's literature based on the contents of the Osborne Collection (q.v.). Mr. de Vries has emphasized the instructional and moral quality of writings in the eighteenth and early nineteenth century, which frequently serve only to amuse modern children. His *Little Wide Awake* (Barker, 1967) is an anthology from the Anne and Fernand Renier collection of Victorian children's books and magazines.

The Oxford University Press *Juvenile Library* includes early children's books of special interest and is directed at students and other interested adults. It includes facsimile editions of John Newbery's *A Little Pretty Pocket Book* with an excellent introduction by Mary F. Thwaite; *The Penny Histories*, in which Victor E. Neuburg traces the development of the chapbook with representative examples; and

Sarah Fielding's *The Governess* with an introduction by Jill Grey. The series is edited by Brian Alderson.

Other examples of the interest in early children's books have been evidenced in series from various publishers. The Rupert Hart-Davis *Keepsake Library* includes Frances Crompton's *The Gentle Heritage* and Flora Shaw's *Castle Blair;* the Gollancz series of *Revivals* includes Mrs. Ewing's *A Great Emergency and a Very Ill-Tempered Family* and G. E. Farrow's *The Wallypug of Why;* and the Hamish Hamilton series of *Reprints* includes F. W. Farrar's *Eric; or, Little by Little* and Talbot Baines Reed's *The Fifth Form at St. Dominic's.* Individual titles which have been reissued include Silas Hocking's *Her Benny* (Liverpool Gallery Press), Richard Henry Horne's *Memoirs of a London Doll* (Andre Deutsch), and George MacDonald's *Sir Gibbie* (Blackie).

At a time when editions of early children's books are becoming more and more difficult to obtain from second-hand booksellers at reasonable prices, the series of reprints and new editions provide research material for the social historian, a consolation prize to the collector, and in many cases an introduction to modern children of the almost forgotten literary treasury of their more recent ancestors.

CHAPTER 9

Current Fiction for Children, from 1900

THE flow of new children's books continued unabated into the twentieth century, the first decade of which witnessed the emergence of a number of outstanding writers. These included Sir James Barrie, Walter de la Mare, Kenneth Grahame, Rudyard Kipling, Edith Nesbit, and Beatrix Potter.

Owing to the First World War (1914–18) there was a pause in the production of children's books, although it was during this period that Eleanor Farjeon's first work *Nursery Rhymes of London Town* appeared in 1916. The trickle of new names continued in the 1920's with only one author of note in the person of A. A. Milne.

Then the trickle became a river once more in the 1930's. So much so that it moved Marcus Crouch in his *Treasure Seekers and Borrowers* to write that "more interesting books and authors made their first appearance even than in the decade of E. Nesbit". These writers included Edward Ardizzone, Eve Garnett, C. Walter Hodges, Hilda Lewis, Arthur Ransome, Noel Streatfeild, J. R. R. Tolkien, and Geoffrey Trease.

Several factors contributed to improved standards in the 1930's. In the first place children's librarianship became a specialized branch of librarianship with the formation of the Association of Children's Librarians, the School Library Association, and the Schools Section of the Library Association in 1937.

There was also an increased interest in children's literature which can be demonstrated by four events. In 1931 the Library Association publication *Books to Read* included a survey of children's books for the first time; 1932 saw the publication of F. J. Harvey Darton's

Children's Books in England; 1936 launched *The Junior Bookshelf*, the first British journal devoted exclusively to the reviewing of children's books; and in 1937 the Carnegie Medal was awarded by the Library Association for the first time.

During the Second World War (1939–45) few writers were able to devote themselves to children's books. Enid Blyton established herself in these years. Possibly no other children's author has received so much publicity. One of the most prolific and popular writers ever in the history of children's books, Enid Blyton has been adversely criticized by many librarians and others. In a number of instances her books have actually been banned from public libraries where self-appointed censors have sat in judgement on her work. It is an injustice to single out the books of one writer for ostracism when so much similar material is still available on those same library shelves.

There was one important development during the war which was to revolutionize children's book publishing. In 1940 the first Puffin Picture Books appeared, which in 1941 were followed by the Puffin Story Books. Thus began two series of inexpensive paperbacks which in the former have a wide scope in informational content and in the latter include many outstanding children's books, not only from Britain but from the United States and European countries.

After the war more important writers began to contribute to this worthwhile field, including Richard Armstrong, Elizabeth Goudge, Cynthia Harnett, Ian Serraillier, and Elfrida Vipont.

The flowering came with the 1950's and early 1960's, and most writers of merit during these decades won the Carnegie Medal. In these years the historical novel was revived in the work of Hester Burton, Rosemary Sutcliff, Henry Treece, and Ronald Welch; and an increased attention was paid to teenagers, as when Penguin's supplemented their well-established Puffin paperbacks with the Peacock Books.

The second half of the 1960's witnessed a vast expansion in the production of books at low prices in paper covers. A hardback book may cost as much as £1.05 but its paper-covered equivalent can be purchased for as little as 15p. Gordon Landsborough sponsored Armada

Books which, having become too large for him to handle, he disposed of to Collins; and went on to launch the Dragon Books with Associated Publishers Ltd. in 1966. Corgi Books began to publish their Collie Books for children in 1966 which consisted of material issued by Hamish Hamilton in their Reindeer Series; Brockhampton's graded Knight Books appeared in 1967; and Macmillan's Topliners for teenagers in 1968. Various other publishers issued existing hardback editions in paper covers: Methuen, slim volumes of A. A. Milne's Christopher Robin and Pooh stories; Faber, books by Lucy Boston, Walter de la Mare, and Alison Uttley; and Allen & Unwin, Tolkien's *The Hobbit*.

It would be impossible to do justice to the many writers of merit who have devoted their attention to children's literature during the twentieth century. For the student who wishes to know more about this subject, histories and criticisms and useful bibliographies have been listed in earlier chapters. The aim here has been to recommend authors whose work if read will give the reader a working knowledge of contemporary children's literature. Having briefly summarized the principal trends of the century a review of some of the most outstanding writers in various types of children's fiction is provided as follows.

FANTASY

The type of fiction which has been awarded the Carnegie Medal most frequently is fantasy. There have certainly been some outstanding contributors in this field, but one wonders whether the judges of medal winners are not overpowered with nostalgia for the lost worlds of their own childhoods in giving it so much tribute.

The date 1900 is an arbitrary one to divide history from current material. The first giant of this century, E. Nesbit, had her book *The Story of the Treasure Seekers* published in 1899. This was a family story but she also wrote fantasies: *The Phoenix and the Carpet* (1904); *The Story of the Amulet* (1906), in which the fabulous Psammead appeared; *The House of Arden* (1908), with the Mouldiwarp; and various others. E. Nesbit did not remove her characters to a fantasy world of their own, and magic incidents happened against an everyday background very often. The strange creations of the Psammead and the Mouldiwarp show the power of this writer's imagination and help to place her in the top rank of children's authors.

Sir James Barrie wrote his *Peter Pan* (1904) as a play which was not turned into prose until 1911. In 1904 only Barrie believed in his now unforgettable characters, but his faith was to be more than justified in Peter, Tinker Bell, Wendy, the Pirates, the Red Indians, and the ticking crocodile in the Never-never Land. His *Peter Pan in Kensington Gardens* (1906) was not so successful and is strictly for devotees.

Perhaps the greatest debt for fantasy in this century is owed to Eleanor Farjeon. She wrote delightful poems and also superb stories. *Martin Pippin in the Apple Orchard* (1921) and *Martin Pippin in the Daisy Field* (1937) were full of magic, as was *Jim at the Corner* (1934). Credit is due to the Oxford University Press for the reissue of these books in the 1950's, as well as for the selection of her best stories in *The Little Bookroom* (Carnegie Medal, 1955). The well-drawn illustrations of Edward Ardizzone have done much to further enhance many of Miss Farjeon's books. She was the first person to be awarded the Hans Christian Andersen Award in 1956.

J. R. R. Tolkien, a scholar in the tradition of Lewis Carroll, in his own way gave us just such a splendid tale in *The Hobbit* (1937). It was originally written for his own family and tells of the adventures of the likeable Bilbo Baggins who, with the dwarfs, went in quest of treasure.

Another scholar, also of Oxford, was Clive Staples Lewis, whose chronicles of Narnia appeared in seven books, commencing in 1950 with *The Lion, the Witch and the Wardrobe*, and concluding in 1956 with *The Last Battle* (Carnegie Medal). Like Tolkien he underlined the eternal struggle between good and evil, a theme which has been common to all folklore. Lewis worked out his conception of the Christian story in excitingly written allegory.

Alan Garner's *The Weirdstone of Brisingamen* (1960) and *The Moon of Gomrath* (1963) are reminiscent of Tolkien and are steeped in legends from the ancient world. Hobbits, however, would keep their distance in books where children play so important a part in the struggle with evil. Mr. Garner used his own locality of Alderley Edge in Cheshire for descriptions of some of the most horrific incidents in children's fiction. In *Elidor* (1965), which should surely have been awarded the Carnegie Medal, the magic moved to Manchester in a slum-clearance area; and in *The Owl Service* (Carnegie Medal, 1967) the lives of three children were affected by a Welsh legend.

Joan Aiken's historical fantasies are set principally in a vaguely early nineteenth century Britain ruled by a Jacobite King and infested by wolves. *The Wolves of Willoughby Chase* (1962) describes the adventures of two girl cousins and their friend Simon, who succeed in bringing about the downfall of the wicked Miss Slighcarp. *Black Hearts in Battersea* (1965), *Night Birds on Nantucket* (1966), and *The Cuckoo Tree* (1971) are concerned with the frustration of Hanoverian plots to overthrow the Tudor–Stuart monarchy; whilst *The Whispering Mountain* (1968) is the setting for a long struggle to return a harp to its rightful owner.

The fantasy stories of Helen Cresswell possess a delicacy of language and a dream-like quality reminiscent of Eleanor Farjeon. *Where the Wind Blows* (1966) and *The Sea Piper* (1968) are fables for younger children, but the creative ability of this author is superbly demonstrated in *The Piemakers* (1967), *The Signposters* (1968), and *The Outlanders* (1970). In the latter book a strange boy grants Piers and his parents their deepest wishes at the end of a long, strange pilgrimage.

Time fantasy has attracted various writers of quality children's books. In *Dream Gold* (1949), David Severn described a dream adventure of two boys with pirates, and in *Drum-Beats* (1953) other children were involved in the fate of an expedition in Africa which had taken place years before. Philippa Pearce's *Tom's Midnight Garden* (Carnegie Medal, 1958) was about the telepathic visit of a modern boy to the latter years of the nineteenth century. The normality of Tom made the experiences most convincing. On the other hand, William Mayne, in his *Earthfasts* (1966) and *Over the Hills and Far Away* (1968), made no attempt whatever to rationalize the events described.

A type of fiction which is difficult to classify is that in which a character creates something out of his imagination, and which does not require the participation of another person for its substance. Mary Norton's *The Borrowers* (Carnegie Medal, 1952) was such a story in which the small beings who dwelt under the floorboards were the product of a boy's vivid imagination. This was followed by *The Borrowers Afield* (1955), *The Borrowers Afloat* (1959), and *The Borrowers Aloft* (1961).

ANIMAL STORIES

Animal stories fall into three categories: where the animal bears little or no relationship to its real-life counterpart as in the work of Beatrix Potter, Kenneth Grahame, and Margery Sharp; where the interest is divided between human beings and animals as with Anna Sewell's *Black Beauty* and L. M. Boston's *A Stranger at Green Knowe*; and thirdly, where the life story of an animal is told in fiction form as with Jocelyn Arundel's *Simba of the White Mane*, and the French writer René Guillot's *Kpo the Leopard* and *Sama*. Outside these groupings is the life story of the animal in which it is not personalized in any way, and which would be classified under Zoology.

Helen Griffiths' stories, many of which are set in Spain, show the response of animals to kindness and their often vicious reaction to cruelty and neglect. Horses are the subject in *Horse in the Clouds* (1957), *Moonlight* (1959), and *The Wild Horse of Santander* (1966); whilst dogs are the focus in *Leon* (1967) and *Patch* (1971).

In *Intent Upon Reading*, Margery Fisher remarked that "humanization can only be successful if something is preserved of the original animal". This is achieved in the books of Beatrix Potter, Kenneth Grahame, and Margery Sharp.

Beatrix Potter wrote most of her children's books before 1913. They included *The Tale of Peter Rabbit* (1902), *The Tailor of Gloucester* (1903), and *The Tale of Jeremy Fisher* (1906). Details of animals and country life were based on the author's first-hand knowledge of specific animals and life at Sawrey near Lake Windermere. The animals are clothed but to some extent follow their natural instincts, as in the case of Peter Rabbit in Farmer MacGregor's garden.

Kenneth Grahame's *The Wind in the Willows* (1908) pictured a riverside world peopled by Mole, Rat, Badger, and Toad, each of them with an individual personality. Sometimes they had human qualities and sometimes not. On one occasion Toad was thrown in a canal as a slimy creature, and on another he was jailed for car stealing. Grahame was familiar with the river animals near to his home at Cookham Dene on the banks of the Thames. The world of nature is well described and rises to a mystic quality in the famous passage on *The Piper at the Gates of Dawn*. This book stands as one of the classics of the present century.

A more recent contributor to the animal story is Margery Sharp, who was well known as an adult novelist before she began to write for children. She tells of the adventures of a Mouse Prisoners' Aid Society in *The Rescuers* (1959), *Miss Bianca* (1962), *The Turret* (1964), and *Miss Bianca in the Salt Mines* (1966). Miss Bianca and Bernard may well achieve the immortality of Peter Rabbit and Mr. Toad, as Margery Sharp is probably the greatest writer of animal fantasy in forty years.

Michael Bond's humorous adventures of a London-domiciled Peruvian bear are recounted in such readable books as *A Bear Called Paddington* (1958), *Paddington at Large* (1962), and *Paddington at Work* (1966). Only initially can Paddington be mistaken for a bear. In all except the outer form he is a small boy. This writer also introduced a mouse in the tradition of Margery Sharp, in *Here Comes Thursday* (1966) and *Thursday Rides Again* (1968).

Three writers who have produced rather different variations on the animal theme require some attention. Rudyard Kipling's *Jungle Books* appeared in 1894 and 1895. In them he pictured the life of the jungle and the boy, Mowgli, who was reared in a wolf pack. Most of the stories concern Mowgli, but others include *Rikki-Tikki-Tavi* the mongoose, and *The White Seal*. In 1902 Kipling's *Just So Stories for Little Children* was published, and he ranked this with the best of his prose work. The stories include *How the Whale Got His Throat* and *The Cat That Walked by Himself.*

Walter de la Mare produced *The Three Mulla-Mulgars* in 1910, the title of which was changed to *The Three Royal Monkeys* in 1935. It contains some of de la Mare's finest writing and tells of three monkeys who were driven into exile and went through harrowing situations. They are real monkeys and never at any time lose their dignity, nor did their creator treat them without due respect.

Winnie the Pooh (1926) and *The House at Pooh Corner* (1928) were very different. A. A. Milne dealt with the adventures of his son's toy animals: Pooh, Piglet, Eeyore, and Tigger. Toys they are, but their characters are as real as those of Grahame. Like all bears, Pooh likes honey, and in the tradition of donkeys, Eeyore is predisposed to be gloomy and sometimes cynical.

In addition to the works described there are a number of well-chosen collections of animal stories. Some of the best include:

DE LA MARE, WALTER (ed.). *Animal Stories.* Faber. 1939.

GREEN, MARGARET (ed.). *The Big Book of Animal Fables.* Dobson. 1965.
One hundred fables ranging from those of Aesop to contemporary writers. The stories are mostly short and are accompanied by illustrations by Janusz Grabianski.

Other selections by Margaret Green and illustrated by Janusz Grabianski are:
The Big Book of Animal Stories. Dobson. 1961.
Mainly folklore for younger children.
The Big Book of Pets. Dobson. 1966.
Twenty-four stories by such outstanding writers as Joy Adamson, René Guillot, Sterling North, and Johanna Spyri.
The Big Book of Wild Animals. Dobson. 1964.
Stories of animals who do not talk. Some are exciting and dramatic while others are fanciful.

KNEEBONE, S. D. (ed.). *Animal Stories of Today*. Hamilton. 1962.
Contributors include Michaela Denis, Gerald Durrell, and Sir
Arthur Grimble.

SHAW, MARGARET (ed.). *The Island of Seals, and Other Stories*.
Methuen. 1957.
Includes tales of seals, swans, monkeys, etc., all based on fact.

ADVENTURE AND FAMILY STORIES

Adventure stories have been the most popular branch of children's
reading for generations, and the most outstanding in the present century have been those which have been related to the home and to the
activities of normal boys and girls.

E. Nesbit's *The Story of the Treasure Seekers* (1899) dealt with the
efforts of the Bastable children to restore the family fortunes, in the
course of which they acted as highwaymen, dug for buried treasure,
and even attempted journalism. Another tale of this kind was *The
Would-be-goods* (1901). E. Nesbit concentrated on telling a good story
but discreetly inserted references to good manners.

In 1930 Arthur Ransome's *Swallows and Amazons* began a series of
twelve adventures in which real life and the imaginative games of
children were subtly interwoven. Understanding adults were helpful
but kept their distance from this middle-class children's paradise.
The characters developed with each book. Ransome's *Pigeon Post*
(1936) was awarded the first Carnegie Medal.

Interest arose in Richard Jefferies' *Bevis* in 1932 when an edition
was published by Jonathan Cape, 50 years after its original appearance. It was illustrated by E. H. Shepard and was introduced by E. V.
Lucas. This book had not achieved success in 1882 but found an appre-
ciative audience in and after the 1930's. In the same holiday-adventure
tradition and modelled on the more recent work of Arthur Ransome,
The Far-Distant Oxus (1937) was written by Kathleen Hull and
Pamela Whitlock. They followed this with *Escape to Persia* (1938) and
Oxus in Summer (1939).

Eve Garnett was one of the first writers to deal successfully with the lives of working-class folk, in *The Family from One End Street* (Carnegie Medal, 1937). Joe Ruggles was a dustman and his wife took in washing. Each child in the family had an adventure which was related to everyday life. As a student, Eve Garnett saw conditions in London's East End and other areas, and was able to record her observations with authenticity. She wrote a sequel in *The Further Adventures of the Family from One End Street* (1956) in which three of the Ruggles family left the town and adjusted to country life.

The working-class story has been widely copied by such writers as Anne Barrett, E. W. Hildick, Elizabeth Stucley, John Rowe Townsend, and Geoffrey Trease. The latter has written two domestic-adventure series in his Bannerdale and Maythorn stories. The former concern the Melbury family and present a complete picture of home, school, hobbies, and holidays. The characters develop in the books from secondary school to university and adult life. *No Boats on Bannermere* (1949), *Under Black Banner* (1950), *The Gates of Bannerdale* (1956), and others were written in the immediate years after Trease's first edition of *Tales Out of School*. It is unfortunate that while they were well written they did not reach the standard which their author himself had set. The Maythorn novels were written much later: *The Maythorn Story* (1960) and *Change at Maythorn* (1962) are interesting but not of the high standard of the earlier series.

Elfrida Vipont's *The Lark on the Wing* (Carnegie Medal, 1950) centres on Kit Haverard and shows the development of her career as a singer, presenting at the same time an authentic picture of the training involved. Other family stories by Elfrida Vipont include *The Lark in the Morn* (1948), to which the medal winner is a sequel; *The Spring of the Year* (1957); *Search for a Song* (1962); and *The Pavilion* (1969).

In the recent decades the most prominent exponent of the family-adventure story has been William Mayne, whose *Follow the Footprints* was published in 1953. Other books in the same vein are, *A Grass Rope* (Carnegie Medal, 1957), *The Rolling Season* (1960), *Sand* (1964) and *Ravensgill* (1970). Mayne's characters are made to speak in the abbreviated form normally used in conversation, which is sometimes difficult to follow. A search is frequently involved in the plots: for the origins of a legend, the discovery of water, the tracing of a tramway, and similar incidents.

Sheena Porter's books are mainly set in the West Midlands and are all mystery stories of one kind or another: *Hills and Hollows* (1962); *Jacob's Ladder* (1963), probably her best; *Nordy Bank* (Carnegie Medal, 1964); *Deerfold* (1966); and *The Valley of Carreg-Wen* (1971). The action in the two latter books takes place in Wales. Most of her books have an interest in the past though set in the present and often reflect the author's interest in archaeology.

The family stories of Barbara Willard usually contain problems of social adjustment. A new road threatened a family with eviction in *The House with Roots* (1959), urban children came to terms with the countryside in *Duck on a Pond* (1962), American and British children resolved their differences in *The Battle of Wednesday Week* (1963), whilst the difficulties of an orphan were resolved in *The Family Tower* (1968) and race relations was the theme in *The Toppling Towers* (1969).

K. M. Peyton demonstrated the conflict between economic need and youthful romanticism when it was proposed to construct a marina in *The Plan for Birdsmarsh* (1965). This author, primarily noted for her historical novels, went on to excel herself in *Pennington's Seventeenth Summer* (1970) and *The Beethoven Medal* (1971), stories of a rebellious talented teenager who was given the opportunity to make good.

North country life has been well described by John Rowe Townsend in such novels as *Gumble's Yard* (1961), *Hell's Edge* (1963), *Widdershin's Crescent* (1965), and *The Intruder* (1969). This author frequently discusses the often undeserving but helpless poor and the conscious and unconscious striving to improve their condition by others and by themselves. In a similar vein to Townsend, Sylvia Sherry told of the boy Rocky in *A Pair of Jesus Boots* (1969), and the poverty of his existence in working-class Liverpool.

HISTORICAL STORIES

In his *Written for Children*, John Rowe Townsend remarked that "one could wish that as many first-class books were being written about contemporary young people as about battles long ago". In fact a big improvement has taken place recently in the availability of modern family stories, but the standard of historical fiction is generally speaking much higher.

E. Nesbit's time-fantasies such as *The Story of the Amulet* (1906) and *The House of Arden* (1908) are histories inasmuch as the characters in them are removed from their present and placed in historical situations. The setting may be ancient Babylon or Egypt, Roman or Stuart Britain. The object of this kind of book is to find the reaction of children to what they see, whilst the historical facts are incidental.

In the early years of the twentieth century the leading historical storyteller for children was Rudyard Kipling. *Puck of Pook's Hill* (1906) and *Rewards and Fairies* (1910) were both set in Sussex and show Kipling's deep love of England. He understood the continuity of history and pictured the Downs at different periods in the stories which Welland the Smith, Sir Richard the Norman, and others told to Don and Una. Unlike E. Nesbit, who transported her central characters to the past or the future, Kipling had historical personages brought to the present through the agency of Puck.

After Kipling there were no outstanding writers of historical fiction until Geoffrey Trease wrote *Bows Against the Barons* (1934) in which he painted a realistic picture of so-called "Merrie England". From 1940 onwards Trease wrote a large number of books on a variety of topics. *Cue for Treason* (1940) was set in Elizabethan times; *The Hills of Varna* (1948) concerned a Renaissance quest for a Greek manuscript; *Mist Over Athelney* (1958) told of Alfred's last stand against the Danes; and *Follow My Black Plume* (1963) was set in Italy at the time of Garibaldi.

The pioneering work of Trease stimulated other writers. Cynthia Harnett's output included *The Great House* (1949), which was centred around the family of a seventeenth-century architect; *The Wool-Pack* (Carnegie Medal, 1951) recaptured the days of the Cotswold wool trade in the Middle Ages; *Stars of Fortune* (1956) concerned ancestors of George Washington in the reign of Mary I; and *A Load of Unicorn* (1959) was set in Caxton's time and includes a Was of the Roses subplot. Cynthia Harnett showed that in the course of time English life changed on the surface but in essentials it has remained unchanged. Great events were kept in the background and the lives of the people recounted in minute detail.

The greatest British historical writer is Rosemary Sutcliff. Some of her books are for middle schoolchildren: *The Armourer's House* (1951) is set in the Tudor period; *Simon* (1953) in the Stuart; and *The Witch's Brat* (1970) in Norman times. In *Simon* she examined the Civil War from a Roundhead point of view and described the personal conflicts involved, whilst in *The Witch's Brat* she showed how a crippled boy came to terms with his disability in tending the sick at the newly built St. Bartholomew's Hospital. Miss Sutcliff has also written books for older children and young adults in which philosophical problems of freedom and friendship, and the importance of maintaining the light of civilization have been discussed. All these books have maintained high standards both literary and historical, and include *The Lantern Bearers* (Carnegie Medal, 1959), *Knight's Fee* (1960), and *The Mark of the Horse Lord* (1965). This author is reminiscent of Kipling in that she has the same understanding of history, and her reading of his books has helped to develop in her the taste for history she now has.

Ronald Welch has either set his plots in Wales or had his characters return there at some stage in them. Most of his work is concerned with the history of the Carey family in such books as *Knight Crusader* (Carnegie Medal, 1954), *Captain of Dragoons* (1956), *Escape from France* (1960), and *The Hawk* (1967). His first book, *The Gauntlet* (1951), is set in present-day Wales but a mailed glove was used as a means of returning to the past, much as E. Nesbit used a Psammead and a Mouldiwarp. His more recent books include *Sun of York* (1970) which is concerned with the Wars of the Roses, and *The Galleon* (1971), which involves a plot to oust Elizabeth I. Ronald Welch is one of many contemporary authors in whose historical stories reaction and romance have given way to realism. As an historian he has written to give boys a sense of history.

Henry Treece was an expert in Celtic history and wrote a number of books about the Vikings: *Viking's Dawn* (1955), *Viking's Sunset*

(1960), and *Last of the Vikings* (1964). He also produced a fiction history of early Britain which covers the period from the New Stone Age to the time of Harold: *Men of the Hills* (1957), *Legions of the Eagle* (1954), and *Hounds of the King* (1955), are among these books. One of his last works, *Swords of the North* (1967), recounts some episodes in the life of Harold Hardrada.

The historical stories of Hester Burton include *Castors Away* (1962), which takes place at the time of Trafalgar; *Time of Trial* (Carnegie Medal, 1963), which deals with the same period from a social angle; *No Beat of Drum* (1966), which spotlights the plight of agricultural labourers in the 1830's and the life which awaited so many of them in Van Diemen's Land; and *Thomas* (1969), a moving picture of the persecution of the Quakers, and the ravages of the Great Plague in seventeenth century England.

Whilst *Castors Away* is a sea story which takes place at the beginning of the nineteenth century, Mrs. K. M. Peyton has chosen the end of the century for two of her sea stories. The two books are *Windfall* (1962) and *The Maplin Bird* (1964). *Thunder in the Sky* (1966) recounts the adventures of a boy engaged in the shipping of freight from Yarmouth to London and Calais during World War I. *Flambards* (1967) and its sequels *The Edge of the Cloud* (Carnegie Medal, 1969) and *Flambards in Summer* (1969), are concerned with the saga of the Russells of Flambards in the early part of the present century.

Leon Garfield has established himself as an outstanding writer of historical novels in literary style, superb characterization, and the apparent (though not always real) authenticity of his settings. He has concerned himself mainly with life in eighteenth century England, and has presented a highly readable and vivid portrayal of the period in *Devil in the Fog* (1966), *Smith* (1967), *Black Jack* (1968), and *The Drummer Boy* (1970). There is a recurring theme of innocent young boys attaining maturity after a series of non-too pleasant experiences.

SCHOOL STORIES

Before the Second World War, school stories were among the most frequently read of children's books, although there were very few writers of distinction.

Stalky and Co. (1899) by Rudyard Kipling was probably the most popular of all school stories for boys and poked fun at earlier tales such as Dean Farrar's *Eric; or, Little by Little* (1858) and *St. Winifred's* (1862). Another example of the art in the nineteenth century was the often sentimental and sometimes vicious *Tom Brown's Schooldays* (1857) by Thomas Hughes.

In the twentieth century boys' stories followed the style of Talbot Baines Reed, the author of *The Fifth Form at St. Dominic's* (1887), in the work of Richard Bird, Hylton Cleaver, Gunby Hadath, and Frank Richards. Probably three generations of girls have read the stories of Angela Brazil, Elinor Brent-Dyer, and Elsie Oxenham.

After the war the school tale almost became extinct in popularity but has been revived in the middle decades of the century in the books of William Mayne: *A Swarm in May* (1955), *Chorister's Cake* (1956), *Cathedral Wednesday* (1960), and *Words and Music* (1963) are set in a choir school. William Mayne was once a pupil at the Canterbury Cathedral Choir School. For girls the writings of Antonia Forest and Mary K. Harris can be recommended. The former wrote *Autumn Term* (1948) and *End of Term* (1959); while the latter wrote *Seraphina* (1960), *Penny's Way* (1963), and *The Bus Girls* (1965). The high quality of some of these books was emphasized in four of them being listed as runners-up for the Carnegie Medal: *A Swarm in May*, *Chorister's Cake*, *Seraphina*, and *The Bus Girls*.

SCIENCE FICTION AND SPACE TRAVEL

As the school story has declined in popularity, so science fiction has improved its position. Even in the 1950s it was not wildly acclaimed, but today there are definite signs that it is regarded with favour by children. After *The Time Machine* (1895), *War of the Worlds*

(1898), and *First Men on the Moon* (1901), by H. G. Wells, there was very little science fiction of any merit until the appearance of Donald Suddaby's *Lost Men in the Grass* (1940). Since those days other reputable writers have contributed such as David Craigie, Hugh Walters, and John Christopher. David Craigie's *The Voyage of the Luna I* (1948) can be recommended, as can Hugh Walters' *Blast off at Woomera* (1957), *Mission to Mercury* (1965), and earthbound *The Mohole Mystery* (1968) in which Chris Godfrey and his friends explored the interior of our own planet.

John Christopher emerged as a leading writer of children's books in the late 1960's. His outstanding trilogy *The White Mountains* (1967), *The City of Gold and Lead* (1967), and *The Pool of Fire* (1968) describe the plight of men dominated by an alien power, and their successful struggle for freedom. *The Lotus Caves* (1969) and *The Guardians* (1970) are also concerned with individual freedom in the face of insidious threats to its attainment. This author brings to science fiction a technical awareness blended with a readable style and reasonably credible plots.

GEOGRAPHICAL FICTION

There is a deficiency of material in this category in British writing for children. Frequently books have foreign or regional settings but the treatment is so superficial as to render them geographically worthless. It is true that regional atmosphere is present in the Yorkshire-based novels of William Mayne and Philip Turner, and that the West Midlands is evoked in the work of Sheena Porter, but the setting is only of secondary importance. The true geographical story may contribute to international understanding, will certainly give its readers a vicarious experience of life in other lands, and may be even used as an aid in the teaching of the subject.

Dr. Alan Boucher has presented a picture of the simplicity of Icelandic village life in *The Hornstranders* (1966). His descriptions of the craftsmanship, fishing, and sheep farming spring from firsthand experience. Similarly authentic are Sylvia Sherry's pictures of Malaysia in *Street of the Small Night Market* (1966) and *Frog in a Coconut Shell* (1968); and of Kenya in *A Snake in the Old Hut* (1972).

Of recent years there has been a fairly large-scale immigration into Britain by people from all over the world. Is it too much to hope that in time they will parallel the pattern in American books for children and write of the lands from whence they came?

PICTURE BOOKS

Having examined the exponents and content of fiction for children, it is of interest to consider picture books for younger children.

In the earlier years of the century Leslie Brooke was one of the leading artists. His work includes *Ring-o-Roses*, his *Johnny Crow* books, and the superb *Golden Goose Book*.

Most of the leading picture book illustrators of recent years have been awarded the Kate Greenaway Medal since its inception in 1955. The Medal is not solely intended for picture books but for any outstanding examples of children's book illustration. However, with few exceptions, the picture books have been selected; and include Edward Ardizzone's *Tim All Alone* (1956); Gerald Rose's *Old Winkle and the Seagulls* (1960); Brian Wildsmith's *A.B.C.* (1962); Victor Ambrus' *The Three Poor Tailors* (1965); and John Burningham's *Borka* (1963) and *Mr. Gumpy's Outing* (1970).

Greenaway Medal winners have been mainly quarto-size volumes, but this is not the only format for a successful picture book. One can call to mind such perennial favourites as the small-size products of Beatrix Potter and Helen Bannerman, Maria Bird and Jane Pilgrim, to realize that size cannot be the primary criterion of selection. In 1967 Faber issued a selection of their picture books in paper covers, some of them being reduced from their original size. Titles include Gerald Rose's *Old Winkle and the Seagulls* and Diana Ross' *The Little Red Engine goes to Market*.

There has been a tendency recently for many picture books to be issued in international editions so that plates are added to editions in different languages. This makes possible a high standard of illustration at reasonable prices. The finest examples are printed in Italy, but work is also undertaken in Czechoslovakia, Austria, Germany, and Switzerland.

A particularly attractive feature of children's books in this century has been seen in the work of a number of talented illustrators from Arthur Rackham, Ernest Shepard, and C. Walter Hodges, to Joan Kiddell-Monroe, William Stobbs, Victor Ambrus, Charles Keeping, and William Papas. The award of the Greenaway Medal in 1964 to C. Walter Hodges' *Shakespeare's Theatre* was the climax of 30 years dedicated work in children's book illustration. It is the illustrations which usually distinguish children's from adult fiction, and it is therefore pleasing that this mark of identification has progressed with the improvement in the standards of the texts.

CHAPTER 10

Poetry and Prose

POETRY

The first introduction of the child to poetry is through the nursery rhyme, and there is no shortage of attractive, well-chosen collections of these rhymes:

BRIGGS, RAYMOND (ed.). *The Mother Goose Treasury*. Hamilton. 1966.
More than 400 nursery rhymes copiously illustrated by Raymond Briggs, in colour and in black and white. This book was awarded the Kate Greenaway Medal for 1966.

IRESON, BARBARA (ed.). *The Faber Book of Nursery Verse*. Faber. 1958.
Caters for children to the age of 7 and contains over 800 rhymes. There are attractive line drawings by George Adamson.

LINES, KATHLEEN (ed.). *Lavender's Blue: a book of nursery rhymes*. Oxford U.P. 1954.
One of the most attractive and colourful editions of nursery rhymes in print. There are about 120 rhymes, and charming illustrations by Harold Jones.

OPIE, IONA and PETER (comps). *The Oxford Nursery Rhyme Book*. Oxford U.P. 1955.
A wide coverage of over 800 rhymes and ditties from "the happy heritage of oral tradition". Some of the wood engravings are by Joan Hassall, but the majority are from chapbooks and toy books.

WALTER, L. E. (ed.). *Mother Goose's Nursery Rhymes*. A. & C. Black. 1924.

John Newbery's fifty rhymes form the basis of this collection, and many of the originals are given in full. The 800–900 rhymes are not well laid out and the print is small, so that the layout does not balance the fine illustrations of Charles Folkard.

WERNER, JANE (sel.). *The Giant Golden Mother Goose.* Paul Hamlyn. 1965.
367 rhymes, illustrated in colour by Alice and Martin Provensen.

Graduation is from the nursery rhyme, whose history is thoroughly examined in *The Oxford Dictionary of Nursery Rhymes*, edited by Iona and Peter Opie (1951), to the poetry anthology. The best anthologies select the outstanding work of all periods. One of the main weaknesses of many British anthologies, even when the content is good, is the inadequacy of the indexes. There are, however, a number of good-quality anthologies from which a choice can be made:

AUDEN, W. H. and GARRETT, J., comps. *Poet's Tongue.* Bell. 1935.
Arranged in two alphabetic sections, it ensures the poems are read with an open mind by only giving the names of poets in the index and not with their work. In his book *English for Maturity*, David Holbrook considered *Poet's Tongue* to be "the best in existence". There are indexes of first lines, poets, and subjects.

BLISHEN, EDWARD (ed.). *The Oxford Book of Poetry for Children.* Oxford U.P. 1963.
The introduction is addressed to children. Some unusual poems are included but there is no mention of Byron, Milton, Pope, or Spenser. Indexes are of authors and first lines. Brian Wildsmith has provided exceptionally fine illustrations.

DE LA MARE, WALTER (ed.). *Tom Tiddler's Ground: an anthology of poetry for children.* Bodley Head. 1961.
The editor has written detailed notes to the poems. Byron, Milton, Spenser are included here, but Dryden, Kipling, and Pope are not represented. Indexes of authors and first lines.

GREAVES, GRISELDA (ed.). *The Burning Thorn: an anthology of poetry.* Hamilton. 1971.

A collection of poems, international in coverage with a twentieth-century emphasis. The arrangement is by topics, flexibly interpreted; and indexes are of poets and titles, and first lines.

GREEN, ROGER LANCELYN (ed.). *A Book of Verse for Children*. Dent Children's Illustrated Classics. 1962.
Among the children's writers whose work is included are R. M. Ballantyne, Sir James Barrie, Lewis Carroll, Walter de la Mare, Eleanor Farjeon, Kenneth Grahame, Charles Lamb, George MacDonald, A. A. Milne, E. Nesbit, and Robert Louis Stevenson. As a contrast Byron, Keats, Shelley, Milton, and Wordsworth are excluded. A very attractive book with author and first-line indexes, and illustrations by Mary Shillabeer.

GRIGSON, GEOFFREY (comp.). *The Cherry Tree*. Phoenix. 1959.
Over 500 poems representative of British poetry. Some are translations from the Gaelic. Indexes of authors and first lines.

HOLBROOK, DAVID (comp.). *Iron, Honey, Gold*. 4 vols. Cambridge U.P. 1965.
First issued in two volumes in 1961, it concentrates on great thoughts by poets under different circumstances, and was compiled "in order to try to remedy the lack of a good anthology".

MCFERRAN, ANN (ed.). *Poems to be Read Aloud to Children and by Children*. Nelson. 1965.
Almost 200 poems are included, many of them selected by the children's library staff of the Philadelphia Public Library. Helpful features are the introductory chapter on Patterns in Poetry, and the brief comments which precede each group of poems. Most standard British poets are represented, although twentieth-century coverage is weak. In contrast modern American poets are included. Illustrations by Roberta Lewis Clark. Index of first lines and authors.

MEYNELL, SIR FRANCIS (ed.). *By Heart*. Nonesuch Cygnets. 1965.
A chronological arrangement which includes many poems not to be found in other anthologies, and representative of the best work of all ages. This is probably the most balanced and well-produced work of its kind to be produced for many years. Well indexed.

Reeves, James (ed.). *Merry-go-round: a collection of rhymes and poetry for children.* Heinemann. 1955.

In four parts, the poems are graduated by age ranges from 7 to 12. There are over 400 poems, and author and first line indexes.

Smith, Janet Adam (ed.). *The Faber Book of Children's Verse.* Faber. 1953.

This caters for children aged 8 to 14, and the poems were suggested by children in this age group. Indexes of first lines, titles, and authors.

Most of the poetry anthologies contain the work of standard poets, but there have been many poets who have written for children during the last hundred years, and whose works are published separately.

Robert Louis Stevenson's *A Child's Garden of Verses* was first published in 1885. Some of the poems in this are very well known, such as "The Land of Counterpane", "Foreign Lands", "The Lamplighter", and "My Treasures". Many of them reflect the world of a delicate child often confined to bed, and in Stevenson's case this was pure autobiography. These poems are available in the Dent *Children's Illustrated Classics*, illustrated by Mary Shillabeer; in the Puffin series, illustrated by Eve Garnett; and there is also the sumptuous Oxford University Press edition illustrated by Brian Wildsmith.

Fascinating interweavings of the real and the fantastic were achieved by A. A. Milne in *When We Were Very Young* (1924) and *Now We Are Six* (1927). These are among the best poetry for all children. Methuen has made them available in separate hard- and paper-covered editions and in the one-volume *The Christopher Robin Verses* (1932). Among the more famous of the verses are "Buckingham Palace", "Daffodowndilly", "Rice Pudding", "If I Were King", "Buttercup Days", and the immortal "Vespers".

The greatest children's poet of all, however, was Walter de la Mare. His outstanding poems were reissued by the Oxford University Press during the 1940's and 1950's, even though most of them were originally published between 1902 and 1930. *Collected Rhymes and Poems* (1944) includes approximately 300 poems from various books such as *Songs of Childhood* (1902) and *Peacock Pie* (1913). His lyrics are said to compare well with those of Campion, Herrick, and Bridges.

The Oxford University Press also collected the poems of Eleanor Farjeon into *Children's Bells* (1957), which was illustrated by Peggy Fortnum. Miss Farjeon's poems were first published during the First World War.

Since the Second World War some first-rate poets have appeared including James Reeves and Ian Serraillier. Reeves' *The Wandering Moon* (1946), *The Blackbird in the Lilac* (1952), and *Ragged Robin* (1961) contain some charming and witty verses which demonstrate both vivid imagination and technical expertise.

Serraillier's *Thomas and the Sparrow* (1946) consists of modern verses based on old nursery rhymes. He has written epic poems which include *The Ballad of the Kon-Tiki* (1952), which recounts the thrilling voyage of Thor Heyerdahl and his companions across the Pacific; and *Everest Climbed* (1955), which tells of the triumphant conquest of Mount Everest by the British expedition of 1953. Ian Serraillier also retold the chief episodes of *Beowulf the Warrior* (1954), *The Challenge of the Green Knight* (1966), and *Robin and His Merry Men* (1969).

In addition to the standard editions of the poets described, there is a Puffin edition of Walter de la Mare's poems (1962); and *A Puffin Quartet of Poets* (1958), which includes work by Eleanor Farjeon, James Reeves, E. V. Rieu, and Ian Serraillier.

Other poets, already honoured for their contribution to adult literature, have written especially for children. These include Robert Graves' *The Penny Fiddle* (1960) and *Ann at Highwood Hall* (1964); Ted Hughes' amusing poems about his relatives for older children, *Meet My Folks* (1961); and John Betjeman's *A Ring of Bells* (1962), which contains some of the passages from his autobiographical *Summoned By Bells* as prefaces to some of his favourite poems.

The Bodley Head series of volumes containing the work of celebrated poets has made an outstanding contribution to the material which is available. Robert Frost was probably the greatest modern poet of the United States, but he found his early success in England. In 1959 was published his *You Come Too: favourite poems for younger readers*, which consists of selections from his earlier work introduced by Eleanor Farjeon. More recent additions to this series are Edward Thomas's *The Green Roads: poems for young readers* (1965), chosen and introduced by Eleanor Farjeon; John Clare's *The Wood is Sweet: poems for young readers* (1966), chosen by David Powell and introduced by Edmund Blunden; and Christina Rossetti's *Doves and Pomegranates* (1969), in which the poems are chosen by David Powell.

A useful guide to children's poetry is the American *Index to Children's Poetry* (H. W. Wilson Co.) which was compiled by John E. and Sara W. Brewton. The first volume appeared in 1942 and indexes 130 collections of poems and nursery rhymes in a sequence of titles, subjects, and authors. Most of the 15,000 poems are American, but well-known British anthologies dealt with include Walter de la Mare's *Poems for Children*; Edward Lear's *Book of Nonsense*; A. A. Milne's *Now We are Six* and *When We Were Very Young*; and Robert Louis Stevenson's *A Child's Garden of Verses*. This volume was supplemented by two others in 1957 and 1965 which index approximately 150 collections of poems published between 1938 and 1963 (Fig. 22). British anthologies include Walter de la Mare's *Bells and Grass*; Eleanor Farjeon's *Children's Bells*, *New Book of Days*, and *Poems for Children*; Robert Graves' *The Penny Fiddle*; Kathleen Lines' *Lavender's Blue*; Ruth Manning-Sanders' *A Bundle of Ballads*; Iona and Peter Opie's *The Oxford Nursery Rhyme Book*; and James Reeves' *The Blackbird in the Lilac* and *Ragged Robin*.

The American Library Association's *Subject Index to Poetry for Children and Young People*, published in 1957, covers 157 anthologies and collected works, and was compiled by Violet Sell.

John Mackay Shaw edited *Childhood in Poetry* for the Gale Research Co. in 1967. It is a catalogue in five volumes of the books of English and American poets comprising the Shaw Childhood in Poetry Collection in the Library of the Florida State University. The first four volumes consist of an alphabetical sequence of authors, editors, and illustrators with biographical and critical annotations, and the fifth is a keyword index. Brief quotations from some of the poems are included with each entry.

INDEX TO CHILDREN'S POETRY

;e upon a midnight dreary,
dered, weak and weary")
  Poe. *SmLg*
lerneath an old oak tree")
or Coleridge. *HoW*
'd as she sate at her meal."
h
on a tree." See The syco-
ind the gullible raven

:he gloom of death is on
wing") Nicharchus. *PlU*
ice upon a midnight dreary,
dered, weak and weary")
;mLg
nderneath an old oak tree")
ige. *HoW*
iic fox and the gullible ra-
:Carryl. *CoH*
:bies. Unknown. *CoSp—*

orbies. *MaB*
mas
ice. *DeT—FeF—JoAc*
n arm-deep into bright
Shells
liss
ere. *HaY*
uchanan
iary rising. *BrL-8*
ooks and reading
ok of hills and seas. T'ao
'r. the Chinese by Arthur

:er. Clarice Foster Booth.

vith one hand to turn o'er."
'y of Rimini
  De Vere. *DoP*
iert Duncan. *GrCc*
rothy Aldis. *AlA—ArTp*
  the pelican." John Ciardi.

ons, but moons not hers."

"The red-brown chipmunk on the wall."
  See The chipmunk
"Red firelight on the Sioux tepees." See
  Cottonwood leaves
"Red gold of pools." See Harvest sunset
The red-gold rain. Sacheverell Sitwell.
  GrCc
Red Hanrahan's song about Ireland. Wil-
  liam Butler Yeats. *SmLg*
Red iron ore. Unknown. *ArTp*
"Red leaves flutter." See Cover
A red, red rose. See My luve's like a red,
  red rose
Red Riding Hood
  Little Red Riding Hood. G. W. Carryl.
  CoH
"Red river, red river." See Landscapes—
  Virginia
Red rooster. Hilda Conkling. *JoAc*
"Red rooster in your gray coop." See Red
  rooster
"A red sky at night." Mother Goose. *LiL—*
  OpO
"Red stockings, blue stockings." Mother
  Goose. *OpO*
Redbirds. See Red birds
Redemption. George Herbert. *HaP*
Reese, Lizette Woodworth
  Bible stories. *DoP*
  A book. *HaY*
  A Christmas folk song. *ArTp—DoP—FeP*
  —JoAc
  The good Joan. *ArTp—FeF—NaM*
  A little song of life. *BrR-6—DoP—FeF—*
  HuL-2
  "Lydia is gone this many a year." *GrCc*
  Thistledown. *HaY*
Reeves, James
  The amperzand. *ReP*
  Animals' houses. *ReW*
  Avalon. *ReR*
  Beech leaves. *ReW*
  Bells. *ReG—ReW*

FIG. 22. Specimen entries from J. E. and S. W. Brewton's *Index to
Children's Poetry. Second Supplement.*
(By courtesy of the H. W. Wilson Co., New York, United States.)

Another useful, but less exhaustive, guide is Helen Morris's *Where's That Poem* (Blackwell, 1967). This indexes poems for children alphabetically, by subject, and by kind; and entries include titles, poets, first lines, and references to anthologies. It is prefaced by an introductory essay on the teaching of poetry, and analyses approximately 150 anthologies and volumes of work by individual poets.

PROSE ANTHOLOGIES

There is a wide selection of anthologies appealing to the varied interests and age ranges of children. Many of them have been written for use in school while others have a more general appeal. Those for younger children are intended to be read aloud by interested parents or other understanding adults or older brothers and sisters.

For Younger Children

BAMBERGER, RICHARD (sel.). *My First Big Story Book*. Oliver & Boyd. 1965.
First published in Austria and translated from the German by James Thin. Seventy-three stories from many lands for younger children.

BAMBERGER, RICHARD (sel.). *My Second Big Story Book*. Oliver & Boyd. 1966.
Fewer but longer stories intended for children who can read for themselves.

BAMBERGER, RICHARD (sel.). *My Third Big Story Book*. Oliver & Boyd. 1967.
Mainly less well known Fairytales.

COLWELL, EILEEN (sel.). *Tell Me a Story: a collection for under fives*. Penguin. 1962.
A wide variety of stories, some anonymous, and others by famous writers. A number of animal stories and tales of personalized objects, such as *Little Red Engine, Little Wooden Horse*, and *The Tale of the Hazel Nut*, are included.

COLWELL, EILEEN (sel.). *Storyteller's Choice*. Bodley Head. 1963.
Twenty stories followed by notes for storytellers regarding telling time, audience appeal, and occasion for use. Miss Colwell, who is one of the most successful storytellers in this country, has also written *A Second Storyteller's Choice* (1965). In this there are eighteen stories for the age group 5–10 with notes and practical suggestions.

FISHER, MARGERY (sel.). *Open the Door*. Brockhampton. 1965.
Thirty-nine extracts and stories by well-known writers. Includes brief comments on the writers and suggestions for further reading from their work.

IRESON, BARBARA (sel.). *The Faber Book of Nursery Stories*. Faber. 1966.
Forty stories for reading by and to children. Most of them are quite short and cover a wide range of topics. Prolifically illustrated by Shirley Hughes.

LINES, KATHLEEN (sel.). *The Faber Story Book*. Faber. 1961.
Seventy-four stories, romantic fairy tales and heroic legends. Sections include Nonsense, Animals, Giants and Witches, and Aesop.

LINES, KATHLEEN (sel.). *Tales of Magic and Enchantment*. Faber. 1966.
Divides into two parts: unusual fairy tales; prose and poetry from medieval literature such as Beowulf, the Volsungs, etc. Illustrated by Alan Howard.

For Older Children

ALLEN, E. E. and MASON, A. T. (eds.). *Twelve Modern Short Stories*. Edward Arnold. 1958.
Chosen for middle grammar school and upper secondary modern forms. Mainly longer short stories by outstanding authors.

BLISHEN, EDWARD (ed.). *Come Reading: a book of prose for young readers*. Michael Joseph. 1967,

A collection of more than fifty extracts from a wide range of literature written for children and adults. Each extract is complete in itself but the editor's aim is to stimulate interest in the sources. The arrangement is by topics.

BRITTON, JAMES (ed.). *Oxford Books of Stories for Juniors.* 3 vols. Oxford U.P. 1964.
Very short stories, mainly extracts from longer works, e.g. Anne Barrett's *Songberd's Grove,* Ian Serraillier's *The Silver Sword.* Some of the stories were written by children. There is a teacher's book with each volume.

The Eleanor Farjeon Book: a tribute to her life and work, 1881–1965. Hamilton. 1966.
A collection of work by twelve well-known children's writers, comprising stories by Ruth Ainsworth, Gillian Avery, Dorothy Clewes, Eilis Dillon, Patricia Lynch, William Mayne, Mary Norton, Rosemary Sutcliff, and Barbara Willard; poems by James Reeves and Ian Serraillier; and a reminiscence of *Tea with Eleanor Farjeon* by Rumer Godden. The contributions are ably introduced by Naomi Lewis and illustrated by Edward Ardizzone.

HOLBROOK, DAVID (comp.). *People and Diamonds: an anthology of modern short stories for use in secondary schools.* 4 vols. Cambridge U.P. 1962–66.
Written to educate the feelings of the 75 per cent of children who do not progress to the grammar school.

LINES, KATHLEEN (ed.). *The Faber Book of Stories.* Faber. 1960.
For older juniors and secondary children. Authors include H. E. Bates, Sir Arthur Conan Doyle, Arthur Ransome, and P. G. Wodehouse.

SANSOM, CLIVE (ed.). *By Word of Mouth: an anthology of prose for reading aloud.* Methuen. 1950.
The 180 pieces are very short and many are only brief extracts. It is appropriate to mention some of the collections of stories by individual writers which include:

BOND, MICHAEL. *Adventures of Paddington*. Collins. 1966.

DE LA MARE, WALTER, *Collected Stories for Children*. Oxford U.P. 1947.

FARJEON, ELEANOR. *The Little Bookroom*. Oxford U.P. 1957.

KIPLING, RUDYARD. *All the Mowgli Stories*. Macmillan. 1964.

MILNE, A. A. *The World of Pooh: containing Winnie-the-Pooh and the House at Pooh Corner*. Methuen. 1958.

UTTLEY, ALISON. *The Sam Pig Storybook*. Faber. 1965.

CHAPTER 11

School Books
and Information Books

DURING the eighteenth and early nineteenth century there were very few school books available which were suitable to the needs of most children, and apart from these there was very little non-fiction at all.

The Society for Promoting Christian Knowledge, founded in 1699, was active in publishing material for use in charity Day schools and in Sunday schools. This consisted of penny spelling and reading books, abridgements of the Bible and the Church Catechism. A further market for books was available in middle-class homes where children were often privately educated, and this resulted in the publication of primers, prose and verse selections, and books on geography, history, and other subjects.

Mrs. Sarah Kirby Trimmer, the author of *The History of the Robins*, wrote spelling books for charity schools as well as Bible abridgements. These were widely used in schools for most of the nineteenth century in the schools of the National Society. Mrs. Barbauld wrote *Lessons for Children* (1778) which set standards as regards style and content in educational literature. So many books at that time were designed to be spelled out rather than read, and very little importance was attached to subject content. In Mrs. Barbauld's *Lessons* the text was made interesting and was related to the world children knew, while the material was attractively printed. Maria Edgeworth, too, made instruction interesting in *The Parent's Assistant* (1796).

The demand for popular education grew, and in 1833 the House of Commons voted £20,000 "for purposes of education". The increasing interest in education drew attention to the lack of suitable textbooks and soon engaged the attention of the Committee of Council on Education which was set up in 1839. In 1847 the Committee's Book Department published a list designed to make school managers aware of different kinds of elementary school books. Money was granted to schools for the purchase of books of a secular nature, a development of importance, because only those of a religious content were available from the educational societies.

While the intentions of the Committee of Council were honourable, numerous accusations of censorship were levelled at it, and on the recommendation of the Newcastle Commission (1861) the list was withdrawn and the Book Department closed. A number of educational publishers sprang up and took over the supply of books, and very seldom conformed to the liberal terms of the Committee of Council.

Through the years the number of schools increased and with them the supply of books. Unfortunately the books were often compiled by incompetent people.

After the passing of the Elementary Education Act of 1870 the vast increase in the number of schools presented publishers with a larger market than ever and the output of books grew enormously. In addition syllabuses were gradually extended and by 1880 could include any subjects which could be properly treated in reading books.

The content of elementary school books changed a great deal between 1870 and 1900. Before 1882 there were various general class readers which differed in size and content but which were all planned to convey a large amount of useful information. After 1882 the readers assumed a more literary character because special books were now required in other subjects. After 1890 the number and variety of reading books increased rapidly to meet the alternative syllabuses.

The Cross Commission Report on *Elementary Education* in 1888 contained many references to the question of books in schools. It rejected the idea of reintroducing official booklists but suggested that "a more or less extended programme should be published for each subject". It criticized the practice of only providing three reading books for each standard for a year, and recommended an increase in the amount of reading material available. This Commission proved itself very forward looking in its statement that "the establishment of school libraries is strongly recommended".

The Code of 1902 contained clear directions regarding the courses of instruction in schools. There were no noticeable results in the supply of school books for many years and they were still used for reading by rote. The principle of collective teaching could hardly contribute to an individual use of a wide variety of books. After the Education Act of 1902 opinion grew in favour of teaching children to read with meaning and not as a technical end in itself. Opinion also grew in favour of learning by discovery and the individuality of children was recognized, so that the choice of a wide variety of suitable books became important.

The 1920's and 1930's were years of prolific thought and the dissemination of new ideas in educational principles and teaching methods. In all the reports of committees which were issued there was a continuous emphasis on the need for more books in schools. For example, in the Hadow report on *Books in Public Elementary Schools* (1928) it was suggested that "not only the supply of books used in schools requires to be increased, but also that their quality not infrequently stands in need of improvement". Similar pleas were made in the Hadow reports on *The Primary School* (1931) and *Infant and Nursery Schools* (1933), and in the Spens report on *Secondary Education* (1938).

After the Education Act of 1944 a great deal of experiment was undertaken in schools. The Ministry of Education pamphlet *The School Library* (1952, revised 1967) indicated the official attitude. A distinction was to be drawn between the type of books under review and "school books" which "have their legitimate purposes but they are useless for the problem before us. The books we are concerned with must in the eyes of the pupils be *real* books; they must be for individual rather than class use; and they must be part of a collection, however small, formed for the encouragement of the pupils as readers."

More recent views on the use of books in schools can be found in the Ministry of Education pamphlet *The Use of Books* (1964), together with the recommendations of the Newsom report, *Half Our Future*

(1963), and those of the Plowden report, *Children and Their Primary Schools* (1967).

Throughout the past decade there have been revolutionary changes in the publishing trade in the field of non-fiction for children. These changes have been made necessary by the greatly increased demand for books of this kind. There has been a rapid growth of school libraries, and the policy has been to stock them with as wide a variety of books as possible related to the age ranges and intelligences of the children who will use them.

The public libraries report an increased readership for non-fiction by children, and the relative proportions of borrowing between this and fiction are gradually changing in favour of the former. Closer co-operation between schools and public libraries have contributed to this factor.

Booksellers are receiving more non-fiction requests from members of the public while the demand for standard fiction editions is decreasing.

Consequently there has been a large increase in the supply of non-fiction from publishers. None of the publishers appear to have any definite subject leanings in children's books as they do with their adult material. Many of the publishers are issuing series on broad subjects which are very similar to one another.

In Science one finds Chambers' *Starting Science*, Heinemann's *Junior Science Series*, Longman's *Science on the March*, Muller's *Junior Science Books*, Wheaton's *Basic Science Series*, all of which are designed to be used in primary schools. Secondary schools are invited to select from Arnold's *Science and You*, Murray's *Junior Scientist Books*, Weidenfeld and Nicolson's *Young Scientist Series*, and many others.

This trend is repeated in other subject fields. There are series, in Geography, for example, which duplicate material in each other: Benn's *Countries of Today*, Burke's *Let's Visit*, Chatto & Windus' *Around the World Today*, Macmillan's *Nations Today*, Methuen's *Children Everywhere*, Muller's *The Kennedys Abroad*, Oldbourne's *Young People*, Phoenix's *Young Traveller Series*, and Ward Lock's *How People Live*, to mention just a few.

The unnecessary amount of duplication is not confined to broad subjects. In Biology, for example, there are Black's *Young Naturalists*, Burke's *Young Specialist Books*, Chatto & Windus' *Play Ideas*, and Oliver & Boyd's *World of Nature*. In Ancient History there are Batsford's *Everyday Life*, Chatto & Windus' *Dawn of History*, Muller's *Exploring the Past*, Max Parrish's *They Lived Like This*, and Weidenfeld & Nicolson's *Young Historian Books*.

In view of the very wide choice offered there is a consequent need for selection. Many of the series are not of a high standard either of content or production. With increased competition, however, there are visible improvements in the accuracy of subject matter and the quality of illustrations, but there is a lack of conviction as to the importance of good indexes. Examples can readily be found from the series listed, and from books which in other respects may be of a reasonably good quality. Longman's *Science on the March*, Muller's *Junior Science Books*, and Chambers' *Starting Science* are all attractive and mainly well written, but they do not include indexes. It must be admitted that the situation in this respect often improves in books for secondary schools.

A further reason for better produced non-fiction in this country is due to the influx of material from the United States. In Britain more attention needs to be given to having less rigid boundaries between textbooks and the new information books. The distinctions have been removed in the United States so that good-quality books are now available which have an equal appeal to the school and the home. This too puts into practice the attitude of the various recent official publications on the subject. There is some evidence that educational publishers like Evans Brothers and Arnold are becoming aware of the advantages of this. One of the leading publishers in the field is the American firm of Holt-Rinehart, which has introduced a great deal of outstanding science books into this country. Other publishers of note are the American Book Co. and D. C. Heath.

Holt-Rinehart's books are usually attractively produced with clear type, useful rather than ornamental illustrations; and their graduated sets of books cater for children from infancy to adolescence. They begin with colourful illustrations and captions, and progress through to material for advanced study. A typical example of this is a work in three volumes by Ira C. Davis and others, entitled *Science*. In addition to the graduated text and good illustrations there are lists for further reading, lists of activities, and very useful indexes. The main disadvantage is the American spelling. Similar publications are the American Book Co. *Thinking Ahead in Science* in six books by Willard Jacobson, and the D. C. Heath *Science Series* in eight volumes written by Herman and Nina Schneider.

It has been pointed out that the development of English literature for children entered a new and more prolific era in the 1930's. Together with an improvement in content this has been maintained. A similar development took place in the United States in the 1920's, giving the Americans an ascendancy which they preserved for many years. In the field of picture books and novels the British and American productions compare well in quality, but in non-fiction this has not yet been realized. A number of publishers are endeavouring to close the gap with some success and will be further encouraged to do so by popular demand and healthy competition. The duplication of series on similar topics by British publishers will foster the desired competition, but during the process those responsible for the selection of books for children will require a carefully worked out selection policy.

Very few non-fiction books have been awarded the Carnegie Medal. The successful ones have been Eleanor Doorly's *The Radium Woman* (1939), a biography of Marie Curie; Agnes Allen's *The Story of Your Home* (1949); Edward Osmond's *A Valley Grows Up* (1953), which shows the development of a valley from the earliest times to the present day; and Dr. I. W. Cornwall's *The Making of Man* (1960), a study of evolution for children. In addition, C. Walter Hodges' *Shakespeare's Theatre* (1964) won the Kate Greenaway Medal for illustration but it must also be recognized as an outstanding contribution to non-fiction. The proportional increase in the number of Carnegie Medals awarded to non-fiction reflects the trend in publishing so that in time their incidence may well be as frequent as that of fiction.

This study of the development of school books and information books is necessarily brief, but the subject can be pursued in much greater depth in the author's *A History of Children's Reading and Literature*, which is the only British book to discuss this aspect of the field (q.v.).

Together with the development of the information book has been that of the work of quick reference. An attempt has been made to give some indication of leading works and details of others can be located by reference to the appropriate guides evaluated in earlier chapters. Dr. Muriel Lock's *Reference Material for Young People* (Clive Bingley, 1966, 2nd edn., 1971) provides a wider selection of material than is represented in this volume.

ENCYCLOPAEDIAS

There are two kinds of children's encyclopaedias: one is designed for consultation by the student and is usually in an alphabetical sequence; while the other is for browsing purposes. Neither purpose can be satisfied adequately in any one encyclopaedia.

Children's editions differ from those for adults in range of vocabulary, the level of knowledge included, the relatively short articles, and the presence of numerous illustrations. Indexes and lists for further reading should also be a feature to look for.

The better-quality alphabetical encyclopaedias include:

Black's Children's Encyclopaedia. 2 vols. 3rd edn. 1971.

Edited by William Worthy and R. J. Unstead for younger children. Also published in a 12-volume school edition. Well produced and illustrated.

Children's Britannica. 20 vols. 1969.

This caters for older juniors and early secondaries and is based on the American *Britannica Junior.*

It sometimes shows a tendency to write down, a feature which is not to be commended in any children's book. Many of the illustrations are decorative rather than informative and the maps vary in quality, but the paper, type, and binding are good. Volume 20 includes a detailed index and atlas of the world. The *Children's Britannica Extension Library* commenced in 1964 and interprets current events.

Oxford Junior Encyclopaedia. 13 vols. 1948–56. New edn. 1964.

For secondary schools and colleges. This is not in an A–Z sequence throughout, but each volume covers a particular area of knowledge with articles alphabetically arranged in each.

No article consists of more than 2000 words and the stress is on the modern world. Volume 13 is an index. Good paper, type, binding, and illustration.

Junior World Encyclopaedia. 16 vols. Sampson Low, Marston. 1960.

Originally an American publication which is written for juniors. Short articles range from 60 to 1200 words with cross references. There is a full index.

Purnell's New English Encyclopaedia. 12 vols. 1965–9.

This was issued weekly. It is the first serial encyclopaedia to be arranged alphabetically and is the first all-colour production.

It is a worth-while contribution to this selection. One disadvantage is that it is printed on art paper.

The World Book Encyclopaedia. 24 vols. Field Enterprises Educational Corporation. 1969.

Twenty volumes are concerned with "the world of man and the fields of science, history and the arts", whilst two volumes are devoted to the British Isles and two to Australasia. The appeal of this work is to a general readership but it is of use to junior and secondary school children. Very well illustrated and arranged and reasonably up to date. There is no index but cross-references are included.

Of the browsing type of encyclopaedia the following are representative:

Children's Encyclopaedia. 10 vols. Grolier Society. 30th edn., 1963.

Designed for younger children and attempts to answer the questions children are likely to ask.

Originally published in serial form between 1908 and 1910 under the editorship of Arthur Mee, but the text has been rewritten in the new edition and the layout and illustrations have been greatly improved.

There is a separate Collins' atlas section, a useful index of poets and poems, and a general index.

Knowledge. 16 vols. Purnell. 1964.

Issued in weekly parts for juniors. The colour plates were printed in Italy and are very well produced. Some of the articles are quite lengthy. Good paper and clear type.

DICTIONARIES

Dictionaries may be assessed on a number of counts such as the period of language covered, the extent of the vocabulary, the inclusion of syllabication, pronunciation, etymological details, definitions and illustrative quotations. Additional features may be included such as synonyms and antonyms, abbreviations, informative illustrations, and general information regarding foreign words and phrases, forms of address, christian names, place-names, and weights and measures.

There is a sufficient selection of children's dictionaries from which to choose, some of which are as follows:

Cassell's First Picture Dictionary. 1952.

Compiled by Mary Waddington, it attempts to bridge the gap between an alphabetical word book and a dictionary. Vocabulary is related to the needs of children who are learning to read, and each word is set in a sentence to demonstrate its use. Pronunciations are not given nor other details of that kind.

Cassell's Second Picture Dictionary. 1957.

Compiled by Mary Waddington for older children.

Chambers' Children's Illustrated Dictionary. 1958.

Over 30,000 entries give pronunciations and parts of speech. Appendices list famous mountains, rivers, foreign words and phrases, and abbreviations. There are illustrations too.

The Hamish Hamilton Children's Dictionary. 1963.

Edited by Arthur J. Arkley to appeal to young children. Some guidance is given as to the use of dictionaries. Confined to modern words and includes some technical terms. Brief definitions and some encyclopaedia information are also given.

Nelson's Junior Dictionary. 1965.

Compiled for children in junior schools by F. R. Witty, who has carefully selected the 14,000 words included. Pronunciations, parts of speech, and idioms are given.

Oxford Illustrated Dictionary. 1962.

Edited by Jessie Coulson and others. A successful dictionary encyclopaedia. Details of spelling, definitions, pronunciations, and abbreviations.

Oxford School Dictionary. 2nd edn., 1960.

Compiled for secondary schools by Dorothy Mackenzie. Pronunciations and etymological details are given and in the appendices are listed prefixes, suffixes, foreign words, and abbreviations.

Thorndike Junior Dictionary. London U.P. 1955.

Contains over 25,000 words most commonly encountered by children in their reading. No derivations are included but pronunciations are shown. Useful in secondary schools.

ATLASES

The atlas is the third main group of children's reference books. There are various criteria which can be applied in selection: accuracy in the location of detail, as up to date as possible, legibility of printing and the absence of too much information, a conventional and consistent use of colour, a good index, a physical format attractive to children, and some explanation as to its use. Other factors may include adequacy of coverage of countries likely to be used most, a double-page map of the world suitable for tracing routes in junior geography, and an arrangement which commences with the homeland and leads children from known to new experiences.

A good selection of atlases is available from which a choice may be made:

Collins–Longman's Series of Atlases. 5 vols. 1965–9.

This series has been produced in the belief that atlases for young people should be linked to age groups: *Atlas One* is for younger children; *Atlas Two* for upper primary and lower secondary forms; *Atlas Three* for G.C.E. students; *Atlas Four* for fifth forms; and *Atlas Advanced* for sixth forms. Attractively produced.

Hamlyn's New Relief World Atlas. 1966.

A well-produced atlas in which shadow relief maps have been used throughout for the first time. Place names not always legible. A good index.

Nelson's School Atlas. 1964.

For secondary schools and in detail. There are many diagrams and illustrations. The colours are mainly green and yellow. Edited by J. Wreford Watson.

Nelson's Junior Atlas. 1962.

Does not include too many place-names and the maps of oceans for the planning of journeys are shown. Instructions for use are given and the index includes gazetteer information. Edited by J. Wreford Watson.

Philips' Modern School Atlas. 1969.

First published in 1906 and continuously revised. Most maps have more detail than in previous editions. It includes climate graphs. Whilst it was prepared for the G.C.E. student it is useful at earlier stages.

In addition to ordinary atlases there are some useful historical atlases:

Hammond's Historical Atlas. 1963.

Covers from the earliest times to the present day. There is more detail than necessary and there are no explanations for use. A flimsy paperback.

Philips' Intermediate Historical Atlas for Schools. 1962.

First published in 1921 as *The Junior Historical Atlas.* It is sponsored by the Historical Association and caters for children at secondary school level. A comparison with earlier editions shows how maps have been simplified, due to the fact that children today are not expected to know so many facts. Covers from the earliest times to 1962. If there is any criticism it is that the maps are too small.

SELLMAN, R. R. *The Student's Atlas of Modern History*. Arnold. 1952.
In this a wide use has been made of the *Cambridge Modern History* and other works of historical reference. Covers from the medieval period to the twentieth century, but there is very little after 1945. Diagrams are provided for military events, and alternative spellings of place-names are shown in the index. The maps are not coloured.

Wheaton's History Teaching Atlas. 1968.
Compiled by C. K. Brampton, it covers from the earliest times to 1960. It only attempts to be an outline, and includes notes on various topics, diagrams, graphs. There is a stress on the Far East. The notes are not printed in clear type.

There are not many reference books of other kinds for children, and one may question their necessity. The standard reference books can be used by juniors and older children, such as Brewer's *Dictionary of Phrase and Fable*, *Everyman's Dictionary of Dates*, Harvey's *Oxford Companion to English Literature*, Grove's *Dictionary of Music and Musicians*, *Whitaker's Almanack*, and *Who's Who*, and other authoritative works which can be easily consulted in the public or school library.

CHAPTER 12

Commonwealth Literature

VERY few new children's books are published each year in Commonwealth countries, where reliance is placed on imports from Britain and the United States. However, from time to time outstanding work by Commonwealth authors has been made available to children in this country.

CANADA

Akin in spirit to Richard Jefferies' *Bevis* was the Canadian Ernest Thompson Seton's *Two Little Savages: being the adventures of two boys who lived as Indians and what they learned* (1903), which was reissued in 1960 in an edition published by Edmund Ward. In this book were described the camping holiday adventures of Sam and Yan in the forests of Ontario. In addition, a collection of Seton's stories was published in the series of Dent's *Children's Illustrated Classics* in 1966, the title being *The Trail of the Sandhill Stag and Other Lives of the Hunted*. Eight stories are included in this volume which were selected by Roger Lancelyn Green.

In the tradition of *Two Little Savages*, Roderick L. Haig-Brown recounted the winter and summer trapping and fishing adventures of Don Morgan in British Columbia, in *Starbuck Valley Winter* (1943) and *Saltwater Summer* (1948).

Cliff Faulknor's *The White Calf* (1965) and *The White Peril* (1966) are stories of Indian life on the Montana–Alberta border in the 1850's. The first describes Eagle Child's encounter with and care for a white buffalo calf, and the second the threat of the white settlers in their search for buffalo, furs, and gold, and the end of the white calf.

AUSTRALASIA

Due to the enterprise of publishers such as Angus & Robertson, a number of books by authors from Australia and New Zealand have been made available to British children in recent years.

Historical Stories

A portrayal of the coming of the Maoris to New Zealand was made by Roderick Finlayson in *The Springing Fern* (1965), who went on to tell of their relationship with the white settlers. He traced the story through successive generations of one Maori family and utilized a subtly changing style as he moved from the sagas of the past to the civilization of the present.

In the early years of the nineteenth century Australia was settled by convicts who were transported there from England, often for petty crimes. In *A Secret to Sell* (1965), Melva Lear described the first convict settlement in Western Australia in 1826. Eleanor Spence's *The Switherby Pilgrims* (1967) and *Jamberoo Road* (1969) are concerned with emigrants from a small English village to New South Wales in the 1820s.

The attraction of Australia increased substantially in the 1850's when gold was discovered at Ballarat, an episode which has been well documented by Denys Burrows in *Fight for Gold* (1966). He also traced the development of railway communications across the country in the 1860's in *Stagecoach West* (1965). Eleanor Spence's *Lillipilly Hill* (1960) showed the continued growth of Australia and the creation of a patriotic people in an account of the adjustment of an English family to a new life at the end of the nineteenth century.

Adventure and Family Stories

The best literature for children has been in this category and has frequently been more realistic than British stories of the same kind.

Intense feeling for rural Australia was shown by Nan Chauncy in whose work a recurring theme has been the secret refuge. *They Found a Cave* (1949) was set in Tasmania, as was *Tiger in the Bush* (1957). In the latter, Mrs. Chauncy introduced Badge, the country boy of the Tasmanian bush, who reappeared in *Devil's Hill* (1958) and *The Roaring Forty* (1963). This author also wrote two books about lighthouses: *Lizzie Lights* (1968) is the story of a girl who lived on a Tasmanian lighthouse island and describes how she conquered her fear of heights and the mainland, and *The Lighthouse Keeper's Son* (1969) is concerned with the life as seen through the eyes of a nine-year-old boy.

Eleanor Spence's family stories have been of a consistently high quality and have presented a faithful picture of Australian life. These include *Patterson's Track* (1959), *The Summer in Between* (1959), *The Year of the Currawong* (1965), and *The Nothing-Place* (1972).

Ivan Southall wrote adventures stories for many years which featured his heroic character Simon Black in successive thrilling situations. Among these stories were *Simon Black in China* (1954) and *Simon Black at Sea* (1959). In the 1960's, however, he matured remarkably in such realistic documentaries as *Hill's End* (1962) in which he combined a search for Aboriginal art with a terrifying disaster. He pictured a remote village wrecked in a storm and young people confronted with violent death and the stark struggle for survival. In *Ash Road* (1966) he recounted the horrors of a bush fire, and in *To The Wild Sky* (1967) children bound for a birthday party in an aeroplane lived through a harrowing ordeal. *Josh* (Carnegie Medal, 1971) is the story of a boy's visit to his aunt and the reaction to him of the local children.

Ivan Southall's books are ideal for teenagers, as are the adventure stories of Mary Elwyn Patchett. She is well known as a writer of books about horses but set out to capture the imagination of the adolescent in *Warrimoo* (1961). In this, Jeff James underwent hardship and excitement among Aborigines and also among South American Indians. *The Terror of Manooka* (1966) describes how a teenage boy went on an expedition in North Australia in a successful attempt to overcome his fear of creeping creatures.

One of the leading writers for teenagers at the present time is H. F. Brinsmead. A girl featured in a New South Wales farming community in *Pastures of the Blue Crane* (1964), and a boy undertook vacation work, weed-spraying in Tasmania in *Season of the Briar* (1965). The latter underlined the problems of living in an isolated community. *Listen to the Wind* (1970) deals with the relationships and problems of young people in a multi-racial society.

A versatile treatment of the family adventure theme is given by Patricia Wrightson. Notable examples of her work are *The Rocks of Honey* (1961), a description of the finding by three children of an aboriginal axe; *The Feather Star* (1962), an account of a holiday by the sea and the discovery of a delicate star-fish in a rock pool; and *I Own the Racecourse!* (1968), a study of Andy, a retarded child who thought he had purchased the local racecourse for 3 dollars, and the reactions of his friends to the situation.

Joan Phipson's *Peter and Butch* (1969) is a truly outstanding book for teenagers in which a boy develops his sense of values and learns to distinguish between the worthwhile and the superficial. The contrasting characters of the delinquents and the boys of the youth club underlines the moral purpose of the author.

Many of these stories have an added interest in their descriptions of the Australian topography, flora and fauna. Lyndon Rose, however, has not confined himself to Australia. In *The Parting of the Mist* (1963) he examined the Maori tradition, and *Tungi of the Big Reef* (1965) is set in Samoa. Not only does the background achieve a feeling of geographical authenticity, but the plots weave a web of adventure and romance.

Australians and New Zealanders often tend to be preoccupied with the Aborigine and Maori tragedy for which all whites must share the guilt. This is evident in the work of Roderick Finlayson, Nan Chauncy, Mary Elwyn Patchett, Lyndon Rose, Ivan Southall, Eleanor Spence and Patricia Wrightson. Sometimes the attention is paid to the old traditions, and at others to the survivors. It could be argued, of course, that this does not arise from guilt but represents the only source of history to which many of the later white settlers and their descendants may consider themselves heirs.

Animal Stories

The most celebrated Australian writer of animal stories is Mary Elwyn Patchett who tells of her life in the bush in the *Ajax* and *Brumby* books. Horses have been the dominant theme in such tales as *Tam the Untamed* (1954), *Ajax the Warrior* (1953), *The Brumby* (1958), and *Brumby Foal* (1965). These are among the best horse stories in existence.

Una Rothwell's *Where Are the Cattle Gone?* (1966) shows that the legendary difference between town and country people has been over-drawn, as Don Peters was gradually accepted by the children of the Roper cattle station in Queensland. Drought followed by deluge and a cattle-rustling incident all combined to ensure that on future holidays Don would be a welcome member of the group.

Also set in Queensland is Elizabeth O'Connor's bird book entitled *The Chinee Bird* (1966). The dollar bird brought the romance of far-off lands into the lives of two children as they nursed it back to health when it had been injured by a stone from a boy's catapult. The author shows that the bird should be free, and against a vivid Australian background the message of kindness to animals is underlined.

Joan Phipson has concerned herself with sheep farming in New South Wales in such stories as *Good Luck Rider* (1953), *The Family Conspiracy* (1962), and *Threat to the Barkers* (1963). In contrast her *Birkin* (1965) was a black calf who was cared for by two children.

WEST INDIES

Andrew Salkey has recounted the terrifying events of disasters which all too often overtake the West Indies in *Hurricane* (1964), *Earthquake* (1965), and *Drought* (1966). In exposing children to topics of this kind the author claims to push them "one step nearer the harsh realities of the adult world". There is a wholesome realism in his treatment of death, an infrequently encountered feature in modern children's books, which contrasts well with the morbid death-bed scenes in nineteenth-century stories such as Catherine Sinclair's *Holiday House* and Frederick Farrar's *Eric*.

C. Everard Palmer's contribution to literature from the West Indies lies in such lively accounts of village life as *The Cloud with the Silver Lining* (1966), *Big Doc Bitteroot* (1968), and *The Hummingbird People* (1971). The latter book spotlights the petty rivalries which can exist between neighbouring villages, but shows how common sense prevails.

Events in the life of a boy and his sister on a Carribean island are described by Shirley Gudmundson in *The Turtle Net* (1965) and *The Hurricane* (1966). The first related how the boy brought back a turtle to his village, and the second tells of the terrifying havoc created by a hurricane and the endeavours of the villagers to return to normality.

AFRICA AND ASIA

Very little literature is as yet available from other parts of the Commonwealth. The African Universities Press (Nigeria) has published numerous works, distributed in Britain by Ginn, which show at times aggressively nationalistic tendencies. An example is D. J. M. Muffett's *The Story of Sultan Attahiru I and His Brave Fight Against the British in 1903*. An African Reader's Library, distributed in Britain by Methuen, includes folk-tales such as *Twilight and the Tortoise* by Kunle Akinsemoyin; stories of contemporary life such as *Eze Goes to School* by Onoura Nzekwu and Michael Crowder; and adventure stories, such as *Juju Rock* by Cyprian Ekwensi. The East African Publishing House (Kenya) has issued similar books for young people, which are distributed in Britain by Heinemann.

Some books too are available from India, a typical example of which is Rama Mehta's *Ramu: a story of India* (1966). It presents a vivid portrayal of life in Udaipur in North-west India, and Ramu's family and friends against a background of customs such as Divali, the Festival of Lights. The poverty of India is contrasted with the ideal of education, the key to the future in this and other developing countries.

As the more populous Commonwealth countries in Africa and Asia develop their social, economic, and educational resources, we may anticipate an increasing flow of outstanding books from countries both inside and outside the Commonwealth.

CHAPTER 13

American Literature

EIGHTEENTH AND NINETEENTH CENTURIES

Since the nineteenth century when editions of famous authors were pirated on both sides of the Atlantic Ocean, the works of the leading American writers have been available to British children. Increasingly, during the twentieth century the best, and sometimes the worst, specimens of American literature have been sent to this country, so that the influence of good children's books has been counterbalanced by the now illegal horror comics which provoked such a storm in responsible circles during the 1950's.

In the seventeenth century, reading in the American colonies was influenced by imports and translations sent from Europe, and by the cultural background of the immigrant races. The first influences on children's reading were British and mainly consisted of Puritan literature. James Janeway's *A Token for Children* was a popular import and a Massachusetts edition of it was published in 1700. One of the early American books was *The New England Primer* which was issued by Benjamin Harris of Boston between 1687 and 1690. It was a devout and instructional work preoccupied with sin, death, and salvation.

Puritan books did not hold the monopoly for very long and in the second half of the eighteenth century John Newbery's publications began to reach the New World. Hugh Gaine of New York issued some of them in the 1770's, as did Isaiah Thomas of Worcester, Massachusetts, between 1785 and 1788. Gaine introduced *Robinson Crusoe* too.

Unfortunately, Thomas was imbued with the spirit of extreme Puritanism and added 163 rules of behaviour for children to *A Little Pretty Pocket Book*.

Towards the end of the eighteenth century some Tract and Sunday School societies were established. These circulated cheap and edifying material for children.

In the nineteenth century the number of books published for children increased, and, as in Britain, books of instruction developed alongside recreational literature.

Many of the instructional works were fairly interesting to read. Instruction was conveyed through the *Peter Parley* books by Samuel Goodrich. There were also the *Rollo Books* by Jacob Abbott which commenced in 1837 and outlined a scheme for learning and entertainment. The *Rollo Books* were full of useful knowledge and guidance in practical living, for example, *Rollo Learning to Talk*, *Rollo Learning to Read*, and others. Abbott's best work was to be found in his *Franconia Stories* (1850–3), which related the life of young people in a primitive American community. He also wrote illustrated histories about *Cyrus the Great* and other leaders of the ancient world. In all, Jacob Abbott wrote over 180 titles.

The greatest American writers of the nineteenth century were those who concerned themselves with adventure and domestic stories. They include names as well known in Britain as in the United States: Washington Irving, James Fenimore Cooper, Harriet Beecher Stowe, Richard Dana, Louisa M. Alcott, Susan Coolidge, Mark Twain, and Mrs. Frances Hodgson Burnett.

Irving, Cooper, Stowe, and Dana did not write their books for children, who adopted them in the absence of good literature especially written.

Washington Irving used the pseudonym Geoffrey Crayon for his *Sketch Book* (1819–20). It consisted of a series of essays, mainly about British life and customs, but also included yarns which Irving had heard in his youth: *Rip Van Winkle* and *The Legend of Sleepy Hollow*.

From the pioneering days to the present, Americans have been fascinated by the primitive life of their fathers in the backwoods. As civilization has achieved a greater hold, so the nostalgia for the old times has become more profound. James Fenimore Cooper wrote stories of the wild forests and prairies which were not only a success in the United States but were popular also in Europe. Cooper inspired a line of lesser writers who drew less authentic pictures. His most famous book was *The Last of the Mohicans* (1826) in which he described the adventures of Hawkeye and Chingachgook. He also wrote *The Deerslayer* (1841) which was set in the region of Otsego Lake where its creator had spent his boyhood.

Harriet Beecher Stowe is remembered for her *Uncle Tom's Cabin* (1852) which was a topical study of slavery in the United States. Its unforgettable characters included the simple, good, Uncle Tom and the mischievous Topsy who "never was born" and just "growed". Many of the incidents are gripping and harrowing, as when Eliza escaped over the ice floes with her child. Apart from this it was a sentimental and a pious book.

Pathos, emotion, and a heavily religious point of view tended to dominate American tales in those days. Typical of these is Maria Cummins' *The Lamplighter* (1854) and Elizabeth Wetherell's *The Wide, Wide World* (1851), which has been shorn of its moralizing and issued by London University Press in an edition by Joyce Lankester Brisley. Orphans often led very unhappy lives in this kind of literature, but they just as frequently surmounted their difficulties with Christian fortitude.

Only one outstanding British children's book of the nineteenth century attacked social conditions as one of its main features. It was Charles Kingsley's *The Water Babies*, in which the author exposed the plight of chimney boys. In American literature Harriet Beecher Stowe attacked slavery, and Richard Dana campaigned for naval reform in one of the best sea stories ever written: *Two Years Before the Mast* (1840). Dana gave a masterly description of a sailor's existence as he had seen it on board ship.

It was in the last three decades of the century that three great children's writers emerged: Louisa M. Alcott, Mark Twain, and Mrs. Hodgson Burnett.

The stories of Louisa M. Alcott were much less intense than those of Cummins and Wetherell. She described her own family life in such books as *Little Women* (1868), *Little Men* (1871) and *Jo's Boys* (1886). Jo March is *the* girl of children's literature and was in reality Louisa herself. The gentle Beth was Louisa's sister Elizabeth who died in 1859. *Little Women* has been translated into many languages and it led a fashion in family stories which was copied by a number of writers. Martha Finley created the *Elsie* books between 1867 and 1890 in which her heroine grew from childhood to old age. Susan Coolidge wrote of the Carr family in *What Katy Did* (1872) and *What Katy Did at School* (1873).

As Louisa M. Alcott presented *the* girl of children's literature so Mark Twain introduced *the* boy in the person of *Tom Sawyer* (1876). This and *Huckleberry Finn* (1885) are among the greatest of boys' stories. They are realistic and highly humorous and imaginative tales based on Twain's memories of his boyhood in Missouri. They present an authentic picture of life along the Mississippi River a century ago.

Frances Hodgson Burnett was born in England but emigrated to the United States in her youth. Numerous editions were published of her *Little Lord Fauntleroy* (1886). Harvey Darton remarked that "the odious little prig in the lace collar is not dead yet" but a more favourable view has been taken by other writers such as Roger Lancelyn Green and John Rowe Townsend. Mrs. Hodgson Burnett's *The Secret Garden* (1911) has had a more lasting appeal, as has her *A Little Princess* (1905).

In England there were many outstanding authors in the nineteenth century who wrote books of fantasy, but this was not paralleled in the United States. One of the earliest was Clement Moore, whose *The Night before Christmas* (1822) has become a classic. It is a delightful poem though not great poetry.

Nathaniel Hawthorne retold some of the Greek myths in his *A Wonder Book* (1852) and *Tanglewood Tales* (1853); and Joel Chandler Harris immortalized American Negro folklore in his *Uncle Remus* (1881) which gave Brer Rabbit to the world.

Howard Pyle was the first great American author–illustrator of children's books. He was also an authority on myths and legends.

His work included *The Merry Adventures of Robin Hood* (1883) and *King Arthur's Legends* (1903–10). In addition he wrote fairy tales among which was *The Wonder Clock* (1886).

Most of the American classics of the nineteenth century can be obtained quite easily in this country in both hard- and paper-covered editions.

TWENTIETH CENTURY

With few exceptions the outstanding American writers of the twentieth century have been awarded the Newbery Medal, which is similar in intention to the British Carnegie Medal and was inaugurated in 1921. The chief proposer of the Medal was the late Frederic Melcher, who, in 1938, suggested a similar award for picture books, which was called the Caldecott Medal. Thus have the pioneer of entertaining books for children and the great illustrator of children's literature in Britain been honoured on the other side of the Atlantic.

The publishing of children's books has not followed the same pattern in the United States as in this country. The flow of good writing began and was encouraged in the 1920's, and was only followed in Britain 10 years later. On the other hand, in proportion to the population of the United States, fewer children's books have been published each year than in Britain.

It would be impossible in a survey of this kind to undertake an exhaustive review of twentieth-century United States literature for children, but it is possible to give some indication of the work of many of the writers which is available in this country and most of which has been published in British editions.

FANTASY

As in the nineteenth century only a small number of fantasy stories have emerged from the United States apart from those in which animals are included.

Two outstanding books which were awarded the Newbery Medal were *Hitty* (1929) in which Rachel Lyman Field described the life and adventures of a wooden doll; and *The Twenty-one Balloons* (1947) in which William Pene du Bois reported an imaginary balloon voyage of 1883, incidents of scientific authenticity being interwoven with sheer nonsense.

The Chronicles of Prydain, with roots in the Mabinogian, are recorded in four books by Lloyd Alexander: *The Book of Three* (1964), *The Black Cauldron* (1965), *The Castle of Llyr* (1966), and *The High King* (Newbery Medal, 1968). These are concerned with the meeting of Taran and Gwydion, the destruction of the evil cauldron, the rescue of Eilonwy from Achren, and the final struggle between the forces of good and evil, culminating in the union of Taran and Eilonwy. Moving incidents, both violent and romantic, are balanced with subtle humour.

New variations of old British legends are contrived by André Norton in *Steel Magic* (1965) when three American children find themselves in Avalon and retrieve Arthur's treasure. In *Fur Magic* (1968) she turned her attention to Red Indian legends of a world peopled by animals, and the adventures of a boy after his transformation into a beaver.

The struggle of good against evil is waged in the fifth dimension in Madeleine L'Engle's *A Wrinkle in Time* (Newbery Medal, 1962), as the Murrys tesseract to rescue their father from IT. In *The Young Unicorns* (1968) the powers of evil seek to produce instant goodness by means of lasers, and the struggle to prevent them takes place in and around a cathedral in New York. The author's message is that, praiseworthy as the intention may seem, it would result in an end to freedom, even the freedom to be evil.

ANIMAL STORIES

Hugh Lofting was born in England and emigrated to the United States in 1904. He wrote ten books about Doctor Dolittle, commencing in 1920 with *The Story of Doctor Dolittle*. His *Voyages of Doctor Dolittle* was awarded the Newbery Medal for 1922. Doctor Dolittle learned how to speak like animals and healed them when they were sick. Lofting's animals are humans in animal form and the humour of the books depends on such characters as Dab Dab the duck, Jip the Dog, and the Two-headed Pushmi-pullyu, behaving like humans.

One of the best stories in this category of animal fantasy is Robert Lawson's *Rabbit Hill* (Newbery Medal, 1944), where lived the rabbits, field mice, and other small creatures.

Elizabeth Coatsworth's *The Cat Who Went to Heaven* (Newbery Medal, 1930) is based on a Chinese legend that a cat can never enter heaven. The appearance of the English edition is made more attractive by the beautiful illustrations of Joan Kiddell-Monroe.

In addition to the fantasy animal stories some outstanding books have been concerned with animals in realistic situations. Will R. James's *Smoky* (Newbery Medal, 1926) and Marguerite Henry's *King of the Wind* (Newbery Medal, 1948) are both stories of horses; whilst D. G. Mukerji and Meindert Dejong have written about birds in *Gay-Neck: the story of a pigeon* (Newbery Medal, 1927) and *The Wheel on the School* (Newbery Medal, 1954), the latter of which was set in Friesland where the author was born and described the attempts of children to entice storks to make their nests in the village. Dejong wrote of animals in *Shadrach* (1953), *Along Came a Dog* (1958) and various other books. He won the Hans Christian Andersen Award in 1962.

Nicholas Kalashnikoff was similar to Dejong in that he emigrated to the United States having spent most of his boyhood in Europe, and it is of Siberia and of the life he knew there that he told in his books. Many of them are about animals and show great sensitivity: *Jumper* (1944), *Toyon: a dog of the North and his people* (1950), *The Defender* (1951), and *My Friend Yakub* (1953). *Toyon* in particular brings out the qualities of a dog in the tradition of R. M. Ballantyne's *The Dog Crusoe* and Jack London's *White Fang*. Dogs are also featured in Eleanor Estes' *Ginger Pye* (Newbery Medal, 1951) and William H. Armstrong's *Sounder* (Newbery Medal, 1969).

Reference has been made to the American Library Association's Aurianne Award which from 1958 to 1966 was awarded each year with one exception (1959) to the author of a children's book on animal life in which a humane attitude was adopted (q.v.).

ADVENTURE AND FAMILY STORIES

There is a deep interest in family stories in the United States. Because it is such a big country, life in one part is likely to be very different from another. The life of New York is so very different to that on a farm in the mid-West, and this will bear little resemblance to life in the deep South.

The traditions of the various peoples who have contributed to the growth of the country are also a subject for study in these books. They serve to demonstrate the difficulties which had to be overcome before a mass of individuals, many of whom could not understand the tongue of their fellows, could become a united community.

One of the earliest writers of family life in this century was Gene Stratton Porter, whose *A Girl of the Limberlost* (1909) has been popular with generations of girls both in the United States and in this country. It describes the difficulties of a mother and daughter in their personal relationship, and examines with a wealth of description the flora and fauna of the Limberlost.

Roller Skates (Newbery Medal, 1936) introduced Ruth Sawyer's character Lucinda, a 10-year-old who did not want to grow up and to whom "elegant" was the finest adjective which could be applied to almost anything. *Lucinda's Year of Jubilo* (1940) takes place in Maine after the death of her father. Ruth Sawyer has shown a masterly ability in her treatment of the development of her heroine's personality from a small girl to a teenager. She won the Laura Ingalls Wilder Award in 1965.

Elizabeth Enright recounted the life of a Wisconsin small farming family in *Thimble Summer* (Newbery Medal, 1938). In 1941 she published *The Saturdays*, the first of a series of stories about the four Melendy children who were very modern and independent young people. There is a great deal of humour in Elizabeth Enright's books, as where Zara the jungle dancer who was performing at a fair forgot to remove her pince-nez, in *Thimble Summer*.

Eleanor Estes' *The Moffats* appeared in 1941. It describes the life of the Moffat family and the other very interesting inhabitants of the small town of Cranbury. In two other books about the same family the characters develop and remain identifiable: *Middle Moffat* (1942) and *Rufus M.* (1943).

An author who is noted for her treatment of social history is Lois Lenski. She invariably visited the localities she was writing about in order to gather local colour. *Strawberry Girl* (Newbery Medal, 1945) was set in Florida, and *Prairie School* (1951) was set in South Dakota, and in these books she showed how immigrant traditions have survived in rural places. The problem is that these features of the United States are disappearing as in other countries, and authors like Lois Lenski are undertaking a very useful task in preserving the dying culture for the interest of posterity.

Laura Ingalls Wilder's stories are autobiographical and recount the events of her childhood. *The Long Winter* (1940), *These Happy Golden Years* (1943), *Little House in the Big Woods* (1956), *On the Banks of Plum Creek* (1958), and others, evoke the thrilling spirit of adventure in the advance to the West. Since 1954 there has been the Laura Ingalls Wilder Award which has been presented every five years by the American Library Association to an author or illustrator who has made a lasting contribution to children's literature. It was first awarded to Laura Ingalls Wilder (1954), then posthumously to Clara Ingram Judson (1960) and latterly to Ruth Sawyer (1965) and E. B. White (1970).

The first writer to be awarded the Newbery Medal on two occasions was Joseph Krumgold. In 1953 *And Now Miguel* appeared, and in 1959 *Onion John*. The central character in the latter was an immigrant from central Europe and the book describes how the people of an American township wished to integrate him into the community. Krumgold pointed out the dangers of both self-projection and making decisions regarding what people ought to want, rather than asking them what in fact they do want for themselves.

Apart from *Berries Goodman* (1965), which has a suburban background and is partly concerned with anti-semitism, Emily Cheney Neville's stories for boys are set in New York. *It's Like This Cat* (Newbery Medal, 1963) and *The Seventeenth-Street Gang* (1966) demonstrate a true feeling for city life and are made the more convincing with well-rounded characters and dialogues which are phrased in the vernacular.

HISTORICAL FICTION

A writer with a similar sense of history to Rosemary Sutcliff was Elizabeth Janet Gray whose *Adam of the Road* (Newbery Medal, 1942) was one of the few American historical stories of great merit to be set in England. It describes the journey of a minstrel boy from London to Winchester during the thirteenth century. This author also wrote biographies of *The Young Walter Scott* (1935) and *Penn* (1938).

Most of the American historical stories are set on that continent and reasonably enough over a short period of time. Common themes are the War of Independence and the Civil War. Esther Forbes wrote one of the best in *Johnny Tremain* (Newbery Medal, 1943), the plot of which took place in Boston in 1773. She was already recognized as an adult novelist, having won the Pulitzer Prize for History in 1942 for *Paul Revere and the World He Lived In*, which was also set at the time of the War of Independence.

Harold Keith dealt with the Civil War in *Rifles for Watie* (Newbery Medal, 1957). It was centred on the life of a young volunteer in the Union Army who was sent as a spy among rebel Indians under the notorious General Watie. It is a gripping story which captures the life of its period, as does *Komantcia* (1965). In the latter, Pedro, a Spanish boy, was captured and adopted by Comanche Indians to whom he proved himself a warrior. Keith's realism occasionally verges on the horrific as when Pedro's mother was scalped before his eyes, and barbaric Indian practices are described in detail. These stories are for teenagers and are strong medicine indeed.

Having already written *Calico Captive* (1957), a story based on a true account of an English girl's capture by Indians and sale to the French at Montreal during the Anglo-French struggle for Canada, Elizabeth G. Speare became the second writer to win the Newbery Medal on two occasions. *The Witch of Blackbird Pond* (Newbery

Medal, 1958) is a story of Puritan times and presents a dramatic and exciting picture of the revolting practice of witch-hunting in the early New England settlements. Quite different in period and setting is *The Bronze Bow* (Newbery Medal, 1961) in which the spirit of Jewish resistance to the Roman conquerors in Biblical times is confronted with the teachings of Jesus Christ.

In addition to *Adam of the Road* and *The Bronze Bow*, other well-recommended historical stories which have their setting outside America include Eric P. Kelly's *The Trumpeter of Krakow* (Newbery Medal, 1928), a tale of fifteenth-century Poland; Marguerite de Angeli's *The Door in the Wall* (Newbery Medal, 1949), a tale of fourteenth-century England; and Elizabeth B. de Treviño's *I, Juan de Pareja* (Newbery Medal, 1965), a fictional portrayal of a Negro slave of the Spanish painter Velasquez.

SCIENCE FICTION AND SPACE TRAVEL

As in Britain, space fiction has in the more recent decades become popular on an increasing scale. Among more competent writers, in a field which unfortunately lends itself to a vast amount of mediocrity, are Alan E. Nourse, the author of such exciting yet sensitive books as *Scavengers in Space* (1964) and *Raiders from the Rings* (1965); and André Norton, author of *The Beast Master* (1959), *Lord of Thunder* (1962), and *Victory on Janus* (1966).

GEOGRAPHICAL FICTION

This group is far more frequently encountered in the United States than in Britain, and writers in the field have won the Newbery Medal on a number of occasions. Many of the immigrants or their descendants have written of their homelands and have kept alive the traditions handed down for their good keeping.

In the mid-nineteenth-century, Mary Mapes Dodge wrote of Holland in *Hans Brinker* (1865). It describes the cities and customs of the country and combines much very palatable instruction with adventure and children's amusements and problems. For its period it is an outstanding book and is available in the series of Dent's *Children's Illustrated Classics*.

Lucy Fitch Perkins' "Twins" series appeared in the years before and after the First World War, and included such titles as *The Dutch Twins* (1911), *The Japanese Twins* (1912), and *The French Twins* (1918). These books were intended to create an undertanding of foreign nations and of their contribution to American culture, but are no longer a reflection of the countries which they describe.

Newbery Medal winners have been representative of geographical fiction such as Elizabeth Foreman Lewis's *Young Fu of the Upper Yangtse* (1932); Monica Shannon's Bulgarian *Dobry* (1934); and Meindert Dejong's Dutch *The Wheel on the School* (1954). The latter author also described Holland in *Journey from Peppermint Street* (1968), and attention has been drawn to Nicholas Kalashnikoff's descriptions of Siberia. It will be observed that the rate of progress in the present century very quickly renders geographical fiction out of date.

An author who is noted for her treatment of various aspects of American life is Lois Lenski, whose *Strawberry Girl* and *Prairie School* have been discussed. In varying degrees, writers whose work has been noted under "Adventure and Family Stories" have presented similarly authentic pictures of American life. These authors include Elizabeth Enright, and Emily Cheney Neville.

PICTURE BOOKS

The standard of American picture books has been high for many years, and in the 1930's the firm of Woodfield & Stanley introduced many to Britain. The first Caldecott Medal was awarded to Dorothy P. Lathrop for her illustrations to H. D. Fish's compilation *Animals of the Bible* (1937). It has been awarded each year since its inception and through the years the quality of picture book illustration has been maintained. Outstanding figures who have won the Caldecott Medal have included Robert Lawson for *They Were Strong and Good* (1940); Maud and Miska Petersham for *The Rooster Crows* (1945); Roger A.

Duvoisin for his work in Alvin Tresselt's *White Snow, Bright Snow* (1947); Leo Politi for *The Song of the Swallows* (1949); Feodor Rojankovsky for his work in John Langstaff's *Frog Went A-Courtin'* (1955); Barbara Cooney for *Chanticleer and the Fox* (1958); Maurice Sendak for *Where the Wild Things Are* (1963); and Ed. Emberley for his work on his wife's *Drummer Hoff* (1967). Three illustrators have won the Medal on more than one occasion: Robert McCloskey for *Make Way for the Ducklings* (1941) and *Time of Wonder* (1957); and Marcia Brown for *Cinderella* (1954) and *Once a Mouse* (1961); and Nonny Hogrogian for *Always Room for One More* (1965) and *One Fine Day* (1971).

Attention has been drawn to the high quality of non-fiction from the United States in the chapter on "School Books and Information Books". All of the twentieth-century American authors represented in this survey are available in Britain and many of them are to be obtained in paper covers.

CHAPTER 14

Translations

THE bookshelf of the British child has been greatly enriched by translations of literature from the continent of Europe. The main influx has been from the northern and central countries such as France, Germany, Sweden, Switzerland, and to a lesser extent from Denmark, Finland, Holland, and Norway.

In the seventeenth century, France led the field with books which were to be adopted by children, and translations from the French have remained to the fore.

Charles Perrault's *Histoires ou contes du temps passé avec des moralités* was published in Paris by Claude Barbin in 1697. The original eight tales included *Blue Beard, Cinderella, Hop o' My Thumb, Puss in Boots, Red Riding Hood*, and *The Sleeping Beauty*. It was necessary for them to draw morals to pass the scrutiny of the social convention. None of the tales had appeared in English as far as is known but they were very quickly issued in chapbook form. Samber's English translation was probably published in 1729, but the earliest extant edition is the third, dated 1741.

Another French writer was Countess d'Aulnoy, whose *Diverting Works* included *The Yellow Dwarf* and *Goldylocks*.

The forty-one volume *Le Cabinet des fées* (1785–9) contained a great deal of worthless material but included Mme de Beaumont's *Beauty and the Beast*.

Fairy tales were very fashionable in France and were read in the literary salons. The characters in them were far too sophisticated for children and they reflected the life of the French court. This did not prevent children from adopting them for themselves

as their adult devotees forsook them for the latest social tran-
sience.

Current editions of French fairy tales include:

Cape. Eleven Perrault tales translated by Anne Carter, includes three
verse tales which appeared before the original collection was rendered into prose. Illustrated by Janusz Grabianski.

Longman Young Books. Translated by A. E. Johnson and others, with
illustrations by Heath Robinson. Fourteen tales: eleven by Perrault;
Mme de Beaumont's *Beauty and the Beast;* and Countess d'Aulnoy's
The Friendly Frog and *Princess Rosette.*

Roger Ingram. *The Hind in the Forest and other tales*, being a selection
of nine tales from Countess d'Aulnoy retold by Hilda McGill and
illustrated by Sylvia Green. Very few of the tales of Countess
d'Aulnoy are suitable for children but this volume is well recommended. It was first published by the Manchester firm of Roger
Ingram in 1950 and issued in a new edition in 1965.

Penguin. Includes a very good introduction to Perrault's work. Eleven
tales translated by Geoffrey Brereton.

In 1818 Sir Richard Philips produced a volume of *Popular Fairy
Tales* which included all the well-known stories from Perrault together
with *Aladdin, Beauty and the Beast,* and *Tom Thumb.* As a sign of changing ideas in presentation, morals were excluded.

Early in the nineteenth century the German romantic movement
began to make its influence felt. Jacob and Wilhelm Grimm were interested in the light which could be shed by folk-lore on early traditions.
Their *Märchen* were collected and written down in the simple language in which they had first heard them and appeared in separate
volumes between 1812 and 1824. Edgar Taylor's English translation
appeared between 1823 and 1826 and was entitled *Grimm's Popular
German Stories.*

Current editions of *Grimm's Fairy Tales* include:

Dent. Forty-seven tales based on Edgar Taylor's translation of
1823–6. The illustrations by Charles Folkard capture the spirit of
Grimm.

Eyre & Spottiswoode. Seventy-five stories. Colour plates and drawings by Mervyn Peake. Entitled *Household Tales*.

Faber. Sixteen tales translated and illustrated by Wanda Gág who
heard them in the German as a child. An ideal edition for younger
children.

Folio Society. A faithful translation of the original tales with twelve
of George Cruikshank's etchings. This edition was first published
in 1949 and was out of print for many years until it was reissued in
a redesigned typography and binding in 1966.

Oxford U.P. A reprint of Edgar Taylor's translation. Fifty-five stories.
Illustrations by Ulrik Schramm.

Routledge. Two hundred and ten tales edited by Joseph Scharl from
the text of the Bohn edition of 1884. More useful to students than
to young children.

Hans Andersen wrote four fairy tales which were published in a
pamphlet in 1835: *Big Claus and Little Claus, Little Ida's Flowers,
The Princess and the Pea*, and *The Tinder Box*. He followed these with
many more, and in 1846 his tales were translated into English by Mary
Howitt, with the title *Wonderful Stories for Children*. Some of Andersen's stories are folk-tales retold by him, but most of them were his
own invention. In Germany the Grimm Brothers wrote their tales in
order to preserve the remnants of a fast disappearing tradition, but
the Danish Andersen's main purpose was to comfort himself and
escape from reality.

Current editions of Hans Andersen's work include:

Bodley Head. Forty-eight stories including the well-known ones.
Scraperboard illustrations by Rex Whistler.

Cape. Three hundred and twenty tales. Adapted from Caroline
Peachey's translation, but misses the ease of Andersen's
style.

Dent. Includes the stories in the Bodley Head edition plus *The Chimney Sweep* and *The Shepherdess*. Translated by Mrs. E. Lucas in
1899, and true to Andersen.

Faber. Entitled *Forty-two Stories* and first published in 1930. Translated by Dr. M. R. James and contains some tales not in other editions. Andersen's work is discussed in the preface.

Oxford U.P. Thirty-two stories selected and translated by L. W. Kingsland. Illustrated by E. H. Shepard.

Edmund Ward. A pocket-size translation by R. P. Keigwin with many stories not contained in Dr. James' edition. The illustrations by Vilhelm Pedersen are taken from the originals in the Hans Christian Andersen Museum at Copenhagen.

Collected editions of fairy tales began to be published in Britain in and after the 1840's, and included Anthony Montalba's *Fairy Tales of All Nations* (1849); Annie Keary's translation of *Tales from Asgard* (1857); J. R. Planché's *Four and Twenty French Fairy Tales* (1858); and Sir George Dasent's *Popular Tales from the North* (1859), which has formed the basis for all later collections of Scandinavian tales.

Italy and Spain are both countries associated with romance, but historically they have not been recognized for outstanding children's books. The only books one can call to mind are Carlo Collodi's *Pinocchio* (1881) and Miguel de Cervantes' *Don Quixote* (1605) which was translated into English in 1612. There are, however, signs that the situation may be changing.

By the end of the nineteenth century most countries had begun to produce their own literature for children, but comparatively little was translated. The writers of merit included Johann Wyss and Johanna Spyri of Switzerland, Heinrich Hoffmann of Germany, and Jules Verne of France.

Johann Wyss' *Swiss Family Robinson* (1812–13) was in the tradition of *Robinson Crusoe*. It described the adventures of a family shipwrecked on an island and how they overcame their domestic difficulties. An English translation was made by William Godwin in 1814. Johanna Spyri's *Heidi* (1880–1) has been widely translated and shows the tremendous affection the author felt for her homeland.

Heinrich Hoffmann's *Struwwelpeter* or *Shockheaded Peter* arrived in England about 1848. It was a moral tale and showed the results of naughtiness by Cruel Frederick, The Inky Boys, Suck-a-Thumb, and other rather pasteboard characters. It has now lost its moral significance and is simply amusing to the more sophisticated young of today.

The science fiction stories of Jules Verne were well established in France before they were translated into English. Much of Verne's work was published in periodicals such as *The Boy's Own Paper*, as well as in book form. They include *A Voyage to the Centre of the Earth* (1864), *From the Earth to the Moon* (1865), *Round the World in Eighty Days* (1870), and they appeared in England during the 1870's. Verne's heroes tend to be English which no doubt assisted him in achieving the success he did. The British were not particularly pro-French in those days!

TWENTIETH-CENTURY LITERATURE

The twentieth century has witnessed a two-way traffic in children's books between Britain and the other countries of Europe. In the nineteenth century the main contribution from Europe was the folk-tale, while British and American adventure stories by Ballantyne, Fenimore Cooper, Kingston, and Marryat were welcomed in exchange. Today, no particular group of stories from Europe predominates and there is an availability of material from Europe and elsewhere which equals in quality, and frequently surpasses, the work of the best British writers. In the account which follows, the first date after a title is that of the original publication, whilst the second is that of the translation.

AUSTRIA

Viva Mexico (1959) (1960), *The Day of the Bomb* (1961) (1962), *The Hour of the Robots* (1963) (1964), and *Child of the Swamps* (1960) (1965), are representative novels by Karl Bruckner, which deal with modern conditions and have an authentic background. The canvas is wide: revolution in Mexico in 1910; Japan after Hiroshima; the cold-war; and the development of the Po Valley in Italy. Karl Bruckne is typical of a large number of Continental writers in their portrayal of realistic situations in children's books to an extent seldom evident in British literature. Fritz Habeck accomplished this in his historical novel *Days of Danger* (1960) (1968), in which he described the siege of Vienna by the Turks and Tartars in 1683, as seen through the eyes of a boy.

CZECHOSLOVAKIA

Josef Lada's *Purrkin the Talking Cat* (1935) (1966) is an enchanting story for younger children of "Puss in Boots", in which are recorded the exploits of Pete and the talking animals, Purrkin the cat, Ziggibock the goat, Piggiwig the pig, and Fluff the lisping kitten. Hilarious episodes include various encounters with Ted, a nasty boy; and Peter stealing pears from an orchard. Occasionally the animals relate tales to each other.

DENMARK

In *I am David* (1963) (1965), a name was the sole possession of Anne Holm's boy hero when he escaped from a concentration camp behind the Iron Curtain. His journey through Italy, across Europe to Denmark, and how he gradually adjusted to normal living, are described with moving sincerity. He found God, learned to trust and love some of his acquaintances, and escaped from the dreaded "them" in mind as well as in body. Some would complain that the final reunion with his mother was improbable, but there are many who will attest to its credibility.

FINLAND

Finland has produced one of the most outstanding writers for children in Tove Jansson who created the now internationally celebrated Moomins. She won the Hans Christian Andersen Award in 1966. The stories are pure nonsense with an uneasy background of melancholy. Moominmamma is the ideal parent who never fusses, always solves Moomintroll's problems, and no matter how hazardous the adventure, the security of home is constant. The humour in the books lies in these strange creatures doing everyday things. Included in Tove Jansson's work are *The Finn Family Moomintroll* (1949) (1950), *A Comet in Moominland* (1946) (1951), *Moominsummer Madness* (1954) (1955), and *Moominpappa at Sea* (1966) (1966). The books were originally written in Swedish.

FRANCE

Babar, the creation of Jean de Brunhoff, made his entrance in the 1930's in *The Story of Babar* (1931) (1934), *Babar's Travels* (1932) (1935), *Babar the King* (1933) (1936), and *Babar and Father Christmas* (1941) (1940). Jean's son, Laurent, continued the work in *Babar and That Rascal Arthur* (1947) (1948), *Babar's Visit to Bird Island* (1951) (1952), and many others. Babar is a boy in animal form and, in Marcus Crouch's view, "an immortal character can hardly have been established with fewer words or lines".

Among the most successful writers of fantasy was Marcel Aymé. His stories contain talking animals: *The Wonderful Farm* (1949) (1952), and *The Return to the Wonderful Farm.*

Paul Berna has enjoyed outstanding popularity in Britain for his adventure stories which include *A Hundred Million Francs* (1955) (1957), *The Street Musician* (1956) (1960), *The Knights of King Midas* (1958) (1961), and *Gaby and the New Money Fraud* (1961) (1971). Berna has also written space fiction; *Threshold of the Stars* (1954) (1958) and its sequel *The Continent in the Sky* (1955) (1959). His space stories contain a wealth of technical detail which helps to make them the more convincing.

Another great writer about children is Henri Bosco whose stories of Pascalet are told in beautiful language. The stories are set in rural France and include *The Boy and the River* (1955) (1956), *The Fox in the Island* (1956) (1958), and *Barboche* (1957) (1959). A recent contributor to French literature who paints an authentic picture of rural life is May d'Alençon. Her *Red Renard* (1966) (1967) describes how Julian, or Bushy as he was called, cared for a young fox and was instrumental in saving him from the hunt.

There are few children's authors as highly prolific without loss of quality and as versatile without loss of authenticity as René Guillot. Some of his books are set in various parts of Africa and include *The White Shadow* (1948) (1959) (French West Africa) and *Riders of the Wind* (1953) (1960) (North Africa). Guillot's animal stories are probably among his best writing and many of these too are set in Africa. Typical of these are *Sama* (1950) (1952), which is about elephants; *Oworo* (1951) (1954), which is about chimpanzees; and *Kpo the Leopard* (1955) (1955). Books with quite different backgrounds are the Indian *Elephants of Sargabal* (1956) (1956) and the Arctic *Grichka and Brother Bear* (1960) (1965). In all his animal stories Guillot preaches a message of kindness to animals. He won the Hans Christian Andersen Award in 1964.

GERMANY

Three most accomplished German writers are Erich Kästner, who wrote many of his books prior to the Second World War, and Hans Baumann and Barbara Bartos-Höppner who have contributed to the historical novel.

Erich Kästner set a trend in placing real children in a modern setting. *Emil and the Detectives* (1929) (1931) showed life in Berlin as seen through the eyes of a small boy. Kästner was original, too, in that he did not confine his characters to the middle classes at a time when British stories were rather limited in that respect. His *Flying Classroom* (1933) (1934) was set in a boarding school in Bavaria, so that he did not always break with convention; and his more recent *The Little Man* (1963) (1966) and *The Little Man and the Little Miss* (1967) (1969), recount the adventures of a latterday Tom Thumb named Maxie and his fantastic adventures with Professor Hokus von Pokus. Erich Kästner won the Hans Christian Andersen Award in 1960.

The only overseas writer to have rivalled the great British historical novelists of the 1950's and later has been Hans Baumann. He is probably the finest of them all, but it is unfortunate that some of his allusions and psychological overtones do not translate satisfactorily. Among his best works are *Sons of the Steppe* (1954) (1957), which describes the boyhood of Kublai Khan; *The Barque of the Brothers* (1956) (1958), in which Henry the Navigator explores Africa; and *I Marched with Hannibal* (1960) (1961), in which the dangerous crossing of the Alps and the range of mountains itself are described in magnificent language. Examples of Baumann's stories for younger children are *Jackie the Pit Pony* (1957) (1958) and *The Bear and His Brothers* (1961) (1962). This author has also written non-fiction: *The World of the Pharaohs* (1959) (1960) and *Gold and Gods of Peru* (1963) (1963) are told from the viewpoint of archaeologists, and are interspersed with legends.

Barbara Bartos-Höppner has restricted herself in her historical novels to the expansion of the Tsarist Empire in Russia. *The Cossacks* (1959) (1962) and *Save the Khan* (1961) (1963) are concerned with the conquest of the Tartars during the sixteenth century. *Storm Over the Caucasus* (1963) (1968) is an account of the struggle for control of the Caucasus between the Tsar's troops and the army of Imam Shamil at the time of the Crimean War.

HOLLAND

One of the best books from Holland is *Avalanche* (1954) (1957) by Rutgers van der Loeff. It is extremely readable and shows the courage of children of the Pestalozzi International Village matched against the terrible avalanche. *Vassilis on the Run* (1962) (1965) is concerned with refugees, and recounts the problems of Greeks repatriated from Albania after the Second World War, the poverty of their existence, and the efforts made by experts from other countries to rehabilitate them.

Johan Fabricus based his *Java Ho!* (1926) (1933) on the logbooks of a seventeenth-century sea captain. It is a tale of four boys on a voyage to the Far East who undergo fire and shipwreck and many other hardships.

A writer of a different kind is Mrs. C. E. Pothast-Gimberg. *Corso the Donkey* (1959) (1962) is an animal story of donkeys for sale in Holland, and of Toni who went with them and loved them. The plea of kindness to animals is emphasized continually, and also sacrifice when Toni gave her beloved Corso to a blind friend. It is unfortunate that more of Mrs. Pothast-Gimberg's books have not been translated into English.

HUNGARY

Géza Gárdonyi in *Slave of the Huns* (1901) (1969) follows the fortunes of Zeta, a Greek, who chose slavery in the camp of Attila the Hun to be near Emmo with whom he was in love. The author describes Attila's bloody conquest of Europe, but gives a sympathetic portrayal of the warlord which contrasts sharply with the popular view. As a historical novel this book is as well written as any and better than most.

ITALY

Angela Latini's *Za the Truffle Boy* (1955) (1960) is a delightful picture of rural Italy and a boy who followed in the family tradition of digging for truffles. In time he became aware of agricultural developments and learned to grow them scientifically.

Progress was further underlined by Renée Reggiani in *The Sun Train* (1962) (1966), the account of a Sicilian family's move from its Mafia-ridden peasant background to industrial Turin. The growth of Agata from a child to a woman is sensitively described.

NORWAY

It is unusual for humour to translate well, but it does so in Thorbjorn Egner's *The Singing Town* (1951) (1959). This is a tale in which a gang of thieves eventually learned the error of their wicked ways and became model citizens. The story is interspersed with verses, and the whole production is rather reminiscent of a musical comedy.

Johanna Bugge Olsen has provided a story in the tradition of the English *Bevis* in her *Stray Dog* (1963) (1966). She recounts the adventures of Erling, Magnus, and the dog Sancho for whom they find a home. In the course of the book the boys observe animals and plants.

A somewhat sad book with a message to most children is *Kersti* (1964) (1966) by Babbis Friis. Following a car accident, Kersti had to adjust to a world of thoughtless cruelty with a scarred face. The children at school were particularly hard on her at a time when her mother was in hospital with a new baby. The author is unusually frank in her examination of attitudes and motives.

SOUTH AFRICA

Wild Goose Summer (1959) (1964) by P. H. Nortje pictures Henk and his friends on holiday in a farming community. The work is enhanced by William Papas' humorous illustrations, but the barbaric baboon hunt leaves a nasty taste. *Dark Waters* (1964) (1965) describes school activities and contains a mystery of missing diamonds which threw a shadow over the friendship of two families.

SWEDEN

Swedish literature is represented by Selma Lagerlöf, H. J. Kaeser, Harry Kullman, Astrid Lindgren, and Maria Gripe.

The Wonderful Adventures of Nils (1906–7) by Selma Lagerlöf did not make its appearance in Britain until 1950. The English translation was published in two parts, the second of which was called *The Further Adventures of Nils* (1953). It is a tale of a farmer's son who was cruel to animals and was turned into an elf and hounded by Smirre Fox as a punishment. One can learn much of Swedish folk-lore and natural history from the exploits of the boy who even had the experience of migrating with wild geese.

H. J. Kaeser, a German, most of whose books have been translated into Swedish, drew memorable pictures of a boy in *Mimff* (1937) (1939). Mimff tried to find the meaning of the word "fear" and had many hair-raising adventures. The excellent characterization and sense of humour were perpetuated in other books about the same boy in various situations, such as *Mimff Takes Over* (1954) and *Mimff-Robinson* (1958).

Harry Kullman has presented a complicated situation of class conflict produced by adults but resolved by children from different backgrounds in *The Secret Journey* (1953) (1959). The lives of lower and middle classes are brilliantly contrasted. His subject in *Runaway* (1957) (1961) is a working-class boy in Stockholm.

One of the best modern children's writers is Astrid Lindgren. She was awarded the Hans Christian Andersen Award for *Rasmus and the Tramp* (1958) (1961). In it she described the sad lot of orphan children hoping to be chosen by foster parents. Astrid Lindgren has also written books about six Bullerby children; and various others about a girl named Pippi, such as *Pippi Longstocking* (1945) (1954) and *Pippi in the South Seas* (1955) (1957). The latter books are extremely fanciful and full of fun.

Maria Gripe's *Pappa Pellerin's Daughter* (1963) (1966) concerns a girl named Loella, whose father figure was a scarecrow until she found her real father. In a lighter vein are *Hugo and Josephine* (1962) (1969) and two other books about a wild, woodcarving boy and his friend, a clergyman's daughter. The author's ability to evoke childhood with its joys and sorrows helps to place her in the first rank of Swedish writers for children.

SWITZERLAND

Tales in verse by Selina Chönz have been translated into English by Anne and Ian Serraillier. They are *A Bell for Ursli* (1946) (1950) and *Florina and the Wild Bird* (1952) (1952).

Manfred Michael portrayed a Swiss town in which the children behave so badly that the adult population move out. *Timpetill* (1937)

(1951) gives an account of how the children managed their own affairs for the brief period of a week.

There is evidence enough of a growing export of literature from other countries throughout the world, from countries which have made no significant contribution previously as well as from those which have produced some of the greatest children's authors of the past century and a half and earlier. Through these writers whose work is easily available in British editions, both hard- and paper-covered, children in this country have been and will continue to be influenced by culture from other lands. The presence of these books in our libraries and on the shelves of personal collections can do nothing but good in spreading a greater international understanding of the customs and outlook of different countries. It must be remembered, however, that the parts of the original works which reach readers in this country are the plot, the setting, and the characters. The style must be the translator's, and intangible things like humour may or may not be translatable. In the hands of an indifferent translator a great work will suffer and its hidden truths be lost to all who are unable to read it in its original tongue.

CHAPTER 15

Retellings

IN THEIR original editions the fairy tales collected by the Grimm brothers were, in fact, retellings. They evoked a spirit of magic and wonder as they were passed down through the generations and lost none of their quality in the hands of Jacob and Wilhelm Grimm. Less able recorders would have failed to preserve the tales and the culture they represented. In less able hands many of them would have ceased to exist except as curiosities.

It is not only the popular lore of Germany which has been immortalized, but also that of many countries, including that of our own. The heroes of legend are still hailed and their deeds absorbed in awe by fresh generations of children. Beowulf, Roland, King Arthur, and Robin Hood have been known and loved far back into the Middle Ages. The interest of the Renaissance in the ancient world resulted in translations of the classics of Greece and Rome, which have since been retold in excellent editions for children. Then, returning to the present, one can consider the many folk-tales of countries far from Europe and the Western world, which have been recorded by students of foreign culture and collectors of tales; and not only by these, but also by the inhabitants of the developing countries, imbued with an awakened pride in their national heritage.

BEOWULF

Beowulf is probably the most ancient epic of the Teutonic world, and is the only poem which attempts a picture of the primitive age on a large scale. The setting is the Danish island of Seeland, and the country of the Goths in south Sweden, whilst the story recounts the victory of the Franks over the Goths between A.D. 512 and 520. Beowulf, a young warrior of the defeated army, distinguished himself in the battle, but later became a saintly personage and his court became a centre of wisdom.

This then is a national epic and is probably an adaptation into Anglo-Saxon of a Scandinavian legend. The later chivalrous romances are foreshadowed in *Beowulf*.

In this and in each instance where a particular legend is described it will be followed by a short list of retellings for children:

NYE, ROBERT. *Bee Hunter: adventures of Beowulf*. Faber. 1968.
A prose interpretation in which considerable changes are made to the content of the original. Poorly reproduced illustrations.

PICARD, B. L. *Tales of the British People*. Edmund Ward. 1961.
Nine folk-tales spanning 1000 years. Included are Beowulf, Hereward the Wake, Sir Bevis, and Gawain.

SERRAILLIER, IAN. *Beowulf the Warrior*. Oxford U.P. 1954.
Follows the pattern of the original and retells the chief episodes in spirited verse.

SUTCLIFF, ROSEMARY. *Beowulf*. Bodley Head. 1961.
A dramatic retelling which recounts the three great battles: with Grendel, with the Sea-woman, and finally with the Fire-Drake.

STORIES OF BRITAIN AND THE NORTH

Recent outstanding contributions to this field are:

HOSFORD, DOROTHY. *Sons of the Volsungs*. Bodley Head. 1965.
A prose retelling from William Morris's epic poem *Sigurd the Volsung*.

NYE, ROBERT. *Taliesin*. Faber. 1966.
One of the stories in the ancient *Mabinogion*. Well written for children.

PICARD, B. L. *Celtic Tales: legends of tall warriors and old enchantments*. Edmund Ward. 1964.

202   HOW TO FIND OUT ABOUT CHILDREN'S LITERATURE

PICARD, B. L. *German Hero Sagas and Folk Tales*. Oxford U.P. 1963.

SUTCLIFF, ROSEMARY. *The High Deeds of Finn MacCool*. Bodley Head. 1967.
Tales of a glorious period in Irish history when the Fianna of Erin led by Finn kept the peace throughout the land.

SUTCLIFF, ROSEMARY. *The Hound of Ulster*. Bodley Head. 1963.
Another well-told Irish story, this time of Cuchulain.

TREECE, HENRY. *The Burning of Njal*. Bodley Head. 1964.
Henry Treece was an expert on the period and brought his scholarship to bear in retelling the eleventh-century saga of Njal's burning.

TREECE, HENRY. *Vinland the Good*. Bodley Head. 1967.
Recounts incidents from the Icelandic sagas *Eirik the Red* and *The Greenland Saga*, which describe the discovery of America by the Vikings in the tenth century.

ROLAND

Le Chanson de Roland is an eleventh-century work and is typical in its clarity and colour of the early French writers. It is a song of disaster in the eighth century and was perpetuated by the Normans, who preserved it, while playing down the Anglo-Saxon traditions until they virtually disappeared.

In the twelfth and thirteenth centuries French became the first of the European literatures and one of its primary spheres of influence was Britain.

CLARKE, E. *The Song of Roland*. Legacy Library. 1962.
Written in straightforward prose for younger children.

PICARD, B. L. *French Legends, Tales and Fairy Stories*. Oxford U.P. 1955.
The stories of Roland and Oliver, and Aucassin and Nicolette are included.

SERRAILLIER, IAN. *The Ivory Horn*. Oxford U.P. 1960.

A prose rendering of the Song of Roland and the great battle of Roncesvalles. Roland's friend Oliver urged him to blow his ivory horn to recall the French forces but Roland fought on and blew his horn too late.

ARTHURIAN LEGENDS

The Arthurian legends are derived from the distant past. Geoffrey of Monmouth mentioned Arthur in his *History of the Britons* in 1147, and he is to a large extent the creator of the legend. Arthur was represented as the defender of the Britons who conquered Anglo-Saxons, Picts, Scots, Irish, and Scandinavians. He went to destroy Gaul and Iceland, and even humbled the mighty Rome itself. Patriotism indeed!

Geoffrey's fables were accepted by Normans and Saxons and the result was that both adopted a racial enemy as their own hero. In this way English patriotism was born.

From time to time fresh material was added to the original, and although Sir Thomas Malory claimed to be translating a French book, his *Morte d'Arthur* (1470) was in fact a compilation. Malory has portrayed a strange world in which all is battle and tournament, all residences are castles, and economics is quite unknown.

COOKE, B. K. *King Arthur of Britain.* Edmund Ward. 1946.
Contains the passages of *Morte d'Arthur* which relate specifically to the King, and is as far as possible in Malory's words.

GREEN, R. L. *King Arthur and His Knights of the Round Table.* Puffin Books. 1953.
A retelling from Malory and other sources arranged as a legendary history of Britain. The picture of Arthur's kingdom retains its essential magic.

HADFIELD, A. M. *King Arthur and the Round Table.* Dent. 1953.
A simple version of the quest for the Holy Grail. It is a highly rationalized account, however, and loses the mystic atmosphere one would expect to find.

KNOWLES, SIR JAMES. *Legends of King Arthur and His Knights.* Warne 1952. (Original 1862.)
Mainly an abridgement of Malory with some of Geoffrey of Monmouth. An effort has been made to arrange the tales into a consecutive story. This is an excellent edition for children.

PICARD, B. L. *Stories of King Arthur and His Knights.* Oxford U.P. 1955.
Twenty-seven independent stories. A well-written and well-chosen selection of material.

A variation of the Arthurian theme is the fragment of manuscript in the Lancashire dialect known as *Sir Gawain and the Grene Knyght*, which has been dated 1360–70. The author is unknown but it is considered he must have been familiar with the life at court. Gawain owes a great deal to all the earlier Arthurian legends but its particular subject is not encountered elsewhere. The Gawain of Malory is a frivolous, bragging oaf, but here he is chaste and unstained. Praise of purity and chastity are dominant.

BORROFF, MARIE. *Sir Gawain and the Green Knight: a new verse translation.* Longmans. 1969.
A competent rendering of the poem which is closer to the original than most other versions.

RIDLEY, M. R. *Sir Gawain and the Green Knight.* Edmund Ward. 1950.
This version preserves the spirit of the fourteenth-century poem and has been retold for older children.

SERRAILLIER, IAN. *The Challenge of the Green Knight.* Oxford U.P. 1966.
A retelling with illustrations by Victor Ambrus.

As was noted earlier, the story of Gawain is also retold in Barbara Leonie Picard's *Tales of the British People.*

ROBIN HOOD

A number of heroes were cherished in fourteenth-century England: heroes whose ancestry was to be found in French and Latin books, and who appeared in their English form towards the end of the thirteenth century. These included Bevis of Southampton and Guy of Warwick. During the fourteenth century the popular rhymes of Robin Hood developed, and by the sixteenth century ballads were being written of his splendid exploits. The legend was changed and enlarged through the years. Maid Marian was a late arrival.

Children have adopted these stories with their philosophy of plundering the wicked rich and passing the spoils to a deserving poor. During the seventeenth century and eighteenth century Robin Hood and other romances were widely issued in chapbook form.

KING, DOROTHY. *Greenwood Tales: stories of Robin Hood*. Blackie. 1965.
Nine stories for children over 7. Simple language but a tendency to be pseudo-archaic. Illustrated by William Stobbs.

OMAN, CAROLA. *Robin Hood Prince of Outlaws*. Dent. 1937.
Taken from the earliest printed ballads and set in the reign of Edward II. There is some discrepancy between the various editions as to which king was on the throne. Well written, and archaic expressions are absent.

PYLE, HOWARD. *Merry Adventures of Robin Hood*. Peveril Classics. 1957.
Includes all the well-known Robin Hood stories in pseudo-archaic language. Illustrated by Howard Pyle. Based on the original United States edition of 1883.

SERRAILLIER, IAN. *Robin in the Greenwood*. Oxford U.P. 1967.
A retelling in verse of twelve of the more well-known stories in a style which recreates the romantic atmosphere of Sherwood. His *Robin and His Merrie Men* (Oxford U.P., 1969) extends his contribution to the presentation of the legend.

SUTCLIFF, ROSEMARY. *Chronicles of Robin Hood.* Oxford U.P. 1950.
Shows the growth of the band of outlaws and how Robin was eventually pardoned by King Richard. For younger children.

GREEK MYTHS

A large number of translations of ancient literature were made during the Renaissance. Chaucer translated parts of Virgil very badly.
By 1579 many of the great works had been translated into English.
The translators did not use the originals but retranslated from French
and Italian versions.

The prose translations were often remarkable for their literary
merit but the verse translations were more uneven. The masterpiece
of verse translation was George Chapman's *Homer* (*Iliad*, 1611;
Odyssey, 1616). Later came John Dryden's *Virgil* (1697); and
Alexander Pope's *Iliad* (1715–20), which he followed by *The Odyssey*
(1725–6).

Thus has the genius of Homer, a Greek poet who lived prior to 700
B.C., and Virgil, a Roman poet who lived from 70 B.C. to 19 B.C., been
preserved for modern generations. Homer's *Iliad* and *Odyssey* are
thought to have developed out of earlier legendary material. Virgil in
his *Aeneid* continued the history of the Trojan War after the death of
Hector, which is the point at which the *Iliad* ends.

HOMER

BUTCHER, S. H. and LANG, ANDREW (trans.). *Homer's Odyssey.*
Macmillan. 1879.
The standard prose translation. It consists of the complete text.

CHURCH, A. J. *The Odyssey of Homer and the Iliad of Homer.* Macmillan. 1951.
First published towards the end of the nineteenth century in simple,
dignified prose. A. J. Church also retold *The Aeneid for Boys and
Girls.*

PICARD, B. L. *The Odyssey of Homer.* Oxford U.P. 1952.

Attempts to convey the spirit of adventure faced by Odysseus on his voyage. Barbara Leonie Picard also retold *The Iliad.* Delightful illustrations by Joan Kiddell-Monroe.

VIRGIL

TAYLOR, N. B. *The Aeneid of Virgil.* Oxford U.P. 1961.

A companion volume to B. L. Picard's *Odyssey* and *Iliad.*

Other Greek myths have been retold in the following works:

BAKER, GEORGE. *Realms of Gold.* London U.P. 1954.

Retells in one narrative the *Iliad,* the *Odyssey,* the *Aeneid,* and many other myths and legends. In so doing, George Baker demonstrates the essential continuity of the story.

BULFINCH, T. *Age of Fable.* Everyman. 1912.

The material for this was acquired from the poems of John Keats and Lord Tennyson, and is intended to provoke further inquiry by older children into more scholarly editions.

HAWTHORNE, NATHANIEL. *The Wonder Book.* Dent. 1952. (Original, 1852.)

Various stories retold as fairy tales to a group of children. Hawthorne continued his work in *Tanglewood Tales* (1853).

KINGSLEY, CHARLES. *The Heroes; or, Greek Fairy Tales For My Children.* Dent. 1964. (Original, 1855.)

No one has outrivalled Kingsley in his manner of telling the stories of Perseus, Theseus, and Jason and the Argonauts.

WARNER, REX. *Greeks and Trojans.* McGibbon & Kee. 1951.

The main episodes of the Trojan War. Based on the *Iliad,* but helped by E. V. Rieu's translation. Divided into broad sections: Greeks and Trojans, Wrath of Achilles, and Fall of Troy.

AESOP'S FABLES

Probably the best known of the ancient stories which have appealed to children are the Fables of Aesop, who lived as a slave in Phrygia about 200 years after Homer. William Caxton translated the Fables from the French into English in 1484 and from that time to the present there have always been two kinds of edition: for recreation and for school work. John Ogilby translated into verse the first version for children in 1651, but a more successful translation was that by Sir Roger L'Estrange in 1692. Current editions include:

Black. About 200 of the fables, illustrated by Charles Folkard.

Dent. A definitive translation by John Warrington, and illustrated. by Joan Kiddell-Monroe.

Hamlyn. A quarto-size edition of forty fables selected and adapted for children by Louis Untermeyer. Illustrations by Alice and Martin Provensen.

Heinemann. A translation by S. Vernon Jones and illustrated by Arthur Rackham.

ARABIAN NIGHTS

From outside Europe a popular collection has been the *Tales from the Arabian Nights*. The first European translation of quality was into French by Antoine Galland, whose work was published in twelve volumes between 1704 and 1717. Shortly afterwards Galland's edition was translated into English and reached the chapbook market. Children especially enjoyed the stories of Ali Baba, Aladdin, and Sinbad the Sailor.

The English version most used or adapted for children today is Lane's text of 1838–40. There are attractive editions in the Dent *Children's Illustrated Classics*, illustrated by Joan Kiddell-Monroe; and the Oxford *Illustrated Classics*, illustrated by Brian Wildsmith.

MISCELLANEOUS COLLECTIONS

There are also other recent publications which cover a very wide field of myths and legends, and which contain much of the work already mentioned:

GREEN, R. L. *The Book of Myths.* Dent. 1965.
Divided by country to include myths from Babylon, Egypt, Greece, Rome, and Scandinavia. Illustrated by Joan Kiddell-Monroe.

HOPE-SIMPSON, JACYNTH. *The Hamish Hamilton Book of Myths and Legends.* 1964.
Follows the early versions and avoids modern retellings wherever possible. A wide coverage of famous and little known material from Greece, Rome, Scandinavia, and other parts of Europe. The retellings are accurate but sometimes rather tedious. ˙

WHITE, ANNE TERRY. *Myths and Legends.* Golden Pleasure Book. 1959.
A quarto-size volume which includes Greek legends, Beowulf, Roland, Tristram and Iseult, and Sigurd of the Volsungs. Fine illustrations by Alice and Martin Provensen.

The next group of material is the fairy tale. Translations of Andersen, Grimm, and Perrault have been examined, but in Britain there were two retellers of prominence towards the end of the nineteenth century. They were Joseph Jacobs and Andrew Lang.

Joseph Jacobs' *English Fairy Tales* (1890) and *More English Fairy Tales* (1894) include *The Three Little Pigs, The Three Bears, Jack and the Beanstalk, Dick Whittington, Tom Hickathrift, Tom Thumb,* and many others. Jacobs said that his tales "must serve as the best substitute that can be offered for an English Grimm". There were eighty-seven tales in all. Sixty of the original number were included in an edition by Frederick Muller dated 1942 and entitled *English Fairy Tales.* A complete edition which includes Jacobs' prefaces, notes and references was published by Bodley Head in 1968, with illustrations by Margery Gill.

Andrew Lang compiled books of fairy tales from many sources. The series commenced in 1889 with *The Blue Fairy Book* which contained favourites from Grimm and Perrault. The other volumes were also named after colours; for example, *The Crimson Fairy Book* (stories from Finland, Hungary, Japan, Russia), *The Olive Fairy Book* (India), *The Rose Fairy Book* (France, Italy, Spain). Longman issued an edition of the *Fairy Books* in 1949, edited by Mary Gould Davis. In 1963

Bodley Head published *Fifty Favourite Fairy Tales from Andrew Lang* in its series of *Nonesuch Cygnets*. These were selected from the twelve colour fairy books by Kathleen Lines and illustrated by Margery Gill. This volume was followed in 1967 by *More Favourite Fairy Tales from Andrew Lang* in which is contained an epilogue by Roger Lancelyn Green.

SERIES OF FAIRY TALES

There are numerous well-produced series of fairy tales available from publishers today:

Edward Arnold. *Folk Tales of the World.*
Edited by A. W. Crown and illustrated by Dean Mitchell. Volumes are included on Australia, Greece, India, Israel, Japan, and North America.

Bodley Head. *Favourite Fairy Tales.*
A series designed for younger children and selected by Virginia Haviland. Six stories are included in each book which is attractively designed and printed in large type. Volumes are included for Italy, Japan, Poland, Scotland, and Spain, and have been illustrated by high-quality artists such as Barbara Cooney and Felix Hoffmann. Originally published in the United States.

Muller. *Fairy Tale Collections.*
Includes Celtic, Chinese, French, German, Persian, Polish, Russian, Spanish, Swedish, and Swiss tales. An attractive series.

Oxford U.P. *Myths and Legends.*
This series includes English, French, Indian, Irish, Japanese, Red Indian, Russian, Scottish, Welsh, and other tales. Mainly illustrated by Joan Kiddell-Monroe. Very attractive.

Routledge. *Folk Tales of the World.*
Edited by Richard Dorson, a world-celebrated scholar in history and folk-lore. Wide coverage includes Hungary, Israel, Poland, the Philippines, and West Africa, retold by nationals of the countries concerned. Explanatory notes, glossaries, and bibliographies are appended.

Finally there are specific volumes representative of the folk-lore of the developing countries of which a selection is:

APPIAH, PEGGY. *Tales of an Ashanti Father*. Andre Deutsch. 1967.

BARASH, ASHER. *A Golden Treasury of Jewish Tales*. W. H. Allen. 1966.

DE LEEUW, ADELE. *Indonesian Fairy Tales*. Muller. 1966.

GHOSE, SUDKIN. *Folk Tales and Fairy Tales from India*. Golden Cockerel. 1961.

WELLS, ANN E. *Skies of Arnhem Land* (Australian Aborigines). Angus & Robertson. 1965.

It is an exciting thought that the literary and folk traditions of the world are so readily available for British children. One particular aspect of international relations in which books can play an important role is in the publication in all countries of the stories which typify the traditions and attitudes to life of other countries. Thus, in the case of a small child, a book can do much to assist him in his individual development and in relation to the community in which he lives. Literature which tells in an interesting manner of the life of people perhaps living at the other end of a child's world can assist him by affording the opportunity for him to compare the similarities and differences of his own and other cultures, and equip him with a maturity of social outlook and a sympathy and understanding for those who do not live and think in an identical manner to himself. It is on such a basis that world peace can be built.

CHAPTER 16

Purpose in Children's Reading

LEFT to themselves children have a preference for authors like Enid Blyton, Richmal Crompton, and Captain Johns, and this author must confess that he derived a great deal of pleasure from them in his youth. In most aspects of their lives, however, children are not left to their own devices. For most of their waking hours they attend school, and are, or should be, educated so that in time they will take their place in the community. Such guidance and exercise in the development of the learning and thinking processes is considered necessary, and in an ideal situation they will be taught how to use books and perhaps derive some enjoyment from them. It seems reasonable that children should be introduced to the great works of literature and particularly those authors who have regarded the young as their audience. There can be no doubt that children's books can play a real part in the individual development of the young. If they are to be introduced to appropriate material at the various stages of their growth, then those who seek to guide them must know something of the principles of child development.

The growth of children follows a continuous and orderly sequence, but each stage does not progress at a steady pace. In infancy children grow quickly and what are called "Maturity Indicators" appear in rapid succession. During the immediate pre-school and the school years, the rate of growth loses its impetus, while certain aspects are accelerated in adolescence.

All aspects of growth—physical, emotional, mental, and social—do not develop at the same rate at the same time. School work, for instance, is sometimes affected adversely while a child is growing taller and heavier. If this is to be properly understood, interested adults must know something of the stages and the patterns of growth. With such knowledge it should be possible to provide experiences which help children, not only to make the best of one phase, but also to prepare for the next.

Reading can be an important contributor to child development. It can help a child to understand and live a healthy life in his immediate environment. The stories of William Mayne, Sheena Porter, John Rowe Townsend, Geoffrey Trease, Philip Turner, and Barbara Willard, and others, are invaluable in this respect. Reading may help a child to appreciate life in the larger world. The books of folk-lore which explain the culture of other people, the authentic geographical stories, and the translations of life in a contemporary setting, are of great assistance in fostering a more objective understanding of those whose differences are mainly superficial.

The historical stories of Rosemary Sutcliff, Hester Burton, Esther Forbes, Elizabeth G. Speare, and Hans Baumann, and many more, provide pictures of earlier days and introduce the child to his heritage and its relationship with those of boys and girls from other countries. These stories help a child to understand that he cannot reasonably allocate Romans, Tudors, Roundheads, Girondins, Chartists, and Boers to historical pigeon-holes, but that they all belong to one pattern of which the young reader is part, and who is likely to take steps to ensure its continuity in the fullness of time. It is right that a child's life should be meaningful to him through these stories in which he undertakes a vicarious role.

Some have gone so far as to claim that historical stories can be used as a teaching aid. In the upper forms of primary schools and the lower and middle forms of secondary schools, interest can be aroused by the teacher reading extracts from suitable novels to his class. The principal value of these will be as a stimulant to kindle the imagination, to give a vivid impression of life in other times, and to stress the point that people in the past were real human beings. Background accuracy is naturally desirable, but errors in detail can be allowed providing they do not distort the truth. Helen Haines in her *Living with Books* remarked that the historical novelist "may transpose time or reshape minor events to fit into his plot's scheme; but he may not falsify history's fundamental record". Most of the stories have a point of view and may tend to be sympathetic to one faction or another. This is especially likely if the period under discussion is fairly recent or if political or religious disputes are being settled. In many books a note is added to distinguish fact from fiction. Cynthia Harnett is a writer who has contributed greatly to the material for history lessons through the wealth of domestic and social detail she includes in her books.

Ideas may be presented and attitudes which are associated with good citizenship and sound character be suggested in books. The American author, Eleanor Estes, who was awarded the Newbery Medal in 1951 for her delightful family story with its canine hero *Ginger Pye*, has attempted to define a good book. She considers it is one which "makes a child laugh or cry, makes him feel some emotion, makes him feel like going out to correct the evils of the world, to accomplish something ennobling; that creates in him a feeling of identity with the most sublime thoughts and ideals of our thinkers, writers and doers; that makes him feel compassion for the unfortunate and the unhappy; that makes him know that by what he thinks and says and does and is, he may in some measure contribute to the understanding of people one for another, and insist that people be kindly and generous".

One can readily call to mind the social purpose in Hester Burton's *No Beat of Drum* and *Time of Trial*; the forthright attack on ignorant attitudes to foreigners in Frederick Grice's *The Moving Finger*; the call for tolerance to minorities in R. F. Chandler's *Ladder to the Sky* and Emily Cheney Neville's *Berries Goodman*; the recognition of an individual's right to live his own life in his own way in Joseph Krumgold's *Onion John*; the splendid lessons of human endurance and triumph in the face of unleashed elements in Ivan Southall's *Hill's End*, Hester Burton's *The Great Gale*, and Rutgers van der Loeff's *Avalanche*; and the plea for kindness to animals which has been the message of so many authors from Mrs. Trimmer to René Guillot and the numerous winners of the American Library Association's Aurianne Award. All of them contribute in some way "to the understanding of people one for another and insist that people be kindly and generous". Not only fiction titles can be quoted in this connection. There are numerous outstanding biographies of the world's heroes which set standards of bravery, intellectual curiosity, and common humanity very often in the face of seemingly overwhelming odds. Numerous series are available which recount the exploits and way of life of great men and women, including the Batsford *Makers of Britain*, Black *Lives to Remember*, Faber *Men and Events*, Lutterworth Press *Stories of Faith and Fame*, Methuen *Story Biographies*, Weidenfeld and Nicolson *Pathfinder Biographies*, and many others.

David A. Shavreen defined a bad book in a stimulating article in the Spring 1965 issue of *Use of English*. He suggested that bad books spring "from immature minds, that gloss over difficulty and danger, that ignore frailty and fear, that pretend that children are goody-goodies or that fame is easy, or that are otherwise written to please rather than to communicate experience". There is a need to teach children right attitudes to cruelty, violence and intolerance, and to encourage them in kindliness, tolerance and good citizenship. Such traits cannot be developed too early in childhood and their acquisition can be helped by the picture books and stories first encountered at a mother's knee. It would be quite easy in view of what has been suggested so far to incur the charge of censorship, but by no stretch of the imagination can it be wrong to uphold attitudes of humanity, and pillory those which corrupt and debase.

A further value of reading in development is to be found in the satisfaction of a child's curiosity about topics of interest to him and in the answering of those questions which arise in the course of study. Many children will never know the value of books in any other connection. It is nonsense to believe that *all* children can be filled with a love of literature, but it is even more nonsensical to believe that books cannot find a place of any kind in the lives of many children. Those who have found difficulty in reading proficiently and do not regard this activity with pleasure can still be taught how to use books as a means of practical assistance throughout their lives. They can even be introduced to great literature through the agency of the story-teller.

The reading of literature, however, will only help some children, but information and reference books have a potential appeal to all.

It is to be recognized that childhood is unique. Each child has his own needs, interests, and capabilities. The characteristics of the different levels of maturity should be understood and books provided which relate to the stages through which a child will progress at his own speed. All normal children follow a predictable order of development but at different rates. Such children can all learn to read, but there is a time when each of them is ready. Reading readiness develops during the pre-school years; and in the primary school, children learn the techniques which lead to the perfection of fundamental skills and meaningful reading. In the secondary school the reading interests and tastes and habits are refined. If this is accomplished successfully, young people will wish to continue their reading when the disciplines of school have been abandoned for the adult world.

CHAPTER 17

Reading and Child Development

WHILST it is possible to identify broad stages of development in children, it is not wise to assume that because a child has not reached one of them at a particular age he is therefore backward. Conversely, a child reaching a stage before he is a given age cannot be assumed to be a potential genius. Some children's books and guides to the literature contain suggestions as to the ages of children for whom authors are writing. In view of the comments made in the last chapter regarding the development of children, it is obvious that such dogmatism is misleading, and may well result in harm to a youngster whose parents panic when he proves himself unable to read a book "prescribed" for his age.

Children of a particular age are not expected to be physically or emotionally alike and there is no reason why they should be identical intellectually. Thus, anyone who asks for a book for a boy of 10 without explaining the capabilities of the child for whom it is intended, is talking arrant nonsense. If the interest age and the reading age coincide there is no problem, but so often they do not equate, and what is more, where there is no marked variation the child concerned would not be regarded as backward.

Therefore, while the following examination of particular age groups and the books which are likely to help them and interest them will involve suggestions of ages, it should be remembered that a child or a group of children may vary by a year or more from the arbitrary norm, and in the case of backward readers the variation will be even greater. What is certain is that children progress through the stages of development individually and in their own time.

After babyhood has been left behind and the instincts and potentialities of a child have begun to emerge, the next stage of development
is concerned with the organization of his personality. This stage usually
takes place between the ages of 2 and 4 years. In this period a child
learns by imitating those with whom he comes into contact, and by
identifying himself with their personalities. If the models are good
the child will build a healthy personality but if they are bad the reverse
may happen.

Gradually, the child ceases to imitate his models but retains their
characters which become part of his own personality. In addition,
the child may in imagination ascribe his own characteristics to others,
even to toy animals and trains, as did Christopher Robin with Pooh
his toy teddy bear. Children's apperception tests have shown that
young children respond more readily to animals than to other human
beings.

Children between 2 and 4 cannot usually read, and parents are advised not to teach them to do so. The kind of book which does not
require the ability to read is the picture book. Such literature contains
stories of other young children with whom the infants may identify
themselves. Edward Ardizzone's *Tim* is a case in point. He is aged 5
and goes on wonderful adventures on land and sea. Another well-
known character is Helen Bannerman's *Little Black Sambo*.

Very often animals are endowed with human personalities, such as
Beatrix Potter's *Peter Rabbit* and other tales, Leslie Brooke's *Johnny
Crow*, Jean de Brunhoff's *Babar*, and John Burningham's *Borka*,
Trubloff, and *Humbert*. Toys can be personalized just as successfully,
as with Diana Ross' *Little Red Engine* and Hardy Gramatky's *Little
Toot*.

The plots of most of the picture books are self-evident from the
pictures but the most satisfactory situation is where the text is read
to the child by some understanding adult. With the collusion of sympathetic adults the possibilities are widened immeasurably. Fairy tales
like *Cinderella*, *Red Riding Hood*, *Jack and the Beanstalk*, and the
easily remembered nursery rhymes can be introduced to the child, as
can such delights as J. M. Barrie's *Peter Pan*, Michael Bond's *Padding-*

ton, A. A. Milne's *Winnie the Pooh*, Alison Uttley's *Sam Pig*, Ursula Moray Williams' *Little Wooden Horse*, and many others. The activities of the child in endowing inanimate objects and animals with human attributes can, therefore, be harnessed and his horizons extended at the same time.

With careful selection of the material which can be understood by a particular child, an adult can lead him quite early in his development to appreciate the treasures of literature. Sometimes difficulties arise, such as explaining the difference between the ball with which a child plays and the event of the same name at which Cinderella met her Prince Charming. Incidents of this kind can be used to extend the child's knowledge of his world and meet with particular success as the child asks the question of his own volition.

Pre-school children can have books read to them which relate to their own environment and experience. Particularly useful in this connection is the Ladybird series which is published by Wills & Hepworth. Children born before the advent of television had not the advantages of pre-school children at the present time. These children can watch stories and documentaries which include objects completely outside the experience of their predecessors of 20 years ago. Therefore, this must be kept in mind when material is being provided for children "within their experience".

In this country most children begin school at 5. Whilst their experiences increase with the widening environment, they will still think much as they did before they commenced their new life. The beliefs in animals and objects with human personalities persist and, by the age of 7, many children are beginning to read simple story books by Joyce Lankester Brisley and Helen Cresswell, and find no difficulty at all in reading many of the picture books at which they could only look in earlier years. Selected fairy tales of Grimm and Andersen with their talking animals and articles of furniture reach a peak of interest between 6 and 7. Children between 4 and 6 may not be interested in fairy tales because of their symbolic significance, and at this stage children are preoccupied with concrete ideas. Most children will not be unduly disturbed by some of the horrific incidents, but many will be upset by them and should not be cajoled or compelled to read of things which frighten them. Girls admit to reading fairy stories for a longer period of their lives than do boys, but this does not mean that boys stop reading them. It is just not considered masculine to confess to it!

Children of the 1960's are fortunate in having access to the useful and usually attractive Ladybird Books which have been mentioned earlier. In this series children can read Bible stories such as *Jesus the Helper, Children of the Bible,* and *A First Book of Saints.* They can read about everyday people like *The Fireman, The Policeman,* and *The Builder.* Ladybird Books are also used in schools, not only in the teaching of reading for which they are obtainable in both traditional spelling and also in the Initial Teaching Alphabet, but also as supplementary reading books which include such topics as *The Farm, Numbers, Telling the Time, Shopping with Mother, The Party, The Zoo,* and an exciting range of others.

An increasing amount of material is available in the Initial Teaching Alphabet apart from reading primers. Well-known works which have been produced in this way include stories by Beatrix Potter and A. A. Milne. I.T.A. is in use in a substantial minority of schools in this country, and in an endeavour to cater for the leisure reading of children who are involved, many public libraries lend books in this medium for home reading. The public library should cater for all children who can read (as well as those who cannot) and the provision of books in I.T.A. not only furthers co-operation with the schools but also helps to ensure that children who visited the library as infants will continue to do so as they learn to read.

Hamish Hamilton publish various series of books for children of 7 and younger. Gazelle books are intended to follow on from picture books, and include work by Christine Pullein-Thompson and William Mayne. The Star Books series is for children beginning to read for themselves and is related to the everyday world: *Man Makes Roads, Man Makes Towns, Man and the Sun.* Reading of the everyday world is an important contributory factor in a child's social development.

Other series by Hamish Hamilton are the Antelope and Reindeer Books, the latter of which is now in a paperback edition entitled Collie

Books and is published by the proprietors of Corgi Books. Collie Books first appeared in 1966 as did the Blue Dragon Books of Associated Publishers Ltd., which are designed for children aged 6–8. In 1967 Brockhampton commenced the Red Knights series for younger readers, representative authors of which are Kate Seredy, Armstrong Sperry, and Rosemary Sutcliff.

An increasing number of hard-back series for younger children is available, both fiction and non-fiction. The former includes the Bodley Head Acorn Library, Brockhampton's Brock Books, Burke's Wren Books, and Methuen's Pied Piper Books; whilst in the latter category are Black's Junior Reference Books, Burke's Our World Series, Longman's All About Things We Use, Muller's Junior True Books, and Max Parrish's Colour Books.

As a child absorbs stories of small boys triumphing over mighty giants, and of small girls outwitting cruel witches, so his emotional development is nurtured. There is so much he cannot do in his real world and he is so dependent on adults, that it is necessary for him to occasionally visit a world in which boys like himself are in control. This kind of situation is well described in Kenneth Grahame's adult book about childhood, *Dream Days*. The danger of escape into fantasy is only when the child constantly abandons his real world for the land of make-believe.

Children of 4–7 are often very self-centred and in their own interests must mix with others of their age in order that they may reach the next stage of development. In becoming accustomed to the company of other children and learning to share and cooperate with them, a child comes to realize that he prefers to act in a group. Before the "gang" stage of 8–12, children play in shifting groups which will not be disturbed by the secession of one or more members. However, 8-year-olds like to belong to organizations such as Boy Scouts and Girl Guides and have passwords and indulge in rituals. It is an especially rewarding age group for youth leaders and librarians, and others concerned with group activities. In contrast, it is a stage when children like to score over adults, a factor which is not conducive to the self-esteem of the pompous or the conceited. Adults must of necessity be sympathetic and understanding, and not be easily hurt or shocked if a particularly blunt remark is made. It is only in the adult world that opinions are cloaked in blow-softening verbiage.

Adventure stories are very popular with boys. In these they find an outlet for their aggressive tendencies in facing danger, triumphing over difficulties, and being undeterred by temporary setbacks in their struggle with evil, whatever form it takes. Intelligence is required in the unravelling of situations, and the discovery of treasure or some unknown territory. Thus the stories of Richard Armstrong, R. M. Ballantyne, Paul Berna, Fenimore Cooper, Erich Kästner, William Mayne, Arthur Ransome, Robert Louis Stevenson, Donald Suddaby, and Geoffrey Trease, which contain the possibilities of projection on the part of children, can be utilized in their development. The good things must inevitably triumph, and cynicism, cruelty, and selfishness must be defeated.

Girls in our society do not look for violence in their lives. This does not denote a sexual difference but a social one. Family-adventure stories answer their needs in the solving of mysteries and the rewarding of courage, but without recourse to fighting. In this connection appropriate authors are Philippa Pearce, L. M. Boston, some of William Mayne such as *Follow the Footprints* or *A Grass Rope*, and Sheena Porter. Also of appeal to girls are stories in a domestic setting by authors such as Eleanor Estes, Elizabeth Enright, Eve Garnett, E. Nesbit, Noel Streatfeild, and Laura Ingalls Wilder. School stories, too, have a message for girls, and are concerned with personal relationships rather than education in its narrower sense.

None of the foregoing is intended to imply that girls should not read adventure stories and that boys should not enjoy family stories. There is nothing necessarily abnormal in a child who does not allow himself to be restricted by convention. It is relevant too in discussing tendencies to remember that 51 per cent can be a majority and 49 per cent a minority.

Animal stories are read by both boys and girls but they tend to differ in the type of stories they choose. The interest in the personalized animals of infancy has long since lost its importance, and has given place in the case of boys to books about wild animals, and with girls to those about ponies and other domesticated animals. Such creatures may be given the power of speech, but the important thing is what they have to say rather than the fact that they talk. Dialogue is a necessity in stories for children and gives them the opportunity to take part in the action. The animals of Beatrix Potter, A. A. Milne, Ursula Moray Williams, and Michael Bond are replaced by those of Helen Griffiths, René Guillot, Nicholas Kalashnikoff, Mary Elwyn Patchett, and those included in the books of animal stories at the same level of interest. Some animal fantasies are relevant, such as Margery Sharp's mice and Kenneth Grahame's water folk, who would not make their full impact earlier. Girls read pony tales of Monica Edwards, Mary Treadgold, and the Pullein-Thompson sisters, and horse stories like M. E. Patchett's *The Brumby*, Anna Sewell's *Black Beauty*, and Joyce West's *Drover's Road*.

Fantasy is much sought after especially among girls. Many boys deny any interest at all. There is a great deal more to folk tales than the plots, and they can inculcate healthy attitudes and introduce their readers to the people of other lands. Many of the nineteenth- and most of the twentieth-century fantasy stories have their devotees. Lloyd Alexander, Lewis Carroll, Walter de la Mare, Eleanor Farjeon, Alan Garner, Madeleine L'Engle, C. S. Lewis, Mrs. Molesworth, E. Nesbit, Mary Norton, and J. R. R. Tolkien are representative writers in this field.

Some authors of books which would normally be placed in other categories include elements of fantasy in various of their works. Rosemary Sutcliff's historical stories for young children, as for example, *The Armourer's House* and *The Queen Elizabeth Story*, include references to fairies and the supernatural. These features reflect the beliefs of Tudor times and are an enchantment to the youngster of 8–12 in his books even if the make-believe is qualified by the knowledge that it is only a story. Lucy Boston's *Green Knowe* books have a feeling for the past which verges on the supernatural, and Philippa Pearce's *Tom's Midnight Garden* has similar traits. William Mayne's *A Grass Rope* and *The Blue Boat* have their own elements of fantasy

which take the form of unicorns and giants, and in *Earthfasts* he does
not even attempt to rationalize the unusual occurrences.

Even where there is a hint of fantasy, or the story is entirely concerned with it, children of this age will insist that the real world is not
entirely left behind. One can enter the realms of fantasy down a rabbit
hole, through a looking-glass, up the chains of a cuckoo clock, by the
manipulation of a bed-knob or a ring, or by flight on a carpet, but
contact with reality must be, and is, maintained either by a frequent
return to normality or by a remembrance of the code of conduct to
which one is accustomed.

The historical stories of Rosemary Sutcliff which followed the historical fantasies have been found of great value in the upper classes of
junior schools and the lower forms of secondary schools in the course
of project work. Cynthia Harnett's books are another example of historical fiction with educational potentialities. Apart from this they are
naturally of entertainment value, as are those of Leon Garfield
Geoffrey Trease, and Ronald Welch. Discrimination must be shown
in selecting Miss Sutcliff's books for this age range as many of her
later titles are more suitable for adolescents due to their complicated
psychological ideas. That is not to say no food for thought is provided
in books for this stage. Rosemary Sutcliff's *The Witch's Brat* is
concerned with a boy in Norman times who has a severe physical
disability with which he comes to terms tending the sick. Added to
this is a wealth of adventure and battle which is certain to captivate
most boys. Geoffrey Trease often has a struggle in his books between
selfish individuals and others who are motivated by feelings of altruism.
This is shown in *The Hills of Varna* in which an Italian aristocrat cov-
ets a manuscript for his private collection and is outwitted after many
exploits by those who want to give it to the world. Interesting incidents
from the past combined with themes of this kind are of great significance in the social growth of children.

In the junior school it is the practice to undertake imaginary journeys around the world as part of geography lessons. It is, too, of international importance for children to understand more of countries
abroad, and in this they can be assisted by authentic geographical

stories which perhaps will prevent the old ignorant prejudices from taking root. Ruth Miller Elson's *Guardians of Tradition* demonstrates how so often in the past the school books themselves have been responsible for many distortions of truth. Positive action is required to ensure that the present generation does not grow up with the same collection of misleading half-truths as have so many parents.

Numerous geographical stories are available which present a true picture of life and customs of other lands. Among these can be named Akosua Abb's *Ashanti Boy* (Ghana), Alan Boucher's *The Hornstranders* (Iceland), W. M. Levick's *Dry River Farm* (South Africa), Renée Reggiani's *The Sun Train* (Italy), Andrew Salkey's *Hurricane* (West Indies), Eleanor Spence's *The Year of the Currawong* (Australia), and many others.

The "Twins" series by Lucy Fitch Perkins is now very out of date and due to this shortcoming presents a false image of the countries concerned. However, Jonathan Cape have produced a new series by different authors including Daphne Rooke's *Australian Twins*, *New Zealand Twins*, and *South African Twins;* Gillian Tindall's *Israeli Twins;* and Eva-Lis Wuorio's *Canadian Twins.*

Nelson's Salamander Books are appropriate for children in the 8–12 age group, in which titles are included by Richard Armstrong, Leila Berg, Naomi Mitchison, Philippa Pearce, and others.

Good-quality fiction paperback series at this stage include the well-established Puffins, and the newer Black Knights, the latter containing books by Paul Berna, Elizabeth Goudge, Geoffrey Trease and Henry Treece. Series catering for a wider audience include Armada Books, Red Dragon Books, and Green Knights.

Throughout school life, children will use information books either in the furtherance of personal interests or as part of curricular activity. There will be many occasions, of course, when these will be indistinguishable, the one from the other. The best of the information books present knowledge and ideas in an attractive form so that readers will be encouraged to use them. In so doing, children are developing their intellectual and mental capacities both in the acquisition of information and in the thought processes which make it meaningful.

Appropriate series include Batsford's Junior Heritage, Hamish Hamilton's Look Books, Methuen's Outlines, and Warne's Observer Books. Brockhampton's White Knight paperbacks include practical books on hobbies and other interests.

Biographies are helpful in presenting patterns for possible emulation. The subject may be a Saint, a social reformer, a scientist, a technologist, an artist, a musician, or a man of letters, each one of whom will have something to contribute to the emotional and social growth of a child. There are, however, dangers which should be recognized. It is possible for a child to identify himself with someone whose standards are excellent but not appropriate to himself. When the child finds it impossible to behave successfully, as did his hero, the result may be a sense of failure, and emotional disorders may follow. A child may also identify himself with a famous person and imagine himself to be that person. If such a situation is taken to excess it represents an escape from reality into a world of day-dreams, which is of no help at all, and the refusal to accept reality may have a detrimental effect on the child's development. Refuge is usually taken in continuous day-dreams when a child finds himself a failure in one or more ways in the real world.

In its report published early in 1967, the Plowden Committee commented on "children's appetite for fact in a world in which knowledge is increasing at an astounding rate", and drew the conclusion that this explained "the dominating place of informative books in many school collections". On the other hand, fiction was "often represented by a random collection of books lent by the public library", and the Committee called for the inclusion of this category of literature as "part of the permanent collection of books in every school". It was suggested that teachers are "not sufficiently informed about the excellence of many contemporary children's stories or their availability in cheap editions" and the recommendation was made that this situation should be rectified. Action must be taken to ensure that children in primary schools have access to suitable books, adequate both in quality and in quantity to meet their needs, for in this they may "be choosing their future and the values that will dominate it".

It is during the years spent in the primary school that children should not only be introduced to books for their profit and pleasure, but ought also be given some initial tuition in their use. The habit of reading cannot be inculcated too early, and while as an end in itself it can be exciting, it is of far more value to a child if with suitable guidance it becomes a means to an end. First of all, the under-fives should be allowed to visit the public library to borrow books with their parents, and those children who are fortunate enough to obtain a place at nursery school can have their first introduction to a small collection provided especially for their use. Then, when they start school they should have access to a wide variety of books which in many schools are dispersed to as many parts of the building as they are likely to be used. The idea is to make children think in terms of using books as part of their everyday activities and at the same time to make themselves familiar with the material which is available. Lessons in the use of books can be given at school and visits to the public library can be arranged, where, if necessary, books are changed and a talk given by the children's librarian. The maximum co-operation is desirable between teachers and librarians especially as their clients are the same.

Whichever institution is responsible for the tuition of children in the use of books is not as important as the fact that they receive it. Too often in the past there has been conflict between librarians and teachers regarding the function of each and none of the acrimony has served to benefit the children at all. In this instance it would seem that as children's librarians are expected to study the bibliography of the literature and also the provision of library services for children in depth, then they should give instruction related to their speciality.

Children can be taught how to find out about their own literature and become acquainted with the appropriate bibliographies and guides. They can be taught the techniques by which most may be gained from encyclopaedias and other reference books. Problems of alphabetization can be explained because some works are indexed by words and others by letters. The importance of consulting reference works by first referring to the index can be emphasized. So much in fact can be done with books between the ages of 5 and 12, but, unfortunately, so little is often done, and the children are the poorer for the omission.

Adolescent boys go through three stages of development: puberty, between 12 and 14; a transitional period at 15; and later adolescence between 16 and 18. Girls follow the same three stages but at a year or so earlier. As has been stated, it is impossible to be dogmatic about ages, and those suggested are intended to be no more than approximations.

Group activity is important to children of 12 and bonds of loyalty to both the group and its leader are much stronger than in the "gang" stage. There is a desire to conform to the ideals and attitudes of the group, although acceptance does not necessarily signify agreement. At this stage the idea of rejection by the group is anathema, and those who are unfortunate enough to be rejected often take up some unusual hobby in order to bolster their battered self-esteem. Boys of 12 tend to admire others and to emulate such qualities as goodness, knowledge, skill, and wisdom. Girls at this age frequently have difficulty in making friends and are often sentimental over teenage heroes. It would be a great pity if these were the only models and the heroic lives of Grace Darling, Elizabeth Fry, Florence Nightingale, and the saints of old had no message for them at all.

During the period of transition from the stage when children prefer the company of others of their own sex to the heterosexual entry into adult life, interest in the group diminishes and moodiness and a wish to be left alone become dominant. It is a difficult time of physical and emotional growth for many teenagers which is combined in grammar schools with a demand for intellectual effort. This is probably a good thing as it diverts the mind from other problems which will only be solved in time, and is not improved by overmuch introspection. Dating becomes an important part of many girls' lives after the age of 14 and a year later with boys. However, many observers are able to point to plentiful examples where dating did in fact commence as much as 2 years earlier. A schoolmaster from a working-class area near Liverpool remarked that Beverley Cleary's *Fifteen* would have been more appropriately entitled *Thirteen* in his neighbourhood, and bore no relevance at all to most of his charges of 15. Good quality recreational literature ought to be helpful to teenagers during this transitional period. It can provide an outlet and at the same time solve particular problems or at least show that the individual is not suffering alone.

In later adolescence idealism increases. The call among responsible teenagers is to public service and self-sacrifice. Feelings of dissatisfaction and inadequacy preoccupy many as the realization dawns that the reality so seldom equates with the high ideals they have set for themselves. The search is for a perfect world which does not exist in reality and it is only when the situation has been accepted but the endeavour continues that young people can become mature adults. This is all very different from accepting the situation and abandoning hope.

It is useful at this point to consider educational organization at the secondary level. There is a widespread movement towards comprehensive education, a system which places all the educable children of a district into one school. After the Education Act of 1944 the general practice was to divide pupils over the age of 11 into grammar schools (for an academic and professional education), technical schools (for those who are talented practically), and modern schools (for the remaining 70–80 per cent). One can readily understand that children who are studying for the General Certificate of Education or the Certificate of Secondary Education may well cease to read children's books due to pressure of work. After school, the reading interests of a large number of young people very often become nonexistent because there is no encouragement to continue with them, and they may even be disparaged for doing so in the workaday world.

When one considers the various features of adolescence which have been described in this chapter, it is obvious that suitable books geared to the needs of the adolescent could be of immense service in bringing him to a state of self-acceptance, in showing that his problems are common to others of his age, and in suggesting a moral code which may well reduce the high rates of delinquency and illegitimacy which are marring the formative years of so many young people. It is of primary importance to understand the ways in which specially written literature may contribute to the needs of this age group.

Whilst the features and problems of adolescence are recognized and it is possible to suggest the kinds of books which could be of value, it is unfortunate that, as yet, relatively few such books have been written in this country. Much more attention has been given to the subject in the United States, where, as will be remembered, there is a separate Young Adults' Services Division of the American Library Association. It has even been suggested that a separate Medal be awarded annually to the outstanding example of literature for young adults.

Many secondary modern boys and girls could well find pleasure in reading the types of adventure, family, animal, historical and geographical stories suggested for the 8–12 age group. A sizeable minority are not avid readers anyway, but they can be taught the value of reference books and other material of an informational nature which it is possible to use in the course of their leisure and occupational activities.

An attempt has been made to reach teenagers through the specially written paper-covered Peacock Books which are published by Penguins. Beverley Cleary's *Fifteen* is an example of this series which is rather pallid in the light of the experience of many teenagers of 15. However, there are some well-chosen books available which have a relevance to teenage problems and point the way to right attitudes and worthwhile ideals. Of particular interest are some of the American titles which have been published as Peacocks, such as Elizabeth G. Speare's *The Witch of Blackbird Pond*, which spotlights the problem of ignorance and inhumanity; arrogance confounded and infirmity overcome are portrayed in Esther Forbes' superb *Johnny Tremain*, as well as a different view of the American War of Independence from that learned in the average British textbook; Gene Stratton Porter's *A Girl of the Limberlost* discusses the kinds of situation which must have worried countless teenage girls. These books deal with matters which teenagers are trying to resolve. An indirect approach of this nature can surely be of far more value than any number of homilies delivered by parents, who, of course, "do not understand"!

Other paperback series for teenagers include Black Knights, Green Dragons, and Topliners. Typical titles in the Green Dragons are Mary O'Hara's *My Friend Flicka* and P. C. Wren's *Beau Geste*, whilst Topliner authors include E. W. Hildick, Reginald Maddock, and Joan Tate. The latter series is especially designed to appeal to the reluctant reader.

Rosemary Sutcliff has catered for the teenager in many of her historical novels. In the trilogy *The Eagle of the Ninth*, *The Silver Branch*, and *The Lantern Bearers*, the struggle to maintain the light of civilization against the ever-encroaching darkness is examined. In each book it is made clear that the light is to be cherished and preserved beyond the lifetime of an individual. The same theme is met with in *Dawn Wind* except that it is apparent that the light is to be carried by the newly introduced Christianity. A second trilogy considered the manner in which youths can win their place in the world of men in *The Shield Ring*, *Warrior Scarlet*, and *Knight's Fee*. Miss Sutcliff's *The Mark of the Horse Lord* considers the price of freedom and its wise use. All these themes are relevant to the topics of discussion which frequently arise among groups of adolescents at any time of the day or night.

Barbara Willard has discussed social adjustment in a contemporary setting in such books as *The House With Roots*, *The Battle of Wednesday Week* and *The Family Tower*. K. M. Peyton departs from her more usual historical writing in *The Plan for Birdsmarsh*, in which she demonstrates the conflict between economic need and youthful romanticism when it is proposed to construct a marina in a small village. Mrs. Peyton deals with the problems of a teenage boy at odds with authority in *Pennington's Seventeenth Summer*, and *The Beethoven Medal*, and underlines the importance of identifying talents which may be developed. Other authors who have written books for teenagers in a contemporary setting include H. F. Brinsmead, Emily Cheney Neville, and Ivan Southall.

Some books are being published for teenagers which are concerned with sexual problems. John Rowe Townsend is one of a small number of British writers who have explored teenage sexual relationships with any sense of reality in his *Good-Night, Prof, Love*. Townsend has a middle-class boy enter into a short-lived elopement with a girl of whom his socially conscious parents would not approve. There appears to be more interest in teenage literature of this kind in the United States than in Britain, and books by Paul Zindel, for example, have been imported by Bodley Head in their series of *Books for New Adults*. Zindel is typical of a growing number of authors who deal forthrightly with the problems of teenagers. *My Darling, My Hamburger* is concerned with teenage love and abortion. Sex is a part of teenage life, and a case can be made for it being included in the literature. A shallow treatment of the subject can already be obtained from picture papers, and good literature can act as a counter to these in presenting a more responsible picture. It is necessary to point out the moral and social consequences which are involved, and which cannot be reasonably isolated from the physical relationship. On the other hand, it can be argued that if teenagers wish to read books of this kind, they can obtain a vast quantity of well-written adult literature without recourse to expurgated purpose-written stories. This is not intended to imply that a literature for teenagers may not be of value both for entertainment and as an aid to development.

A specially written literature for adolescents must cater not only for the avid reader but also the reluctant. Having had adequate training in the primary school, the vast majority of adolescents ought to want to continue their reading after they go to work. The public library has a captive clientele of school children, but they do not continue to use it after they leave school. This is a situation into which much serious research will have to be made. Many argue that teenagers should be left to go their own way. However, before the Second World War and for a few years after it ended, the "Teenager" as an entity did not exist in the popular mind. In spite of this he did exist and the world of commerce, noticing his affluence, has made quite certain that he is very much aware of himself. In these circumstances it is no longer possible for anyone to ignore his presence and the world of books must recognize his real needs.

Until a specially produced high-quality literature is more widely available, the teenager must do as the younger child up to a century ago, and adopt material which is to hand. Many teenagers have read and enjoyed Rumer Godden's *The Greengage Summer*, William Golding's *Lord of the Flies*, Graham Greene's *Brighton Rock*, Ernest Hemingway's *For Whom the Bell Tolls*, and J. D. Salinger's *Catcher in the Rye*. Other authors who will appeal to teenagers include John Braine, Margaret Drabble, Ian Fleming, Hammond Innes, Pamela Hansford Johnson, Iris Murdoch, and C. P. Snow. In addition to hardcovered editions many of the books of these authors are available in such paperback series as Fontana, Pan, and Penguin.

Collins' Modern Authors series is particularly suitable in its provision of adult books for teenagers. The contents of the books, both fiction and non-fiction, have not been abridged. Fiction is represented by Nigel Balchin's *A Sort of Traitors*, Agatha Christie's *The Murder of Roger Ackroyd*, and Hammond Innes' *Campbell's Kingdom* and *The White South*; and typical non-fiction are Alistair MacLean's *The Guns of Navarone* and *H.M.S. Ulysses*, and R. J. Minney's *Carve Her Name with Pride*. Laurel and Gold paperbacks from the same publisher include Paul Brickhill's *Reach for the Sky*, Pierre Boulle's *The Bridge on the River Kwai*, and Eric Williams' *The Wooden Horse*.

It is possible that a special literature is not required for adolescents. Whether this is or is not so cannot be known until such a literature has been provided. If the attitude of not attempting to meet specific needs had been dominant in and after the eighteenth century then it is very likely there would be no children's literature today. One can never know. What is known, however, is that adolescents drift away from reading and most of them never return to it later in life except for examination purposes. If this is to be regarded as unfortunate, then every possible avenue must be explored in finding a solution.

In this book have been examined the sources of children's literature, the development of the literature itself, and its application to different age groups. It may be worth while to be aware of the guides which are available; it may be of interest to follow the evolution of the subject from its small beginnings to the present time; but if the needs of those for whom the literature has been written are not considered, then a knowledge of the first two can be of little more than academic value. It is in the practical application of a knowledge of children's literature, wherever it can possibly have relevance, that the real rewards accrue and a lasting contribution is made to the development of young people. First and foremost, this should be the responsibility of parents, who will be joined by teachers as the children commence school. Librarians can play their part while the children are still infants, provided the parents are sufficiently aware of the contribution they can make. In fact, anyone who is concerned with the well-being of the young can profit from knowing how to find out about children's literature, not least the young themselves.

Useful Addresses

AMERICAN LIBRARY ASSOCIATION: 50 East Huron Street, Chicago, Illinois, United States.

BIBLIOTEKSTJANST: Tornavagen 9, Lund, Sweden.

Bookbird: See INTERNATIONAL BOARD ON BOOKS FOR YOUNG PEOPLE.

Books: See NATIONAL BOOK LEAGUE.

Books For Your Children: 100 Church Lane East, Aldershot, Hampshire.

British National Bibliography: 7 Rathbone Street, London, W.1.

CHILDREN'S BOOKS COUNCIL: 175 Fifth Avenue, New York, United States.

Children's Book Review: 67 High Road, Wormley, Broxbourne, Herts.

EDINBURGH CORPORATION, MUSEUM OF CHILDHOOD: 38 High Street, Edinburgh.

EDUCATION AND SCIENCE, DEPARTMENT OF: Curzon Street, London, W.1.

EDUCATIONAL FOUNDATION FOR VISUAL AIDS: 33 Queen Anne Street, London, W.1.

GEOGRAPHICAL ASSOCIATION: 343 Fulwood Road, Sheffield, 10.

Growing Point: Mrs. Margery Fisher, Ashton Manor, Northampton.

HISTORICAL ASSOCIATION: 59A Kennington Park Road, London, S.E.11.

Horn Book Magazine: Dept. N, 585 Boylston Street, Boston, Massachusetts, United States.

INTERNATIONAL ASSOCIATION FOR RESEARCH IN CHILDREN'S AND YOUTH LITERATURE: George Voigt Strasse 10, Frankfurt am Main, Germany.

INTERNATIONAL BOARD ON BOOKS FOR YOUNG PEOPLE: Fuhrmannsgasse 18a, Vienna 8, Austria.

INTERNATIONAL FEDERATION OF LIBRARY ASSOCIATIONS: c/o British Museum, London, W.C.1.

INTERNATIONAL INSTITUTE FOR CHILDREN'S, JUVENILE AND POPULAR LITERATURE: Fuhrmannsgasse 18a, Vienna 8, Austria.

Junior Bookshelf: Marsh Hall, Thurstonland, Huddersfield.

LIBRARY ASSOCIATION: 7 Ridgmount Street, Store Street, London, W.C.1.

Library Journal: R. R. Bowker Co., 1180 Sixth Avenue, New York, 36, United States.

MATHEMATICAL ASSOCIATION: 22 Bloomsbury Square, London, W.C.1.

NATIONAL BOOK LEAGUE: 7 Albemarle Street, London, W.1.

NATIONAL LIBRARY FOR THE BLIND: 35 Great Smith Street, London, S.W.1.

SCHOLASTIC PUBLICATIONS: 64 Bury Walk, London, S.W.3.

SCHOOL LIBRARY ASSOCIATION: Premier House, 150 Southampton Row, London, W.C.1.

Times Educational Supplement: Printing House Square, London, E.C.4.
Times Literary Supplement: Printing House Square, London, E.C.4.
TORONTO PUBLIC LIBRARY: College & St. George Streets, Toronto, 2B, Canada.
ULVERSCROFT LARGE-PRINT BOOKS: F. A. Thorpe (Publishing) Ltd., Station Road, Glenfield, Leicester.
UNESCO: Place de Fontenoy, Paris VIIe, France.
J. WHITAKER & SONS LTD.: 13 Bedford Square, London, W.C.1.
H. W. WILSON CO.: 950 University Avenue, Bronx, New York, United States.

Addresses of British Libraries can be obtained from *The Libraries, Museums and Art Galleries Year Book*; British periodicals from *Willing's Press Guide*; and British publishers from *British Books in Print* (Whitaker).

Index